Contributions to Regional Science

This book series offers an outlet for cutting-edge research on all areas of regional science. Contributions to Regional Science (CIR) welcomes theoretically sound and empirically robust monographs, edited volumes and handbooks from various disciplines and approaches on topics such as urban and regional economics, spatial statistics, spatial econometrics, geographical information systems, migration analysis, land use and urban development, urban and regional policy analysis, inter-industry analysis, environmental and ecological analysis, and related fields. All books published in this series are peer-reviewed.

Fujio Mizuoka

Subsumption of Space

A Theory of Marxist Geography

Springer

Fujio Mizuoka
Hitotsubashi University
Tokyo, Japan

Contributions to Regional Science
ISBN 978-981-97-7559-0 ISBN 978-981-97-7560-6 (eBook)
https://doi.org/10.1007/978-981-97-7560-6

This Springer imprint is published by the registered company Springer Nature Singapore Pte Ltd.
The registered company address is: 152 Beach Road, #21-01/04 Gateway East, Singapore 189721, Singapore

To the Ukrainian people and Japanese families who are resisting the arbitrary power that is eroding their natural bonds with their land and children.

Introduction

The Core Category of Marxist Geography

Space has increasingly been given its due position in the system of social sciences since the last quarter of the twentieth century, to the degree that "space and time are fundamental components of human experience" (Sack, 1986, p. 216). Yet there is no systematic presentation of the dialectics of space and society.

This book, therefore, aims to fill this conceptual gap by providing a more rigid and dialectical social logic of space to formulate what French sociologist Henri Lefebvre termed "spatiology" (1991, p. 404), by filling the "missing link" in the theory of Marxism that bridges the existing theory of political economy and various spatial phenomena, including social struggles, related to space. It thereby intends to extend and substantiate the discourse that Lefebvre embarked on in his *Production of Space*: "to expose the actual production of space by bringing the various kinds of space and the modalities of their genesis together *within a single theory*" (Lefebvre, p. 16, italics mine), or a "political economy of space" (Lefebvre, p. 104). Although Lefebvre's conceptual contribution is profound indeed, his "single theory" is unfortunately not well systematised.

In building a single "unitary theory of space" (Lefebvre, p. 21), this book adopts the method of a more structured theoretical deduction. This is the theoretical procedure called "ascent" (see Chap. 1) that Karl Marx adopted in formulating the body of theory as presented in *Capital*. Of course, in Marx's mind, there would have been thousands of cases of economic transactions by market agencies or exploitation by capitalists. In the case of geography, presenting inductively from all the socio-spatial processes taking place in space can do little more than demonstrate the melange of disorganised facts, unless it is clear where and how to abstract the theory out of them, which ironically requires guidance from further theory. Therefore, in constructing a new spatial theory of political economy, this book takes the deductive steps of dialectics to explain the socio-spatial processes lacking in conventional Marxist social science. It thereby attempts to bridge the gulley between the existing theory and the actual socio-spatial processes that develop in the real world. Through this theoretical praxis, Marxist social science is elevated to a more affluent whole that includes space as an indispensable logical moment.

"The law of space resides within space itself" (Lefebvre, p. 173). The task of Marxist geography is to prove that there is indeed a logic with which spatial differentiation is created *endogenously* within the social system. Thus, two crucial conditions emerge at the beginning: first, the theoretical body of Marxist geography should *not* assume spatial differentiation at the start of the theoretical *ascent*. That is, Marxist geography attempts to *explain* the existing spatial differentiation based *not* on empirical description but through the logics of space embedded in the property of space and society themselves. They should be duly exposed and integrated into the system of Marxism. Therefore, second, the crucial logical moment of the discipline—space—must not be abstracted away from the theoretical body at any point.

It is a logical error to assume something that is to be demonstrated in the explanation at the outset. To assume a spatially differentiated social product at the beginning of the logical ascent is identical to assuming that such differentiated space is an indispensable logical moment for the genesis of the unevenness of the economic landscape and its unequal development, or claiming that without assuming such differentiated space at the beginning there is no way for capitalism to generate endogenously such spatial unevenness and inequality. In other words, to assume differentiated space at the outset is to assume, as with John Browett (1984), that capitalism is incapable of generating an uneven landscape and an unequal development intrinsically and endogenously.

Browett (p. 156) supports the view that "inequalities in the spatial organisation of society are not *necessary* to, nor *systematic* consequences of, the *logic* of the capitalist mode of production." Browett sees the emergence of unevenness in capitalism as "both spontaneous and socially unplanned" and a "contingent factor", which individual capital or capitalists may, at certain times, "be able to take advantage of" (*ibid*, p. 159). Costis Hadjimichalis (1984, p. 336) makes a claim similar to this, in that in the capitalists' attempt to improve technology, "general conditions of social production across regions and sectors tend to equalise towards a social average, producing at the same time a homogeneous space", which "minimises capitalist expansion since no excess profits can be obtained with equal rates of profit in all sectors and all regions". According to Hadjimichalis, the factor of differentiation to integrate into this tendency of equalisation does not come from the "laws of motion of the capitalist mode of production", but only from "an intervention by a political agent producing changes in the character of the dominant social relations of production, exchange, and consumption" (*ibid*, p. 338).

These claims resemble Doreen Massey's idea that "spatial change" is "understood predominantly *as an effect of the response to non-spatial developments*" and autonomy is not "accorded to the spatial dimension" (Massey, 1979, p. 71, emphasis mine). Hadjimichalis too asserts that the "inner logic of capital" (p. 338) does not have power to create spatial differentiation; but it must be explained by means of such an exogenous factor as "a political agent". For Browett, "uneven regional development is not... something which can be known in advance on the basis of theory" (p. 170).

The three authors share a reluctance to admit a relatively autonomous theoretical sphere dealing with spatial subsumption and unevenness.

The understanding of this book is contrary to these writers. The "inequalities in the spatial organisation" and its unequal development are part and parcel of the inevitable inner logic of capitalist reproduction and accumulation. If the creation of spatial unevenness and differentiation is a part of the necessary logic of capitalism, then capitalism must be capable of generating such unevenness or differentiation endogenously, regardless of the existence or non-existence of differentiated space in the beginning. The economy and society should be capable of creating unevenness in the economic landscape and unequal development, even if it is transplanted onto a featureless plain.

Thus, the dialectics in establishing the core category of Marxist geography lie in the following: we must assume space as the crucial moment of Marxist economic geography from the beginning. Yet, in the meantime, we must not assume spatiality (spatial differences) simultaneously.

The task of Marxist geography is to *explain* the existing spatial differentiation based *not* on empirical description but through building the conceptual blocks of Marxism. Since geography contains space as the indispensable moment, the moment of space must not be abstracted away from the theoretical body of geography.

As pointed out earlier, it is a logical error to assume something that is to be proven in the proof at the beginning. Therefore, since the object of Marxist geography is to prove that spatial differentiation is created *endogenously* within the economic system, the theoretical body of geography should *not* assume spatial differentiation at the starting point of the theoretical ascent. The capitalist mode of production must be capable of creating unevenness in the economic landscape and unequal development endogenously, even if it is transplanted onto a featureless plain. This is the very logic of capitalism this book aims to investigate.

Marx himself paid more attention to the socio-economic character of space than we think. For example, in *Grundrisse* (1973), the well-known phrase "the annihilation of space by time" appears three times, and in relation to it, a long discourse was added on the mysterious character of roads. The *Theories of Surplus Value* (1971 edition) points out that the nature of the two-sided character of material space, which will be mentioned later in this book (Chap. 1), is a metaphor for explaining goods. Space appears in Marx's *Capital* (1977 and 1981 editions) in the description of transportation expenses and distribution periods in Volume 2, as well as in the treatment of location in the ground-rent theory in Volume 3. Of course, these discussions in Marx's own literature are not intended to build a spatial theory of the political economy itself, but form parts of the explanation and critique of the capitalist mode of production, such as the period of circulation of capital and the economic basis of the existence of the class of landowners. Therefore, it is not sufficient to just cut and paste such phrases and to claim it as a Marxist theory of space.

The task of building a spatial theory of political economy is thus still left to scholars of subsequent generations.

Developments Among Past Critical Geographers

This theoretical endeavour has been carried out mostly by critical geographers in North America and other English-speaking countries for a half century. It was also an agenda for Japanese critical geographers up until 1972 (Mizuoka et al., 2005), which will be discussed in more detail in the Afterword of this book.

By the mid-1970s, Marxist geographers in North America had become more concerned with theoretical extensions of Marxist social science, particularly with respect to space, than with mere applications of existing Marxist categories to empirical field research, which characterised Marxist geography before then. According to Richard Peet (1977, p. 257), this is "a second, more innovative" cycle of North American Marxist geography, marked by "creative additions to Marxist theory". As stated above, space was also a major research concern of Lefebvre.

In the first cycle, Marxist geographers had simply applied the existing theory and concepts to empirical research findings to describe problems. Even if this was based on the theory of Marxist social science to some extent, primitive generic propositions had directly been applied to cities or regions. In terms of the theoretical research of social science, nothing was added to the theoretical understanding. No new theoretical categories had been created to explain the spatial processes and structures of society. Various phenomena related to these general propositions had been treated as mere expressions of these general and primitive propositions.

Georg Hegel wrote (2017, paras. 115 and 116): "… beginning cannot be made with anything concrete … If impatience with the consideration of the abstract beginning should provoke anyone to say that the beginning should be made not with the beginning, but straightaway with the subject matter itself, well then, this subject matter is nothing else but the said empty beginning; for what this subject matter is, that will be explicated only in the development of the science and cannot be presupposed by it as known beforehand."

For the impatient first-cycle geographers who claim themselves to be somewhat critical, the path at the introductory level can be negotiated well enough. However, when the path of research passes beyond the inflexion point into the terrain of innovative theorisation, the trail suddenly becomes rugged and unbeaten. Here, the concepts of existing Marxist social science function merely as generic footholds, with which the intellectual enthusiasm to break through drives critical researchers, not content with the established ideas of social science, to proceed. If the rugged path of research started at the very beginning of learning, people would have been more prepared at the outset. Researchers who want to develop elaborate quantum theory, for instance, cannot use empirical and journalistic statements to condemn the current situation.

In this context, the contributions of North American critical geographers were remarkable in the transcendence from the first and second cycles. The real contribution of Marxist geography in North America and of Lefebvre in France is that it succeeded in making this breakthrough, passing through this "inflexion point" and elevating these empirical phenomena of geography into the real categories of Marxist social science. Marxist geography thereby became a real part and parcel of the whole body of Marxism.

Their efforts were essentially centred, of course, around the concept of *space*.

The Structure of This Book

This book attempts to explain the present socio-spatial phenomena as a rich whole in theory, not as mere chaotic representation. This process will bring fresh and open life to Marxist social science. In this sense, this book is an addition to prior innovative theoretical endeavours in its attempt to revive Marxism, as Lefebvre (p. 343) pointed out, "Each of the concepts of Marxism may be taken up once more, and carried to a higher level, without any significant moment of the theory as a whole being lost."

To meet this task, this book builds a sequential set of dialectics.

Chapter 1 identifies two logical moments that should be incorporated in the theoretical body of Marxism in analysing the Marxist theory of space. The first logical moment is *ascent*. Based on Marx's argument in *Grundrisse*, the ascent shows the way to position space within the entire logical unfolding of Marxist economics. The second logical moment is *subsumption*. Originating in the *Results of the Immediate Process of Production* by Marx, subsumption is the Marxist concept of incorporating something external to the theoretical body into Marxism.

Marxism is a social science based on the principle of materialism. Therefore, Chap. 2 presents the material base of the theory—the nature of space in material or pristine form, or physical space free from any human actions in it. Pristine space has the dual and contradictory attributes of *absolute* and *relative*. This chapter discusses generally how pristine space is subsumed into society.

Chapter 3 deals with the dialectics on pristine absolute space and its subsumption into society. The homogenous and all-embracing nature of pristine absolute space has the social implication of liberty, equality and fraternity. It even has homogenising physical power. Absolute space works negatively and can therefore be detrimental to society based on separation and discrimination. State or economic power that is not amenable to this property of absolute space attempts to negate it by bounding the expanse of space with a produced space, that is, by imposing boundaries. Fragmentation and differentiation of spaces thus ensue.

Chapter 4 deals with the parallel dialectics of the subsumption of relative space. Pristine relative space has dividing and individualising properties, which imply discrimination and segregation in society. The divided space functions in contradiction to the integration of society. Relative space has thus to be annihilated through agglomeration as well as through the construction of a network of the means of transportation and communication. However, the network becomes more sparse and uneven as the means of transportation travel at higher speeds or a vehicle for transportation has a larger capacity. The chapter deals with this paradox of spatial integration.

From the processes of the subsuming space, the logical scene by now turns to the absolute and relative attributes of pristine space together with the elements of produced space that came out of the processes of subsumption; that is, bounding, agglomeration and spatial integration. They are combined together to form *relational space*. The fundamental dialectical dichotomy of the relational space is *contiguity* and *separation*. The dominant societal and economic system strives to place the entire system of relational space under its domination and control. Chapter 5 explains the socio-spatial process of this dialectical relation of relational space that leads to the production of a spatial configuration of society overall, which is the subsumption of *relational space*. The configuration of relational space is subsumed into society through two processes: vertically as territorial integration, homologous to Walter Christaller's central-place theory, and horizontally as land-use coordination, in a logic similar to that of Johann Heinrich von Thünen.

The configuration of relational space is etched onto the land surface and the human mind. The former is the built environment, the physical materialisation of space. The huge cost of producing the built environment induces the state power into the production process. It thus becomes social relations made tangible and visible. As the built environment is a part of the material space, it can change its shape only when certain economic conditions are met. The built environment therefore forms a fetter for society in its development and functions to curb the movement of the oppressed to achieve their own autonomy and freedom. Chapter 6 deals with these points, in drawing upon the arguments of David Harvey and Japanese Marxist economists.

Chapter 7 deals with the native as well as contrived bond of space and body in terms of the "autogenous bond of space and body". The configuration of relative space is integrated with the human body in various ways autogenously through the quotidian contact of the human mind with space. However, it is bound to be alienated by the state and capitalist powers. These powers manipulate and destroy the bond such that it will support their domination and control, then displace the bond into contrived ones.

Chapter 8 turns back to the capitalist space, yet this time in its dynamism. The capitalist spatial configuration is always subject to the crisis-prone business cycle. This chapter analyses the cycle in close relation to space. Ultimately, the repeated cycles culminate in a tendential fall in the rate of profit, which triggers global capitalism to mobilise countervailing forces to overcome the profit squeeze. This leads to a new capitalist regime of neo-liberalism and the production of a global configuration of economic space, most notably the New International Division of Labour.

The subsumption of space by the state and capitalist power that this book discusses is never complete. The space that remains unsubsumed can be deployed by the oppressed people, serving as an important strategic element of class, ethnic and other social struggles of the people against the state and capitalist power. Chapter 9 presents various spatial strategies for these struggles in referencing the logics and concepts that this book has developed in the preceding chapters. As a case study, this chapter presents the struggle against human rights infringements committed by the child guidance centre in Japan, in which I have taken part for several years.

The sum of the arguments of this book will confirm the statement that "social relations [and struggles against them], which are concrete abstractions, have no real existence save in and through space. Their underpinning is spatial" (Lefebvre, p. 404). Exposing the spatial underpinnings of power relations and the struggles contesting them is the ultimate task of this book.

References

Browett, J. (1984). On the necessity and inevitability of uneven spatial development in capitalism. *International Journal of Urban and Regional Research, 8*(2).

Hadjimichalis, C. (1984). The geographical transfer of value: Notes on the spatiality of capitalism. *Society and Space, 2*.

Hegel, G. W. F. (2017) (translation). *Science of logic*. Createspace Independent Publishing Platform.

Lefebvre, H. (1991) (translation). *The production of space*. Translated by Donald Nicholson-Smith. Wiley-Blackwell.

Marx, K. (1971) (translation). *Theories of surplus-value. Part III*. translated by Jack Cohen and S. W. Ryazanskaya. Progress Publishers.

Marx, K. (1973) (translation). *Grundrisse*. Translated by Martin Nicolaus. Vintage Books.

Marx, K. (1977) (translation). *Capital*. Vol. 1. Translated by Ben Fowkes. New York: Vintage Books.

Marx, Karl. (1977b) (translation). Results of the immediate process of production. In *Capital* (Vol. 1, pp. 948–1084). Translated by Ben Fowkes. Vintage Books.

Massey, D. (1979). A critical evaluation of industrial-location theory. In F. E. Ian Hamilton, G. J. R. Linge (Eds.), *Industrial systems* (pp. 57–72). John Wiley & Sons.

Peet, R. (1977). The development of radical geography in the United States. *Progress in Human Geography, 1*(2).

Sack, R. (1986). *Human territoriality: Its theory and history*. Cambridge University Press.

Contents

About the Author

Fujio Mizuoka was born in 1951. From 1979 to 1981, he taught as a visiting lecturer at Department of Geography and Geology, Faculty of Arts, University of Hong Kong. He then moved on to the US on the Fulbright Scholarship to conduct his doctoral research at Graduate School of Geography, Clark University for the period between 1983 and 1986. After the conferment of his Ph.D., for which Richard Peet and David Harvey were on the Committee, he was appointed to the associate professorship of economic geography at Faculty of Economics, Hitotsubashi University in 1987, and was promoted to a full professor in 1992. During his tenure, he took his students to various overseas field research. In 2007, he conducted his research as a visiting scholar at the Hong Kong University of Science and Technology, on the critical analysis of the Mass Transit Railway project there, which consists of a chapter in *Contrived Laissez-faireism: The Politico-Economic Structure of British Colonialism in Hong Kong*, also published from Springer. After retirement in 2015, he hosts the JCREC, a human rights organisation against de facto state kidnapping and abuse of children by the Child Guidance Centre of Japan.

Chapter 1
The Fundamental Moments in Formulating Marxian Spatial Theory

Contents

Abstract Two logical moments to be incorporated into the theoretical body of Marxism in analysing space are identified: ascent and subsumption. Based on Marx's argument in *Grundrisse*, the *ascent* is demonstrated in Section 3 in introducing money into *Capital*. Space is positioned in the same dialectical way in the entire logical unfolding of Marxist economics. *Subsumption* originates in the 'Results of the Immediate Process of Production' by Marx. This book expands the application of this concept more generally to incorporate anything external dialectically into the theoretical body of Marxism, from Marx's application only to the labour process. Section 5 testifies to the position of Marxist geography within Marxism, drawing upon Engels' classification of science.

1.1 Introduction

Our first theoretical task lies in identifying in the logics of Marxian social science the fundamental moments upon which the critical theory of space unfolds. Two fundamental moments for this task are identified: ascent and subsumption.

F. Mizuoka, *Subsumption of Space*, Contributions to Regional Science,
https://doi.org/10.1007/978-981-97-7560-6_1

1.2 Ascent and Descent

a. The method of political economy

In the relation between abstraction and reality, there are, on the one hand, abstract categories; and on the other, empirical and concrete facts. The task here is to discover the dialectics between them. Without it, the claim for "dialectics" remains a mere melange of words with little theoretical content. Both reductionism, where every aspect of reality is associated with simplistic theoretical elements, and empirical eclecticism, where the structure of society is considered to be an "eclectic grafting" of various fragmented empirical facts, are inevitable, with a proper understanding of the methodology of abstraction left behind.

Simplified categories are created by reducing chaotic reality; these categories should then work as the conceptual element to reconstitute reality. In this way, the chaotic concrete reality of capitalism is synthesised into a theoretical whole.

This method is concisely summarised by Marx in *Grundrisse*. As a proper understanding is crucial for the discussions to follow, I quote the relevant section in full:

> It seems to be correct to begin with the real and the concrete, with the real precondition, thus to begin, in economics, with e.g. the population, which is the foundation and the subject of the entire social act of production. However, on closer examination this proves false. The population is an abstraction if I leave out, for example, the classes of which it is composed. These classes in turn are an empty phrase if I am not familiar with the elements on which they rest, e.g. wage labour, capital, etc. These latter in turn presuppose exchange, division of labour, prices, etc. For example, capital is nothing without wage labour, without value, money, price etc. Thus, if I were to begin with the population, this would be a chaotic conception of the whole and I would then by means of further determination, move analytically towards ever more simple concepts, from the imagined concrete towards ever thinner abstractions until I had arrived at the simplest determinations. From there the journey would have to be retraced until I had finally arrived at the population again, but this time not as the chaotic conception of a whole, but as a rich totality of many determinations and relations. The former is the path historically followed by economics at the time of its origins. The economists of the seventeenth century, e.g. always begin with the living whole, with population, nation, state, several states, etc.; but they always conclude by discovering through analysis a small number of determinant abstract, general relations such as division of labour, money, value etc. As soon as these individual moments had been more or less firmly established and abstracted, there began the economic systems, which ascended from the simple relations, such as labour, division of labour, need, exchange value, to the level of state, exchange between nations and the world market. *The latter is obviously the scientifically correct method.* The concrete is concrete because it is the concentration of many determinations, hence unity of the diverse. It appears in the process of thinking, therefore, as a process of concentration. as a result. not as a point of departure, even though it is the point of departure in reality and hence also the point of departure for observation and conception. *Along the first path the full conception was evaporated to yield an abstract determination: along the second, the abstract determinations lead towards a reproduction of the concrete by way of thought.* (Marx, 1973, *Grundrisse*, pp. 100–101, emphasis mine)

Note that even though money is ubiquitous and always accompanies the capitalist mode of production, Marx does not assume the existence of money a priori from the beginning.

b. Ascent and Descent

The statement above tells us two important things about the methodology of Marxist social science (Fig. 1.1). First, in formulating the theoretical body of political economy, "the scientifically correct method" is to set out from a more abstract and simpler category, then proceed to more concrete and complex categories; not the other way around. The reason for this is simple: a more complex category always needs to be explained, or supported by preceding simpler categories; otherwise, the more complex category remains hollow and unsubstantiated. In order to substantiate the more complex category, we must turn to a simpler one; and unless the simpler category is already established and explained as such, such substantiation is not possible. This logical process of proceeding from a simpler to a more complex category is called ascent.

The motive power that carries this process of ascent forward is the dialectical relations among the categories as well as the relation between categories and reality. The whole theoretical body of *Capital* forms a continual ascending logical path from the simplest category, the commodity, explained at the very beginning of *Capital*, to the more complicated, the category of social class explained at the end of Volume 3. The categories in this logical path are an interdependent whole forming a systematic theory; thus, none of the categories of this logical path can be isolated from the theoretical body of *Capital* as a whole.

This Marxian method of dialectical materialism is formulated by inverting Hegelian transcendental idealism and bringing this into the material context. Therefore, the categories in political economy are not idealistic products taken from a transcendental world, but are firmly rooted in reality. Marx states as follows:

> My dialectical method is, in its foundations, not only different from the Hegelian, but exactly opposite to it. For Hegel, the process of thinking, which he even transforms into an independent subject, under the name of "the Idea" [*Idée*], is the creator of the real world, and the real world is only the external appearance of the idea. With me the reverse is true: the ideal is nothing but the material world reflected in the mind of man, and translated into forms of thought. (*Capital*, Vol. 1, p. 102)

This being the methodology of Marxist dialectics, a category forming an element in each logical step of ascent is obtained through a process of abstraction from empirical reality. Marx states, "in the analysis of economic forms neither microscopes nor chemical reagents are of assistance. The power of abstraction must replace both." (*Capital*, Vol. 1, p. 90).

The process of abstraction from reality is called *descent*, which constitutes the other element of the methodology of Marxist economics. Consider how many commodity transactions are carried out every day. Clearly the category "commodity" is real, not an imagined one, taken from reality by the abstracting power of the human brain. Although the logical process of the ascent of the political economy may seem to be a transcendental and autogenous unfolding of categories, this "unfolding" is only possible by means of the descent that is repeatedly taking place to obtain these categories. Thus, Marx selected England, where the capitalist mode of production

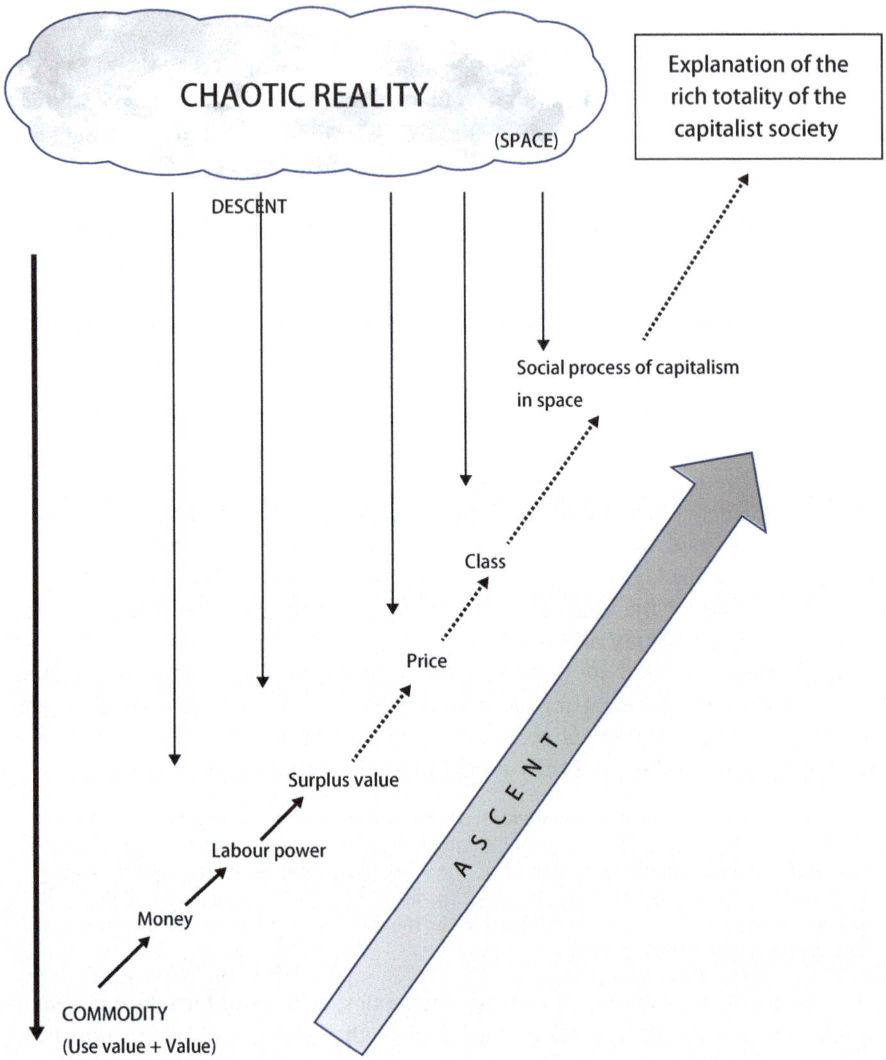

Fig. 1.1 The method of political economy

was developed as a "*locus classicus*" (*ibid*, p. 90), as the geographical area for his "fieldwork".

c. Their dialectical unity

To understand the dialectical unity of ascent and descent is the core of the methodology of Marxist economics that spans the bridge between theory and reality. In the first instance, a "generalised term", or raw material to be transformed into a real category, is taken from "chaotic reality" through the method of empirical observation and generalized through the process of *descent*. Through this process of descent, the eventual category is embodied with material, and the whole theoretical process of ascent is substantiated with the material.

It is not arbitrary to take the empirically generalised "terms" or conceptual moments into the theoretical framework. The order is determined by the logical process of ascent. The moment that is simpler and more basic is to be chosen prior to that which is more complex, presupposing a more extensive logical support of simpler categories. Then all these moments extracted from "chaotic reality" are put into the theoretical system. The moments then turn to be the real category and the chain of categories comes onto the logical path of ascent. Thus, although the logical path of ascent in political economy seems to be the autonomous unfolding of the *Idée* in Hegelian philosophy, this outlook is merely a way to grasp material reality in a systematic manner. This dialectical unity of ascent and descent is summarised by Mita (1963, p. 5):

> [we must acquire] a category by way of an analysis of the given reality. In the ascent from abstract to concrete categories consecutive analysis of reality is conducted at the same time, which eventually reaches the scientific cognition of the capitalist mode of production as a whole or that of a particular nation.

"Category" and "reality", mentioned here, should of course include those categories and realities of economic geography.

1.3 The Unified Dialectics of Ascent and Descent in the Opening Chapter of Capital Volume 1

a. The Marxist way of developing the plan of *Capital*

This book follows Lefebvre's method of following "*Capital*'s plan in dealing with space" (Lefebvre 1991, p. 100), with the addition of more robust logics. Marx's plan of *Capital* is constructed in ascending dialectical steps. In order to develop the spatial theory in line with Marx's plan, it is essential to grasp that the dialectics of ascent and descent is exactly what Marx used to develop the economic theory of *Capital.*

To endorse what I have discussed, let me briefly demonstrate how this unified process of ascent and descent is conducted at the beginning of Volume 1 of *Capital*, where the commodity, "the first category in which bourgeois wealth presents itself" (*Grundrisse*, p. 881), is discussed with respect to commodities in general, and a special kind of commodity—money.

Marx states as follows:

> The wealth of societies in which the capitalist m ode of production prevails appears as an "immense collection of commodities"; the individual commodity appears as its elementary form. (*Capital*, Vol. 1, p. 125)

> The commodity-form is the most general and the most undeveloped form of bourgeois production... (*ibid*, p. 176)

In these statements, the unity of ascent and descent is already clear. The category commodity is taken from the empirical fact that there is an "immense collection" of them in capitalist society. Meanwhile, the commodity logically forms the "most elementary" and "most general" forms of the capitalist mode of production. The two constituent elements of the general form of capital are *M*-*C*-*M*′, where *C* and *M* are both commodities; that is, capital consisting of various kinds of commodity. The category of capital thus presupposes the category of commodity, but the commodity can be explained *without* presupposing the category of capital. For this reason, the category of commodity must precede that of capital.

Nevertheless, the category of commodity, even though it is most general and elementary, does not explain everything, since many aspects of reality in the capitalist mode of production have been distilled away in order to obtain it. In order to accommodate facts that cannot be explained by this most general category, we need to go a step further: introducing a commodity with particular characteristics, that is money.

This process of incorporating more complex terms into a simple category is the process of ascent.

b. How Marx deduced the category of money in *Capital*

The dialectical nature of the process of ascent from a simple category, the commodity in general to money, a more complex one, is demonstrated in Marx's explanation in the following manner.

The process of ascent in this respect involves two different paths: the value-form and the process of exchange.

First, the value-form sets out from "the simple, isolated, or accidental form of value":

> x commodity A = y commodity B or x commodity A is worth y commodity B. (20 yards of linen = 1 coat, or: 20 yards of linen are worth 1 coat), ...[where the] first commodity plays an active role, the second a passive one. The value of the first commodity is represented as relative value, in other words the commodity is in the relative form of value. The second commodity fulfils the function of equivalent, in other words it is in the equivalent form. *(ibid*, p. 139)

Marx then expands this into the total or expanded form of value:

> z commodity A = u commodity B or = v commodity C or = w commodity D or = x commodity E ... etc. (*ibid*, p. 134)

Nevertheless, this form of value has defects. It can never be the exhaustive form to explain the relations among different kinds of concrete "useful labour" which form as a totality "a social division of labour" (*ibid*, p. 133). Nor can the elements constituting this form of value be connected to one another for a total system. In order to acquire a better logical vantage point which commands the social division of labour in totality, Marx introduces "the general form of value" where values of all the commodities are expressed through one single kind of commodity. According to Marx, the simple and expanded forms of value are "a motley mosaic of disparate and unconnected expressions of value" and "the only equivalent forms which exist are limited ones [and] the specific, concrete, useful kind of labour contained in each particular commodity equivalent is only a particular kind of labour and therefore not an exhaustive form of appearance of human labour in general" (*ibid*, pp. 156–157). "The general form of value", which overcomes these defects, has the following formula:

$$\left.\begin{array}{l} \text{1 coat} \\ \text{10 lb. of tea} \\ \text{40 lb. of coffee} \\ \text{1 quarter of corn} \\ \text{2 ounces of gold} \\ 1/2 \text{ ton of iron} \\ \end{array}\right] = \text{20 yards of linen} \tag{1.1}$$

x commodity A etc. (ibid, p. 157)

It is from this formula that Marx obtains the money form, where the universal equivalent of value, "20 yards of linen" in the right-hand side of this equation, is replaced with "2 ounces of gold" (*ibid*, p. 162).

In this argument on value-form, Marx shows why a mere mineral substance, gold, takes the general form of value in a commodity-producing society—the expression of value in money form. For example, "10 pounds of tea equals 2 ounces of gold" is nothing but a developed form of the simple form of value. Therefore, the ultimate secret behind the fetish form of "money" lies in these simple value forms constituted by the social division of labour under commodity production.

Second, Marx considers the explanation not to be complete, however, unless the actual process of exchange, carried out by the economic agencies in various branches of the social division of labour under commodity production, is analysed and the real contradiction in the exchange of commodities is discovered.

In order to complete the explanation, the social process which actually attempts to transcend[1] the contradiction inherent in the social division of labour under commodity production, that is, the contradiction between use-value and value in the commodity transaction, needs to be examined. In the following, the nature of this dialectic and the way of its transcendence are examined.

In a system of the social division of labour, the labour spent in the production process only counts in so far as it is useful for others in society. Under the system of commodity production, all the commodities produced are non-use-values to the producer; but other agencies in the market who do not produce them seek use-values in these commodities.

This relation in the social division of labour under commodity production requires that all the commodities produced in society must change owners. The relation between market agencies in which the commodity is exchanged is mediated only with value. In other words, commodities must be realised as values before they can be realised as use-values. Nevertheless, for commodities to be realised as value, they

[1] *Aufzuheben* in German, sometimes translated into English as "to sublate" or "to suspend".

must prove themselves as having use-value. However, it is only the act of exchange, actions of the market agencies, that can prove whether labour spent in the production process is useful for others, with the product consequently taking part in the social division of labour. Thus, a commodity must prove its use-value before it is realised as value; but in the meantime, the same commodity must prove itself as value before it is proven that the commodity has use-value. This is the dialectic inherent in commodity production.

Hence, the producer expects the products to function as the universal equivalent for all other commodities (i.e. the right term of the Eq. (1. 1.)). But since every market agency hopes this, there is in fact no commodity acting as the universal equivalent. "In their difficulties our commodity-owners think like Faust: in the beginning was the deed. They have therefore already acted before thinking" (*Capital*, Vol. 1, p. 180). Only with the assistance of money, or to be more precise only after relating all other commodities to this particular kind of commodity as the universal equivalent, can the market agencies mutually bring their commodities into relation as values, thus as commodities. As Marx states:

> only *the action of society* can turn a particular commodity into the universal equivalent. The social action of all other commodities, therefore, sets apart the particular commodity in which they all represent their values.... Through the social process it becomes the specific social function of the commodity which has been set apart to be *universal equivalent*. (*ibid*, emphasis mine)

In the social division of labour under commodity production, a particular commodity, which is gold in many societies, yet sometimes also silver or shell, comes to be set out as *money* through the action of society. Marx thus succeeded in explaining money by incorporating the fact in real society that a particular commodity had been extracted and deployed as the universal equivalent—money—since ancient times.

In this process, three things are clear. First, the logical process of ascent is carried out by means of contradiction within a simpler category, in this case the contradiction between the use-value and value of the commodity. Second, it is not ideal speculation but actual human action over centuries that plays a crucial role in transcending the contradiction inherent in the category. Third, the direction in which the contradiction is transcended is determined by means of the process of descent. Money, the universal equivalent, is not the product of an ideal imagination, but is taken from empirical reality through the process of descent.

There are hundreds of thousands of monetary transactions carried out by commodity owners every day. In this sense, a new category, money, is explained by means of the unity of two methods: ascent and descent. Through this process an abstract theoretical category develops towards the theoretical reconstruction of reality, which is not as a chaotic conception of facts, but "a rich totality" of actual social relations determined by the interrelations of categories of various complexities at various stages of ascent. More complex categories crucial in explaining the capitalist mode of production, like labour power, capital, absolute and relative forms of surplus value, wages, capital accumulation etc. are successively introduced into the theoretical framework of political economy in this manner. The framework thus gains in strength of explanatory power, approaching infinitesimally close to the "rich totality of many determinations and relations". Herein lies the logic of the dialectic between concrete reality and abstract theory. Through continued efforts of this sort, the process of theoretical ascent. supported by the abstracting process of descent, is carried out step by step, while maintaining the dialectical relationship between reality and abstract theory. Thereby we can ultimately obtain a theoretical reconstruction of reality without retreating into the labyrinth of eclecticism.

1.4 Formal and Real Subsumption: The Dialectical Process to Incorporate a Fresh Logical Moment into Marxist Theory

Marx did not write much about space, except for a few, albeit insightful passages. The task to bring space as the theoretical moment into the body of Marxist economic theory has been left to later Marxist researchers. Yet Marx left us with the dialectical logic which should be followed when a fresh, so far exogeneous conceptual moment is incorporated into the existing theoretical body of Marxism. Subsumption consists of another logical driving force of ascent.

The two consecutive stages of the dialectic whereby something that existed before the emergence of capitalism is incorporated into the capitalist mode of production are called by Marx *formal subsumption* and *real subsumption*. The concept of *subsumption* was first put forward by Marx (1977) in his *Results of the Immediate Process of Production*. Although Marx theorised subsumption only with respect to production technology that took place at the dawn of the capitalist mode of production, this concept is powerful enough to be extended to wider conceptual moments, including space.

The takeover by capital of something that exists outside capitalism is termed *formal subsumption*. For example, "the formal subsumption of labour under capital" is "the takeover by capital of a mode of labour developed before the emergence of capitalist relations" (*Results of the Immediate Process of Production*, 1977 edition, p. 1021). The labour process itself is an antediluvian social phenomenon, not an invention of capitalism; capitalism rather first inherits the labour processes existing before it emerges. Marx explains this point as follows:

> capital subsumes the labour process as it finds it, that is to say, it takes over an existing labour process, developed by different and more archaic modes of production. And … it is evident that capital took over an available, established labour process. (*ibid*)

Capitalism first takes the labour process for granted and subsumes it formally into it. Capitalism then transforms it into the shape most suitable and fit to be an integral part of the capitalist mode of production. The division of labour in manufacturing, for example, "reacts back upon that in society" and develops and multiplies it further (*Capital*, Vol. 1, p. 473). It creates machines, and eventually large-scale industry. This is the process of the *real subsumption* of the labour process. On the foundation of a formally subsumed labour process, the nature of the labour process is transformed, through the development of the forces of production and the purposeful application of science and technology.

Through the real subsumption of the labour process, the capitalist mode of production establishes itself "as a mode of production *sui generis* and brings into being a new mode of material production" (*Results of the Immediate Process of Production*, p. 1035). In large-scale industry, for example, the labour process is subsumed into capitalism in real terms and transformed into cooperation and the division of labour within a firm which is "specific" to the capitalist labour process (*Capital*, Vol. 1, p. 453). Through this change, technology and organisation in the labour process are totally revolutionised, creating a condition for further development of capitalist relations of production. In short, one of the first tasks of industrial capital is to subsume all these forms existing before the emergence of capitalism in a formal manner, then transform them in a real manner (real subsumption). Marx himself summarises this process:

> Capital encounters these older forms in the epoch of its formation and development. It encounters them as antecedents, but not as antecedents established by itself, not as forms of its own life-process. in the same way as it originally finds the commodity already in existence, but not as its own product, and likewise finds money circulation, but not as an element in its own reproduction. ... [These forms] must first be destroyed as independent forms and subordinated to industrial capital. (Marx, *Theories of Surplus-Value*, Part III, p. 468)

The concept of subsumption can be expanded to the incorporation of many exogenous physical substances and natural systems into society: ecosystem, human body, and such physical landscape features as river or mountain and space, to name just a few. Through subsumption, society transforms the nature and the processes of pre-existing and pristine natural substances into those generating no obstacles to it. One-point, spaceless society thus "reproduces" the property of its configuration in the property of its exogenous physical substances, or space, through subsumption so that the obstacles in the exogeneous pristine space can be negated; thereby the produced space is made to serve to the requirements of the society. It is just like "God created man in his own image." (Genesis 1: 27)

These dialectics exist also with respect to space, the unique logical moment of Marxist geography. The capitalist mode of production, whether it emerges as a transcendence of the contradiction in the feudal mode of production, or is created on a virgin land as in the so-called "New World," has to inherit this pristine space. Capitalism first subsumes pristine, antediluvian space formally, then subsumes it in a real manner in a form suitable to itself, through intentional applications of science and technology and the creation of new social relations.

1.5 The Classification of Science

The body of theory that has subsumed space has a unique set of logic, thus it can set itself as a relatively independent field of discipline in pursuance to the Marxist concept of the classification of science. In Marxist philosophy, each branch of science can secure its relatively independent position if it reflects and studies a relatively autonomous form of motion in the material world. Friedrich Engels states as follows:

> classification of the sciences, each of which analyses a single form of motion, or a series of forms of motion that belong together and pass into one another, is therefore the classification, the arrangement, of these forms of motion themselves according to their inherent sequence. (Engels, 1954 edition, p. 249)

> Just as one form of motion develops out of another, so their reflections, the various sciences, must arise necessarily out of one another. (*ibid*, p. 250)

This proposition comes from one of the three laws of dialectics: "the law of the transformation of quantity into quality and vice versa" (*ibid*, p. 62). Suppose we divide a living creature into smaller portions. The creature divided beyond a certain limit can no longer survive: a living body transforms itself into a non-living organic mass. If we continue dividing the organic mass, we eventually obtain a molecule.

The further division of a molecule ends up with the atom. The part of the body, a molecule and an atom are all the substances with different forms of motion, studied by different branches of sciences: biology, chemistry and nuclear physics. Engels summarises this relation as follows:

> The purely quantitative operation of division has a limit at which it becomes transformed into a qualitative difference: the mass consists solely of molecules, but it is something essentially different from the molecule, just as. the latter is different from the atom. It is this difference that is the basis for the separation of [sciences]. (*ibid*, p. 64)

Thus, the academic division of labour is, according to dialectical materialism, not an ideal product nor a matter of expediency, but is firmly rooted in the objective and material forms of motion and concomitant contradictions. Societal relations and their forms of motion are no exceptions. The particular form of motion mentioned above, dealt with in each section of the academic division of labour, is characterised by a logical moment unique to it: for instance, a molecule or an atom. Marxist geography must have such a moment, a real category intrinsic to the theory of capitalism at the departure of the logical process of ascent. Applying the formulation of Engels, we can infer that Marxist geography has a position as a relatively independent field of Marxist social science, since it has a qualitatively distinguishable "single form" or "a series of forms of motion" related to space in capitalist society, and has its own unique contradiction.

Behind this point of departure in the process of ascent there lies the aspatial theory of capitalism, and beyond this point the theory of Marxist economic geography unfolds.

References

Engels, F. (1954) (translation). *Dialectics of Nature*. Translated by Clemens Dutt. Progress Publishers.
Lefebvre, H. (1991) (translation). *The production of space*. Translated by Donald Nicholson-Smith. Wiley-Blackwell.
Marx, K. (1973) (translation). *Grundrisse*. Translated by Martin Nicolaus. Vintage Books.
Marx, K. (1977) (translation). Results of the immediate process of production. *Capital* Vol. 1, pp. 948–1084. Translated by Ben Fowkes. Vintage Books.
Mita, S. (1963). *Shihonron no Hoho* (*The Methodology of Capital*). Kobundo.

Chapter 2
The Space and Its Subsumption into Society

Contents

Abstract This chapter examines the logical point of departure and the fundamental material base of Marxist geography: physical space. The nature of pristine space free from human action is presented in the Euclidean axioms of geometry, summarised into the dual and contradictory attributes of pristine space: absolute and relative. The *absolute* space has contiguousness, homogeneity and isotropy and accepts anything as a container. However, *relative* space has the property of separation differentiation, which individuates anything in space. These two attributes are thus in contradiction, while they are unified in physical space: the dialectics of separation within unity. In a class society, the physical space with these attributes is placed under power.

2.1 The Space: The Logical Moment of Geography

Pure space itself, or space in its pristine mode of existence is not an invention of capitalism, just as the "original" powers of the land, independent "of the action of human industry" (*Theories of Surplus Value*, Part II, 1971 edition, p. 246) are not. Space in this pristine mode is an antediluvian object in existence since the creation of the universe; thus, pristine space is older than the emergence of the capitalist mode of production.

Space of this nature is most close to the concept of "absolute space", defined by Harvey (1973, p. 13) as "thing in itself" with an existence independent of matter" where "structures, people and land parcels exist in a manner that it is mutually exclusive each of the other in a three-dimensional, physical (Euclidean) space" (*ibid*, p. 168). This is the space "immune to influence" in itself" (Sack, 1980, p. 55), and is still "the space of the physical world". Three-dimensional geometry would be the

F. Mizuoka, *Subsumption of Space*, Contributions to Regional Science,
https://doi.org/10.1007/978-981-97-7560-6_2

most appropriate way to describe this Euclidean space (*ibid*, p. 7). According to Sack (1980, p. 7), space of this nature is what "the physical scientist bequeaths to the geographer and to the social scientist". It is the framework in which their facts and events are located.

Society can never exist in a one-point world. Space is an integral part of social processes and structures, and thus space must be incorporated as an integral part of the system of Marxist social science. Geographers are well-positioned to take up the task of discovering this logic, being in a discipline where the dialectics between society and space have always been a focal point of their research. Discussions and commentaries abound in the contemporary geographical literature. Yet few sufficiently dialectical logics have been provided to offer a comprehensive understanding of socio-spatial relations.

This does not mean that the one-point world premise is wrong, however. At a higher level of abstraction, it is indeed necessary to abstract space away and construct the theory without space. Yet, at some point in research, the system of Marxist social science must subsume space, to rectify and enrich the one-point world premises.

Our first task is to identify the initial logical moment unique to Marxist geography that positions it properly and legitimately in the logical process of ascent in Marxist social science—in other words, the crucial category that differentiates Marxist geography from Marxist social science in general.

To determine this crucial logical moment, the implications of the word "geography" must first be examined. Dietrich Bartels (1969), a German geographer, considers the meanings implied in the word geography, pointing out that the word has four different implications: (1) whatever a researcher belonging to an institutionalised social body representing an academic field called geography is doing; (2) empirical and descriptive field research; (3) theoretical conceptualisation involving space; and (4) the same conceptualisation involving the environment or physical world. In this list of definitions, the first two are naturally irrelevant. An "institution" is merely a product of the academic division of labour (often with strife), not a cause of it. Empirical or descriptive field work is a part of geographical research, but also a part of other academic disciplines.

Yet it is a historical legacy that geography deals with the physical environment and space in its specific area of research. The interest of this book does not lie in tracing the evolutionary path of geographical science to prove how geography has come to deal with these two objects, as it takes them for granted. Marxist geography therefore must demonstrate its uniqueness within the classification of science in the Marxist political economy in that the spatial concept serves as the crucial and basic element of the theory. This book will, however, not deal with the physical environment, because space and the physical environment are physical substances of a completely different nature from each other, abiding by different laws of motion. Thus subsumption of physical environment is classified into a different category of science, which is out of scope of this book.

This book presupposes that Marxist geography has its own unique and indispensable theoretical moment: *space*. The position of Marxist geography should be determined therefore by how space could be placed within the whole system of Marxist social science, and how the uniqueness in its motion is identified.

2.2 The Spatiality Marxist Geography Should Assume at Outset

As discussed in the Introduction, (pp. vii–ix) the real contradiction in establishing the most crucial category of Marxist geography lies in the following: we must assume space as the integral element of Marxist geography from the beginning while also not assuming spatiality at the beginning.

What kind of spatiality should Marxist geography then assume at the beginning of its ascent? The spatiality that fulfils this condition is only a society with a spatial dimension, but without spatial differentiation. This logical point of ascent can be obtained by abstracting the most basic and pristine element of spatial dimension, distance, out of the diverse reality of the spatial differentiations of the capitalist landscape. As discussed in the previous section, spatial distance, "a relation between the one thing and the other", can be expressed in terms of spatial dimension, which has the attribute of distance, but no other spatial differentiation. Here, everything is equalised *sub specie spatii*, and distinguished only in terms of distance from one point to another. This is the space at the logical point of departure of Marxist geography.

The space at the logical departure may therefore be named *pristine space*. The only spatial difference comes from the property of physical space itself, as discussed in the previous section; that is, the attribute of expanse and distance, or what incorporates these two attributes: a "*uniform and homogenous plane*".

Pristine space, the point of departure for ascent in Marxist geography, is one of the moments in the theory of the capitalist mode of production obtained through the process of descent as all capitalism operates over space. Although there is no such empirical existence as a "uniform plane", the logical elements that constitute it, namely spatial distance and expanse, do exist everywhere in capitalism; and in this sense pristine space or the uniform plane is the result of the process of descent.

Furthermore, the assumption of pristine space is deeply rooted in the social process of capitalism as one of the real categories expressing the necessary and intrinsic tendencies of the capitalist mode of production: the "universalising tendency of capital" (*Grundrisse*, p. 540) or the "tendency towards equalisation" (Smith, 1984, p. 113). In this general tendency of capitalism, the existence of local spatial differences is insignificant, as opposed to general tendencies, as the following statement by Marx demonstrates:

> even though the equalization of wages and working hours between one sphere of production and another, or between different capitals invested in the same sphere of production, comes up against all kinds of obstacles. The advance of all economic relations to this mode of production tends nevertheless to bring this process to fruition. Important as the study of frictions of this kind is for any specialist work on wages, they are still accidental and inessential as far as the general investigation of capitalist production is concerned and can therefore be ignored. In the general analysis of the present kind, it is assumed throughout that actual conditions correspond to their concept, or, and this amounts to the same thing, actual conditions are depicted only *in so far as they express their own general type*. (*Capital*, Vol. 3, pp. 241–242)

This book attempts to investigate the "general type" of the logical processes leading to the production of spatial differentiation in the society, especially capitalism. Given this aim, all actual locally different conditions or spatial differences should be abstracted away and assumed as corresponding to the general type.

It is from uniformity of category that heterogeneity develops. This is the condition of the problem, as well as the dialectic, of introducing fresh categories of Marxist geography.

2.3 Pristine Space: The Logical Point of Departure of Marxist Geography

a. Introduction

As stated in the previous chapter (p. 11), geography based on Marxism must be a part of the whole Marxian social science, and it is subject to the unified methodology of ascent and descent.

Lefebvre identified (p. 402) the "initial basis or foundation of social space is nature—or natural physical space". Pure space itself, or space in its pristine mode of existence, is not an invention of capitalism, just as "original" powers of the land, independent "of the action of human industry" (*Theories of Surplus Value,* Part II, p. 246) are not. Space in this pristine mode is an antediluvian object which has existed since the creation of the universe; thus, pristine space is older than the emergence of the capitalist mode of production.

Physical space came into existence with the "Big Bang" of the universe and has existed ever since. Everything in the universe is contained in space, and space is a prerequisite for the advent of the biological and human world, if only because all living beings have a spatial dimension and act across space and the societies that they organise need some form of physical container that supports their existence and functioning.

Interestingly, Marx himself describes the dialectical nature of differentiating physical distance in relation to the equalising pristine space as the container in his work *Theories of Surplus Value* as follows:

> a dimension of space, it is a certain length which may as well express the distance of two other things besides those compared.... In speaking of the distance of two things, we speak of their difference in space. Thus we suppose both of them to be contained in space, to be points of space. Thus we equalise them as being both existences of space, and only after having them equalised *sub specie spatii* we distinguish them as different points of space. To belong to space is their unity. (*Theories of Surplus Value*, Part III, p. 143)

b. Axioms of geometry and the concepts of space

Lefebvre lists Euclidian geometric space as the first "formant" for the critical analysis of space. Philosophy treated the Euclidean space "as 'absolute', and hence a space long used as a space of *reference*" (Lefebvre, p. 285), which is what I call in this book "pristine space". The nature of pristine space in the theory of this book is best explained in regard to the property of the "Cartesian surface"—also called the "Cartesian coordinate system"—which was first invented in the seventeenth century by the philosopher René Descartes, to show any points on a plane with values shown in x and y axes. The nature of this surface has been more intensively studied and developed as Euclidian plain geometry by mathematicians.

The word "geometry", comprising of geo (=land) and metry (=measurement), were derived from quantitative measurements of space, and thus is closely related to geography. Geometry is a theoretical set of theorems providing the regularity with which various linkages of pristine space occur. The fact that geometry is the centrepiece in the drawing of maps and the industrial location theory of Alfred Weber (1929) supports this close relationships between geometry and geography.

Although the earth is a sphere, and three-dimensional space may become a problem in the case of high-rise buildings, geography approximately deals with a two-dimensional plane, where the Euclidean concept of space dominates. This concept starts with the following five axioms, which are treated as self-evident, or should be accepted without proof:

1. A straight line may be drawn between any two points.
2. Any terminated straight line may be extended indefinitely.
3. A circle may be drawn with any given point as its centre and with any given radius.
4. All right angles are equal.
5. If two straight lines in a plane are met by another line, and if the sum of the internal angles on one side is less than two right angles, then the straight lines will meet if extended sufficiently on the side on which the sum of the angles is less than two right angles.

Geometry treats these axioms as *a priori* and does not ask for further proofs of them. However, given the fact that geometry is a science that analyses the system of space, it is obvious that these axioms express the properties of pristine space as an objective existence. Therefore, these axioms are supported by physical substance, even though they have a seemingly *a priori* expression.

Next, I consider how these axioms express the property of pristine space for each axiom.

The first axiom implies the homogeneity of space in the expression "*any* two points" and expresses that it is possible to create a position with relative individuality and discrimination in space by setting a point anywhere in the continuous expansion of the space, and that when two points are set, a line segment always exists between them regardless of their positional relationship. This indicates the existence of the "distance" attribute towards any direction in relation to the original position; that is, the existence of the "location" and the "distance" attributes in the space and the isotropy of pristine space.

The second axiom implies that "distance" can extend infinitely; that is, pristine space is not limited by any external boundaries, or has no boundedness as such, and is infinite in any direction.

The third axiom states that a circle can be drawn anywhere with an arbitrary radius; that is, the radius r of a circle can exist from infinitesimal to infinity, the function $f(r) = \pi r^2$ (the area of a circle) is always differentiable, and there is no discontinuity in space that makes this differentiation impossible at any point. $r = \infty$ shows that the spatial extent is infinite. Additionally, drawing a circle with any given point as its centre means bounding by its radius, which means that the extent of a contiguous plane can be bounded by any "distance" regardless of its relative position.

The fourth axiom expresses that any relative relationships existing in this contiguous pristine space can be compared and reduced to a common measure on a homogeneous basis; in other words, that in pristine space, a common homogeneous property exists everywhere which enables such comparison.

Finally, on the fifth axiom, in the sense that parallel lines can be drawn for any straight line, the first statement of this axiom suggests the exclusivity in which the parallel lines never intersect; that is, pristine space can accommodate only a unique existence at one and the same position, specifically that pristine space is a Euclidean surface with its curvature being zero. That is, only one bounded piece of space consisting of a set of such line segments is possible in pristine space, and this piece of space occupies a part of the universal spatial extent exclusively.

Despite these five axioms being disguised as *a priori*, the five axioms of geometry in fact demonstrate the properties of the Cartesian surface or pristine space as an objective existence. The properties include isotropy, infinity, contiguity, egality, and exclusivity.

This pristine physical space is the space "immune to influence" in itself (Sack, 1980, p. 55), and is still "the space of the physical world". Yet, according to Sack, space of this nature is what the physical scientist bequeaths to the geographer and to the social scientist. It is the framework in which their facts and events are supposed to be located. These properties of pristine space constitute primordial moments which activate when the production of economic and social space enters into the agenda.

c. Einstein's concept of space

Einstein mentioned the nature of space in his Foreword to Max Jammer's *Concepts of Space* (2012):

> … as to the concept of space, it seems that this was preceded by the psychologically simpler concept of place. Place is first of all a (small) portion of the earth's surface identified by a name. The thing whose "place" is being specified is a "material object" or body. Simple analysis shows "place" also to be a group of material objects. Does the word "place" have a meaning independent of this one, or can one assign such a meaning to it? If one has to give a negative answer to this question, then one is led to the view that space (or place) is a sort of order of material objects and nothing else. If the concept of space is formed and limited in this fashion, then to speak of empty space has no meaning. And because the formation of concepts has always been ruled by instinctive striving for economy, one is led quite naturally to reject the concept of empty space.
>
> It is also possible, however, to think in a different way. Into a certain box we can place a definite number of grains of rice or of cherries, etc. It is here a question of a property of the material object "box," which property must be considered "real" in the same sense as the

> box itself. One can call this property the "space" of the box. There may be other boxes which in this sense have an equally large "space." This concept "space" thus achieves a meaning which is freed from any connection with a particular material object. In this way by a natural extension of "box space" one can arrive at the concept of an independent (absolute) space, unlimited in extent, in which all material objects are contained. Then a material object not situated in space is simply inconceivable; on the other hand, in the framework of this concept is quite conceivable that an. empty space may exist.
>
> These two concepts of space may be contrasted as follows: (*a*) space as positional quality of the world of material objects; (*b*) space as container of all material objects. In case (a), space without a material objects. In case (*a*), space without a material object is inconceivable. In case (*b*), a material object can only be conceived as existing in space; space then appears as a reality which in a certain sense is superior to the material world. Both space concepts are free creations of the human imagination, means devised for easier comprehension of our sense experience.
>
> These schematic considerations concern the nature of space from the geometric and from the kinematic point of view, respectively. They are in a sense reconciled with each other by Descartes' introduction of the coordinate system, although this already presupposes the logically more daring space concept (*b*). (p. xv)

The attribute of pristine space (a) is called *relative space*, and (b) *absolute space* in this book.

To avoid confusion, note that "absolute space" defined as such has a connotation different from "absolute space" in Lefebvre. According to Lefebvre, absolute space consists of fragments of physical (natural) space, such as "cave, mountaintop, spring river"; and the natural space politicised or sanctified is also "absolute space" (Lefebvre, 1991, p. 48). Absolute space, in physics as well as in this book, is far more generic: it derives directly from the very nature of pristine and physical space.

Society needs to take the existence of physical space for granted. The "facts and events" of society cannot avoid space of this nature. This is the nature of space that we extract from chaotic reality as the crucial element of Marxist economic geography.

2.4 Two Attributes of Pristine Space: Absolute Space and Relative Space

Based on the conceptualisation of space by Einstein, I now explain the two attributes of pristine space, absolute and relative, in more detail.

a. Absolute space

The attribute of absolute space was put forward by Sir Isaac Newton, who discovered universal gravitation and is sometimes called the father of physics. As the renowned economist J. M. Keynes (1946) pointed out, Newton practised medieval alchemy. Keynes claimed, "Newton was not the first of the age of reason. He was the last of the magicians…". Newton's spatial theory therefore remained mostly a theological compromise. Newton considered space as the "sensorium of God". When God gives judgement to anyone after death, in modern terms, it is necessary for each individual to have a database that records their acts in this world, and for that purpose, God installs "sensors" ubiquitously throughout space. It is necessary to monitor the conduct of all individuals and collect and store information about them because everyone is equal before God, and such a space must have a universal, uniform, and contiguous nature. Newton thus tried to explain the ontology of "space" through the power of theology.

Absolute space is a contiguous and homogeneous spreading, infinitely equal in any direction (isotropic), as a Cartesian surface. Absolute space is the container of every object, human, and thing, including its social and economic processes. Without this "container", no object or social relationship can exist.

Pristine absolute space accepts everything as it is, creating a physical platform for the substances and subjects in the space to interact through its contiguity, resulting in the homogenisation of the materials and subjects contained in absolute space. Suppose that ice at 0 degrees Celsius and boiling water of 100 degrees Celsius with the same mass are placed side by side in a sealed room. In a contiguous space, the hot water and ice exchange heat; the hot water cools down, the ice melts, and eventually both come to have equal temperatures. The same applies not only to substances but also to human and social relationships. If objects with different properties enter a single container, they interact in the container and come to share the same property. In the same way, absolute space thus has an attribute of equalisation in primitive space.

b. Relative space

The idea of absolute space was considered incompatible with modern natural science, which excludes the supernatural "god" from every aspect of it. German mathematician Gottfried Leibniz rejected Newton's alchemical spatial concept and established a new space concept.

In Leibniz's ontology, space can be interpreted as the relative positional relationship of objects. In his correspondence with Samuel Clarke, one of Newton's agents, Leibniz states, "space is nothing else but an order of the existence of things, observed as existing together", while rejecting the Newtonian concept of "an infinite empty space" (Para. 29 of Leibniz's Fifth Correspondence, Alexander (1956), p. 63), which represents God's immensity. As long as this relative order of existence is established and proven, space is proven. He thereby postulated the attribute of *relative space* in defining pristine space.

On a Cartesian surface, for any value of x or y, it is always possible to define a single unique point. Relative space thereby consists of a myriad of positions corresponding to individual points on such a coordinate plane, and these positions are distinct.

A line segment connecting these points defines *distances*, which physically creates a barrier to the interaction between economic agents and social groups. In pristine space, distance is logically the sole attribute to define spatial differentiation.

Distance is the degree of spatial separation between two points. The interaction over these points rapidly weakens with a distance-decay effect, which is inversely proportional to the square of the distance. This relationship is known in physics as the gravity model.

Distance creates uniqueness, individuality and differentiation in the economic system and among social groups. The cost and effort to overcome distance can make the system and groups themselves dysfunctional, and can thus jeopardise their very existence.

2.5 Subsumption of Space

The point of departure for the logical ascent of Marxist geography has thus been identified: *pristine space with the attributes of absolute and relative.*

Society is defined as relationships among more than one person, within which those dominating and dominated contest one another. Although space does not enter as a logical element in the beginning, human beings in society "act and situate themselves in space as active participants" (Lefebvre, p. 294).

The dialectical logic that explains a society acting and situating itself in space is *space subsumption,* which is a part of the logical journey of ascent. The subsumption of space bridges the moments of society and space into a dialectical unity. On one side of the dialectic stands the moment of pristine space, an objective existence created through the "Big Bang"; on the other side, there stands society.

Space and society, both existing initially as *Ding an sich* (a thing in itself), then relate to one another to form the socio-spatial relation in "unity within separation". The dialectical process then transcends itself into *Ding für sich* (a thing for itself). Here, society explicitly incorporates space through the production of space, whereby society and space enter an explicit dialectical interrelationship. Space then becomes capable of bringing the raw materials, finished products, business or "culture" together and enveloping them. Space, then, becomes "less and less neutral, more and more active, both as instrument and as goal" (Lefebvre, pp. 410–411).

This "contradictory character" of space, Lefebvre pointed out, can be put into a dialectical order following Marx's concept of the formal and real subsumption as he put forward in the last chapter.

This dialectic proceeds in two phases:

1. **The formal subsumption** of space. Here, as society deepens its relation with physical space, an increasingly hostile and contradictory relation develops between them.
2. **The real subsumption** of space. Eventually, quantity transforms into quality; that is, the space and society that exist to each other *an sich* lead society to transcend this contradiction purposefully through transforming the physical space itself. This is the process of the *real subsumption of space*, or what geographers and

sociologists referred to as the "production of space". This is an attempt by society to transcend the contradictions of the space formally subsumed.

In the dialectical process of transcendence, society negates the adverse properties of the formally subsumed space and creates a new configuration of space that overcomes the contradiction and supports its needs and requirements. In the theoretical framework of this book, the production of space is taken to mean the process of subsuming space by the power of reconfiguring the property of pristine physical space.

2.6 Space and Power

a. Definition of power

Society is not homogenous but its structure is normally organised in a vertical power structure, while people struggle to achieve a more egalitarian and empowering society.

Max Weber defined power as "opportunity existing within a social relationship which permits one to carry out one's own will *even against resistance* and regardless of the basis on which this opportunity rests" (Weber, 1962, p. 117, emphasis mine); that is, the concept of power presupposes a society in which some people dominate others despite the spontaneous will of those placed under domination. When individual A is restricted in free spatial movement by person B despite A's will, and A has to accept the order set by B to confine A within a certain closed space unwillingly, then B has power over A. The most important entity that emanates power is, of course, the state, with its apparatus to enforce its power, such as the police, courts and prisons. State power sets up a legal system which forces the people to abide by it despite their will. Money is another significant source of power, as Harvey (2012, p. 159) states: "there shall be no serious challenge to the absolute power of money to rule absolutely."

Space itself also has physical power that imposes certain processes upon society, since physical and material relations have their own causal mechanisms. For example, carbon dioxide emissions cause warming of the global atmosphere and raise the levels of shorelines, which may force removal of built facilities, against the will of their owners. The struggle against this physical power of space is in fact the crucial moment in the subsumption of space, which shall be discussed in detail in the following chapters.

b. The processes of space subsumption as an act of power

State and economic power is exerted over space, as Sack states, "human spatial relations are the results of influence and power. Territoriality is the primary spatial form power takes" (1986, p. 26). Indeed, here, "territoriality" should be taken to mean the whole configuration of space produced by society, since the territoriality "is the means by which space and society are interrelated" (ibid, p. 5).

In a class society, those in power play dominant roles in the process of space subsumption. Those in power deploy superior political and planning apparatuses to transcend the formally subsumed space into configurations that facilitate its domination. In the market of neo-classical economic theory, absolute space is supposedly bounded infinitesimally to guarantee the perfect independence of atomic economic agents, spatial integration is infinitesimally perfect, perfect information is available instantaneously everywhere and market transactions occur instantaneously. This is the ultimate picture of space subsumption that neo-classical economists implicitly assume.

Those in power attempt to impose *representationion de l'espace*, in Lefebvre's terminology, onto the subordinated people. It is indeed "the dominant form of space" which "seeks, often by violent means, to reduce obstacles and resistance it encounters" (p. 49).

Sack (1986, p. 17) depicts this power relation using an example of a secretary in an office, as follows:

> Each desk is designed as a work station. The secretary is employed to type, and part of the working agreement is that he be in the office at his desk for a specified number of hours per day, five days a week, fifty weeks a year. The modern secretary may leave the work station. But if he does so often and without permission he may be in violation of the work agreement and stand to lose his job. Even if the secretary is permitted to leave his work station his movements within the buildings are likely to be restricted. He cannot simply wander into any office. Perhaps the only areas to which he is free to go are those designed for "traffic" corridors, and those open to "workers" such as lavatories and coffee rooms.

On the other hand, the higher-level managers can command the much wider space of the company premises and move about the office space freely without restriction. The managers impose the spatial restriction corresponding to the secretary's allowed authority in performing the duties of the company.

In sum, the extent of space subsumption differs depending on one's position in the hierarchy of the company's power structure. As long as the secretary wants to be a part of the company's social structure, he or she must accept and abide by this limited command on space created by the power structure of the company. Indeed, "territoriality for humans is a powerful geographic strategy to control people and things by controlling area.... *Territoriality is a primary geographical expression of social power*" (Sack, 1986, p. 5, emphasis mine).

c. Social struggles against power in space subsumption

Subordinate people may then challenge this dominant way of subsumption and attempt to alter it. If a subject does not want to accept the subservient position in this power structure, or contests it, then there will be social sanctions from those who have power, which would likely trigger a concomitant socio-spatial struggle. This is repressive space, containing symbols of "bureaucratic and political authoritarianism", as in phallic monuments and arrogant towers (Lefebvre, 1991, p. 49).

However, subordinated people also have their own logic in subsuming and producing space. In defying this space of repression, the subordinated classes or ethnic groups attempt to produce their own configurations of space, which challenge the dominant *représentation de l'espace* to break the spatial "straitjacket". Lefebvre called the space thus produced *les espaces de représentation*, or space that represents the subordinated people.

In a class or multi-ethnic society, therefore, the outcome of the real subsumption of space is ridden with contradictions. The methods to subsume space then become a contested terrain. A class or group which manages to produce a configuration of space must constantly make "efforts to establish or maintain" (Sack, 1986, p. 19) the territory and boundary by enforcing control over the boundary. The existing subsumed space can therefore manifest the class nature of the society: the class structure itself and the struggles against it.

Lefebvre (1991, pp. 23–24) depicted the socio-spatial struggles between state power and the people opposing it in the late twentieth century. The situation has indeed been aggravated and continued in the current century:

1 The state is consolidating on a world scale. It weighs down on society (on all societies) in full force; it plans and organizes society "rationally", with the help of knowledge and technology, imposing analogous ... measures irrespective of political ideology, historical background, or the class origins of those in power.... Space in its Hegelian form comes back into its own....
2 In the same space there are, however, other forces on the boil, because the rationality of the state, of its techniques, plans and programmes, provokes opposition. The violence of power is answered by the violence of subversion.... State-imposed normality makes permanent transgression inevitable.... Though defeated, they live on, and from time to time they begin fighting ferociously to reassert themselves and transform themselves through struggle.
3 Nor has the working class said its last word. It continues on its way, sometimes underground, sometimes in the light of day. It is not easy matter to get rid of the class struggle, which has taken myriad forms not accounted for by the impoverished schema usually so referred to—a schema which is nowhere to be found in Marx even if its devotees claim to be Marxists.....

d. The potential to displace the struggle to a multi-scalar configuration

In some cases, however, the struggle may be compromised by shifting or displacing it to a multiple-layer configuration of spatial scales, each of which is dominated by a different class or group. The interrelation between the scales then becomes contradictory and struggle-prone as the relationship between the scales represents that of the classes or groups concerned.

Multiple contesting classes or groups may co-exist simultaneously, with their struggle shifting to an inter-scalar conflict against each other. That is, at a certain period, multiple layers of space make the struggle shift to a spatial configuration. Harvey demonstrated this case using two different scales centred around London (1985, p. 160): "the 'city' of London [or a leading centre of global finance] has a far different kind and range of influence than the [local municipal socialism-oriented] Greater London Council."

Thus, Lefebvre affirms, "(social) space is a (social) product." Space is "a means of control, and hence of domination, of power" (p. 26). Nevertheless, he did not forget to add that space "escapes in part from those who would make use of it. The social and political (state) forces which engendered this space now seek, but fail, to master it completely." The process of subsuming pristine space by power produces social space as a social product; yet it creates a paradoxical outcome of producing the antithesis of contested spatial configuration. For example, as discussed later in this book, attempts to recover spatial contiguity create an uneven configuration of space; yet the configuration of the networks is open for the deployment of the alternative spatial strategy. These configurations of space can be deployed by those placed under domination to counter the dominant social power.

Chapter 9 of this book investigates various antitheses of space production and concomitant spatial strategies with which subservient people can wage a struggle against the dominating power. At this moment, there are two important strategies worth mentioning. The first concerns a piece of space excluded from the attempt of social power to master space: "stray space". Such space can be used as the launch pad for insurgent activity while the dominant power attempts to put it under surveillance and suppress it. The second is "scale jumping", a spatial strategy commonly used by local insurgents to counter the power, where the spatial extent is confined within a territory. Chapter 9 provides a longer discussion on these.

References

Alexander, H. G. (1956). *Leibniz-Clarke Correspondence* (Philosophy Classics). Manchester University Press.

Bartels, D. (1969). *Zur wissenschaftstheoretischen Grundlegung einer Geographie des Menschen.* Franz Steiner.

Harvey, D. (2012). *Rebel cities: From the right to the city to the urban revolution.* Verso.

Harvey, D. (1973). *Social justice and the city.* The Johns Hopkins University Press.

Keynes, J. M. (1946). Newton, the Man. http://mathshistory.st-andrews.ac.uk/Extras/Keynes_Newton.html (Accessed 27 July 2021).

Lefebvre, H. (1991) (translation). *The production of space.* Translated by Donald Nicholson-Smith, Wiley-Blackwell.

Marx, K. (1971) (translation). *Theories of Surplus-Value. Parts I–III.* translated by Jack Cohen and S. W. Ryazanskaya. Progress Publishers.

Marx, K. (1973) (translation). *Grundrisse.* Translated by Martin Nicolaus. Vintage Books.

Marx, K. (1977 and 1981) (translation). *Capital.* Vols. 1–3 . Translated by Ben Fowkes. Vintage Books.

Max, J. (2012). *Concepts of Space.* Dover Publications.

Smith, N. (1984). *Uneven development.* Basil Blackwell.

Sack, R. (1986). *Human territoriality: Its theory and history.* Cambridge University Press.

Sack, R. (1980). *Conceptions of space in social thought: A Geographical perspective.* University of Minnesota Press.

Weber, A. (1929) (translation). *Alfred Weber's theory of the location of industries.* Translated by Carl Joachim Friedrich. University of Chicago Press.

Weber, M. (1962) (translation). *Basic concepts in sociology.* Translated by H. P. Secher. Peter Owen.

Chapter 3
Absolute Space

Contents

Abstract This chapter explains the dialectics of absolute space and its subsumption into society. The homogenous and all-embracing nature of pristine absolute space has the social implication of liberty, equality and fraternity. It also has homogenising physical power. This nature of absolute space works negatively and thus functions adversely to a society based on separation and discrimination between different social groups and exertion of power over the subservient groups. A new configuration of space is then produced; those in power attempt to negate the contagious and homogenising nature through bounding or imposing boundaries. Fragmentation and differentiation of absolute space thus ensue.

3.1 Introduction

This chapter explains the process of subsuming pristine absolute space and the dialectical contradictions embedded in the process of its real subsumption.

As discussed in Chap. 1, the process of the formal subsumption of space entails contradictions. In the dialectical process of transcending the contradictions, a heterogenous configuration of space emerges. Since society has its own power structure of domination and subordination, the configuration thus produced inevitably incorporates the power of domination to contain the contestation.

F. Mizuoka, *Subsumption of Space*, Contributions to Regional Science,
https://doi.org/10.1007/978-981-97-7560-6_3

3.2 Negation of Society by Absolute Space and Externalities

a. Use of absolute space by the body and society

The subsumption of pristine absolute space by economic and social groups and subjects involves three moments:

First, a body occupies space. "Each living body *is* space and *has* its space: it produces itself in space and it also produces that space" (Lefebvre, p. 170). The physical dimension of a body immediately determines the extent of absolute space occupied, and the occupation must be exclusive.

Second, the development of bodily energy generates the action of the body with its spatial scope and necessitates the extension of the area in which the energy is exercised and the extension of space occupied. How and to what extent a social group is involved in subsuming absolute space depends on the technical conditions of the group occupying its space. Space that cannot be utilised under this technical condition is left without being subsumed.

Third, to make the occupation of a piece of absolute space solid and perpetuating, the groups must aim to occupy a piece of space with considerable density, have intense interactions among the members and the area of the space must remain uncontested by other social groups. If the social integration of the members within the domain is weak and the area of space is only sparsely filled, then the marginal reduction or expansion of the frontier may not bring about large social and economic consequences, but vice versa, the consequences can be large.

b. Social properties of pristine absolute space

Pristine space is, initially, "an empty space, a space that is primordial, a container ready to receive fragmentary contents, a *neutral* medium into which disjoined things, people and habitats might be introduced" (Lefebvre, p. 308). The contagious property of absolute space is neutral to society, accepting any substances and any acts equally without discrimination. The pristine absolute space of these properties provides a container that supports the existence of economic bodies, groups and the market mechanisms themselves.

The isotropic property of absolute space allows any subject in absolute space to move in any direction. Together with the isotropic and contiguous properties, absolute space provides a physical relation that makes everything enclosed therein homogeneous.

All subjects and people placed in absolute space move towards homogenisation. The properties of pristine absolute space generate unlimited connectivity, which offers a physical potential to strengthen the dominating class, yet also to empower the subordinated people.

The connectivity and concomitant homogenisation in contagious space would eventually create convergence and equilibrium among the members, agencies or economic variables across space. Together, they have implications for society, especially around the concepts of *Gesamteigentum* and the significance of commons to society.

Indeed, in a positive sense, the expanse of absolute space is a basic existence condition for all economic and social groups. It universally encloses all objects and provides a physical foundation for all objects, subjects and social relationships. It provides human subjects and groups with a container for any phenomena, including the physical equipment necessary for production, living and leisure of the human body itself. It also serves as a container of social relations: the political apparatus of state and the macro-economy. Absolute space thus physically supports production activities and the existence of a state apparatus. Thus, absolute space embraces a social connotation similar to the slogan of the French Revolution: *liberté, egalité, fraternité*.

c. Absolute space comes into contradiction with the social structure

The equalising property of absolute space can disturb existing social relations. Economic and social actors and social groups have their own social structure or organisation. They always strive to maintain their own identities by avoiding any social interference.

This structure and property of society must therefore be defended from any disturbance by other entities or groups. The tendency of absolute space toward homogenisation of objects and social relations contained in the contiguous absolute space has therefore a *negative effect* on economy and society. The pristine property of absolute space, therefore, comes in contradiction with a society because it interferes with the integrity of a social group or a market agency that strives to make itself wealthier than others and that does not want wealth to flow to those who suffer from poverty.

Interference in absolute space threatens the property of the subject or groups and eventually leads them to collapse. Here is a contradiction between the tendency of absolute space toward physical homogenisation and the intention of the social subjects, classes and groups which want to maintain property, power and integrity.

d. Externalities: absolute space destroys the market

This tendency towards physical homogenisation brought about by the contiguous property of absolute space comes in contradiction with the tendency towards homogenisation through the equilibrating process of the market economy. The economists saw this problem as a challenge to their theory, and thus devised a new category.

Neo-classical economic theory presupposes that all economic relations operate through competition among economic agents, leading to an equilibrium in the market. However, when a good is placed within the equilibrating tendency of absolute space, a physical relation without money as the medium of transaction outside the market emerges between economic agencies.

When a service or good is in a contiguous space, an individual or economic entity within the spatial range of a service or good can enter the area in which the service or the good is available without paying a fee and consume the good automatically. Therefore, it is impossible to collect the fee for the service of a lighthouse, and the trade relation between market agents and the concomitant process towards market equilibrium are not established. The tendency of absolute space to homogenisation creates physical relations outside the market, disrupts the equilibration process of the market economy through competition, and gives rise to market failure.

Economists identified this contradiction and call it an *externality*. A commodity of specific property called *public goods* has been set up to deal with this contradiction, which the economists call market failure.

Consider the socio-spatial externalities in the relationship between a sailboat and a lighthouse, which is a seminal example in textbooks of public economics. Goods possessing properties for which "it costs nothing for an additional individual to enjoy their benefits"; and "it is generally difficult or impossible to exclude individuals from the enjoyment" are termed *pure public goods* and the government is invited to supply the good to avoid an undersupply of this good (Stiglitz, 2000, p. 80). Operating the lighthouse incurs expenses for construction, power, maintenance labour and so on. On the other hand, ships may be wrecked if there is no lighthouse. Yet, a market agency operating the lighthouse cannot collect a fee for its service from the operator of a ship each time it navigates into the spatial range in which it benefits from the lighthouse because of the spatial contiguity of the area it serves.

Here, one can discern the problem that the physical action of homogenisation in absolute space is not compatible with the action of equilibration or homogenisation through the market competition.

The market mechanism would collapse in other cases, too. In market competition, it is the level of price which determines whether goods are supplied to the market or not. Here involves the "degree of indivisibility" that James Buchanan (1968, p. 174ff) addressed. The supply of a good implies that each good is physically divisible, such as a car or music CD. If goods are physically indivisible (e.g. digital music data transmitted through the Internet), then those who do not pay the price cannot be excluded from its use without, for example, restrictions through user authorisation with a password. For the Internet in general, there is no mechanism for price determination through competition for each piece of information.

Goods, services and information become "indivisible" when they are spatially contiguous. The contiguity of the formally subsumed absolute space makes it impossible to produce and supply goods through the market mechanism. This is the clear manifestation of the contradiction created by the contiguity of absolute space in a society with a market economy.

In the case of such indivisible or spatially contiguous goods, supply normally occurs through taxes collected by the government from all its members. If the group which needs the service spreads nationally, then the national tax system collects the cost for the service, whereas if it is local, the local tax system does it. For the Internet, information providers earn profits through advertisements, not through direct monetary transaction with the users.

To save the market economy, market fundamentalists have taken up the disturbance to the market system by the indivisibility of spatial contiguity and physical power of equalisation, and addressed it in the famous "tragedy of the commons" by Garrett Hardin (1968). The problem of the "commons" can be solved, unless public goods are created, only by denying the existence of a contiguous space called "the commons", and by dividing it into closed individual slots.

3.3 Types of Territoriality Produced Through the Subsumption of Absolute Space

There are two types of territoriality produced through the subsumption of absolute space: *Wirkungsraum* (literally, "functional space" in German) and action space.

a. *Wirkungsraum* or "field of employment"

Absolute space embraces any subject or object without distinction and welcomes it amicably and warmly. In this egalitarian freedom of absolute space, a subject occupies a piece of it and encloses it such that all economic and social entities need the exclusive occupation of a plot of absolute space on which it stands. This type of bounded space can be called, after Marx, the field of employment (*Wirkungsraum,* functional space). The term "field of employment" derives from Marx's passage of *Capital*: "the earth itself is a universal instrument... for it provides the worker with the ground beneath his feet and a 'field of employment' (*locus standi, Wirkungsraum*) for its own particular process" (Vol. 1, pp. 286–287). The connotation of the term "field of employment" could be expanded to a generic concept referring to a part of the earth's surface, or exclusively bounded space in general.

The most fundamental reason for the necessity of *Wirkungsraum* lies in the sheer size of the human body. The human body, which shoulders economic and social activities, has a certain spatial dimension. If humans were as small as ants, then their homes and land would be just like a child's toy. Correspondingly, the earth would seem much larger to the ant-sized human. A family needs "minimal living-space, as quantified in terms of modular units and speed of access; likewise minimal facilities and a programmed environment" (Lefebvre, p. 316). This space must be occupied only by family members, either nuclear or extended, because a family is the fundamental social group generated out of the biological process, and kinship ties require strong privacy. A family needs their field of employment, too.

For work, an employee needs at least one exclusive desk space to work efficiently in an office. Space for installing machinery and equipment is necessary to carry out a production process. In agriculture, arable land on which to grow crops must be exclusively occupied. For outdoor recreational activity, skiing and golf need to occupy the space for ski runs or fairways.

The examples given above intend to illustrate how space is occupied with exclusivity. In all the above illustrations, once a subject occupies a plot of space having a certain area, another subject can no longer occupy that same plot. The expansion of space required for space allocation is called the area demand of economic and social activities (*Flächenaspruch*) in German social geography (Maier et al., 1977, p. 28).

The need for *Wirkungsraum* also applies to the state power. According to Georg Jellinek (1905, pp. 381–420), a German political scientist and jurist, the three fundamental elements of a state are: state territory, state power and the people. A state can exercise its power only when it secures its space or field of employment of it. Additionally, space is an essential condition for social relations.

In a market economy, for an economic agent to acquire the title of *Wirkungsraum*, the agent must bid for the right by bidding rent by money and pushing aside other entities. Here, the title to the *Wirkungsraum* is determined by the power of money. Given the cost to occupy space, the right to the working space becomes a "necessary evil" for the economy and society in a market economy.

b. Action space

The second of these types is *Aktionsraum* or action space. This term originates in German social geography (Maier et al., 1977, p. 61).

A spatial process may actually be carried out such that different social groups use the same spatial domain at different times, which therefore does not necessitate the standing occupation of a piece of space. Some are durable, yet others are transient (Lefebvre, p. 388). For example, moving cars occupy a road space, where many drivers and passengers co-exist while moving in the same direction. This is *action space*.

There is little exclusivity in action space, since a car constantly on the move occupies road space only momentarily, without occupying a piece of space constantly. Within the extent of the area, space for passage function (e.g. streets, highways, railway tracks or airports) must be secured and stably occupied, but the subjects who pass through the space are constantly changing. The space for traffic and communication which is not occupied continuously by a specific subject is called *right of way*. Different agents or activities can share the right of way, and more than one action space can overlap one another. However, the action space presupposes the right of way available to the general public, or space not occupied exclusively by any particular group or individual.

Action space in itself does not have a fixed boundary, but its limit is delineated solely by a physical constraint: the *distance-decay effect*. Sack (1986, p. 19) therefore excludes action space from his definition of territory, by stating that it is "simply descriptions of the geographic extent of activities in space". Therefore, action space involves no political power that delimits the extent of the territory. The limit of action space is delineated not by the dominating power but by physical distance, which is a property of pristine relative space before subsumption. For example, *commuting area*, a space where workers move between places of working and living, has a roughly circular shape with a radius of about 50 km from the metropolitan centre.

Action space, created by the repeated mobility of agencies, activities or phenomena radiating from the core across the absolute expanse of space towards the periphery, is typically nodal in its configuration, as in the case of commuting or emitting of pollutants. Physical distance, the property of pristine relative space and spontaneous mobility play crucial roles in the production of territory.

Action space occurs for a much larger number of causes: selling labour power every day to the job location, commuting to schools, migration either permanently or temporarily, commodity trade, including contraband, activities of multinational corporations engaged in production or finance, military deployment, tourist activities, and the area within which families are customarily related by marriage. Actions of non-human origin such as the movement of pollutants or of animals and plant seeds in an ecosystem also form action space.

For flow to occur, all the public must be granted the general right to utilise the public right of way, such as the street or highway or the right to use public transportation. Contrary to the *Wirkungsraum*, the removal of exclusivity in the public right of way and acquisition of the right to transportation are the condition for the rights to the action space.

Physical distance spontaneously generates a distance-decay effect of the actions in which the intensity of social or market interaction in the social space diminishes in inverse proportion to the square of distance.

Space for the actions and socio-economic activities of humans and movements across the expanse of absolute space manifests a propensity towards spatial equilibrium and egalitarianism, to seek an opportunity for higher wages or profits.

The movements of the body or physical substances in each action space have a unique spatial range depending on the nature of the substance and trips, as assumed in central-place theory, where the spatial ranges of goods are determined by the order of goods, with higher-order goods commanding wider action space than lower-order goods. The physical extent of a range is rather flexible and can change for various reasons including improvements in the means of transportation, growth or decline of the local economy, fluctuation of land prices in the city centre and changes in perceptions of physical distance among the agents concerned.

The range of action space is subject to the distance-decay effect, discussed in more detail in the next chapter (p. 49), as well as the physical and economic capacity of each actor or social group to overcome the distance in relative space. The higher this capability, the greater the potential for expanding its action space towards the frontier. If it is low, then the distance-decay effect attribute of relative space hinders the spread of the frontier. The strength of the distance-decay effect, and hence the extent of action space, then depends on the disposable resources of the subject or group occupying the territory and the labour or disposable income that can be allocated to overcome the distance. The range therefore inevitably becomes specific to the income levels of the social groups.

Other kinds of spaces possess a similar property to action space. Herding nomads share grazing space, where many herders and livestock freely go in and out. This type of land occupation is called *Gesamteigentum*. In this type of space, the space takes on the property similar to action space. Additionally, in course law, the right of innocent passage in which a ship can pass a foreign territorial sea peacefully so as not to harm the coastal state is recognised, as is the case of action space in marine transportation.

c. Action space in the market and abstract space

Money and goods flow across space, but there is no need to continuously occupy that space, so the space of circulation in a market economy also constitutes an action space. A market area is a typical action space in which money is a measure of commodity value and a means of trading goods. Money as the "means of payment" (*Capital*, Vol. 1, p. 232ff.) is abstracted from any concrete commodity, and enables goods to flow freely in the action space of the market. It makes commodity circulation universal by separating it from specific space and time, and transforms action space into *abstract space* (Lefebvre, p. 49).

Money as the means of trading goods makes barter unnecessary. The owner of a commodity need not find a person nearby who owns another commodity that he or she wants for an exchange. In an abstract space, concrete labour such as clothing production and steel production invested by respective economic entities are all abstracted away with a universal "price" which is impersonated through embodied human labour. All the concrete attributes of production evaporate.

The position of production is one such attribute that is to disappear. In this way, the action space of the market, consisting of the networks of innumerable flows of commodity transactions, stands before us as an abstract space, or absolute space without the properties of location, individuality and concreteness of economic entities.

The ideology of the market economy which supports abstract space is homologous to the ideology of the French Revolution, which supported the freedom and right of businesses of *le Tiers-État* consisting of merchants and handicraftsmen. This freedom in the market is manifested in the market competition equilibrium using dollar bills as "ballots". Thus, the nature of pristine absolute space is homologous to that of the abstract space of the market, which has the universality of abstract human labour.

However, the problem is that in abstract space, money mediates the process towards equilibrium. The more money an economic entity possesses, the more "ballot sheets", which represent monetary power, it can cast. Therefore, individual market entities need to have money to exercise power to win in the battle for equilibrium. Thus, the action space of the abstract market is dominated by those who have enough money to apply impersonal coercion to those who do not. In this respect, abstract space contains the power relation; thus abstract space is clearly different from pristine absolute space.

Abstract space, which neoliberalists praise, is the conqueror of globalism, as Richard O'Brien (1992) calls it, the "end of geography". To end geography, and to further strengthen abstract space, the WTO and the IMF eliminated tariff barriers, ensured the right of goods and money to flow through the world unconstrained by instituting high-porosity borders without controls, and encouraged the world as a whole to function more fully in the "invisible hand" of markets.

Thus, when abstract space controls the extent of absolute space, all the concrete physical and personal rights in absolute space are replaced with the impersonal and reified power of money, which alienates the human being who expresses it concretely.

3.4 Bounding: The Real Subsumption of Absolute Space

Absolute space has the property of being an infinitely continuous homogeneous and isotropic expanse. It has also the potential to equalise the phenomena contained within it. Once subsumed formally into society, absolute space functions both positively and negatively in relation to it. However, if this egalitarian ideal is detrimental to the power that dominates absolute space, then "territorial circumscription" (Sack, 1986, p. 37) is required to establish power effectively and more efficiently.

A body itself cannot exist, and a social group, which is a collection of human bodies, also cannot exist without appropriating *Wirkungsraum* exclusively. If the action space is not at disposal, then the spatial circulation of commodities will not occur and people cannot obtain the goods and services to meet necessities. In this sense, the exclusiveness in occupancy and utilisation of space constitutes the fundamental rights for the subject and groups to exist, survive and take social actions. Bounding is thus called for.

a. The principle of occupation of *terra nullius*

When a person or group continuously and spontaneously occupies a specific space for an extended period, a customary right to the space arises for the occupant, as long as absolutely no one contests it. A typical example is *the principle of occupation of terra nullius* in international law. In the colonial era, this concept was used to legitimise the acquisition of colonies by European powers, which did not recognise the right of indigenous peoples to their land. Even if the space was occupied by indigenous peoples, Europeans occupied and colonised the territory, and resorted to ethnic cleansing to extinguish the indigenous peoples, or would rule them as oppressed peoples, except in cases where the space was truly landless.

This principle of *terra nullius* does exist in daily scenes as well. For example, a passenger who sits on a train seat in a non-reserved carriage has a moral right to remain seated until he or she leaves the seat spontaneously. If all the seats are full, then a passenger cannot have a seat and must stand.

A state could claim sovereignty over "unclaimed" land that did not belong to any other imperialist power, so long as the people of the particular state were long engaged in economic activities and had effective control over the land, again provided that there was no contestation from other parties or from conquering the indigenous people. Title to territory or the exclusive power over a plot of absolute space was thus acquired.

b. From frontier to boundary

Ladis Kristof summarised the socio-spatial process that would take place with two powers intending to occupy the same place as the process of the transformation of frontier to boundary.

According to Kristof (pp. 270–271), "frontier" is "not a legal concept", but rather "a manifestation of the spontaneous tendency for growth of the ecumene [habitable zone]" or "the margin of the inhabited world". In short, it is the frontier where the spatial actions of economic and social processes advance into the pristine space of wilderness. On the other hand, "boundary" is the concept appropriate to the present-day state, defined as "a certain well-established limits (bounds) of a given political unit, and all that which is within the boundary is bound together", which is a suitable concept for the coexistence of a contemporary "state as a sovereign spatial unit".

Kristof explains the transformation from frontier to boundary as the former frontier is "defined more and more exactly until there is … an exact borderline".

The most fundamental process in forming the frontier is the direct and spontaneous expansion of the social and economic subject or social group which occupies *Wirkungsraum*. The frontier is not so much a clear line but a zone of transition where the intensity of socio-economic action is weakening. Beyond that, the space is left pristine. Therefore, in an expanding frontier, there is no conflict with other neighbouring subjects or groups. Real subsumption requires only the labour involved to make the wild pristine space habitable as socio-economic space. The position of the frontier is directly regulated through the spontaneous action of the society and economy of the social group. The frontier expands and contracts arbitrarily corresponding to the spatial expanse of action, and has the possibility of changing its position and form.

The development of society generally augments the intensity and density of space utilisation as to the three moments explained earlier in this chapter and expands its frontier. As is typically seen in the development from a hunting and gathering economy to agriculture and concomitant population growth and the more variegated desire of the people, the density and intensity in use of space increase. As technology advances, and the communal mode of production gradually shifts to a mode of production where the vertical class relationship between those dominating and dominated becomes clear, the intensity and frequency of social interaction for the purpose of exchange of goods and control increase, and the range of activities expands through development of transportation and communication technologies and the increase of social surplus. Furthermore, the spatial dimensions of the means of production and consumption that regulate the spatial dimensions of equipment for their actions grow, which dictates the size of the required piece of absolute space.

When the frontier dominates, the frontier as the circumference of a territory is only an a posteriori consequence of the process of space subsumption by individuals or social groups. As economic and social processes that create frontiers change, the alignment of frontiers expands accordingly. Eventually, two neighbouring frontiers may come to overlap. Here arises the need for the real subsumption of absolute space.

For a piece of absolute space to be consolidated for exclusive occupation of a group circumscribed by a frontier in pristine absolute space, the group must aim for social and spatial integration and close interactions that are self-contained from others and have a large number of members with a high population density in the piece of absolute space to occupy.

Unless the social interaction within the domain is weak and land use in the area is extensive, the marginal reduction of the frontier can bring about large social and economic consequences. In this case, the propensity of agents and groups to maintain and even expand the frontier increases. The development of society and its economy generally works in the direction of expanding the consolidated area and concomitantly pushing the frontier outward. Technological development for the use of space, intensifying social and economic interactions for market transactions and political domination, increasing population, and accumulating social surplus all contribute to the denser use of space. This progress is typically seen in the development from a hunting and gathering economy to agriculture and concomitant population growth.

Through this process, multiple social groups try to share the same spatial position. Now, what lies beyond its frontier is no longer pristine space but "the strange, the foreign, the hostile" (Lefebvre, p. 294) groups, which already exclusively occupied another piece of space. The economic and social processes that create the edge of the exclusively occupied areas now emerge accordingly.

c. Bounding and production of territory

Through this process, a situation occurs in which the frontier of a piece of space is no longer pristine space but abuts other social space already exclusively used by other social, economic power or social groups.

When two neighbouring frontiers overlap, the exclusivity and heterogeneity of the neighbouring areas provide exogenous spatial constraints on socio-economic processes. If each subject or social group involved in the contact of two overlapping frontiers happens to share the same idea as to the delineation of the space of their functioning, a boundary is peacefully established according to their common idea. However, such a situation rarely occurs spontaneously, and if they do not share the same spatial idea, either friendly or hostile social interaction arises between the social groups that occupy the two abutting areas. The frontiers can be adjusted in one of the following three ways.

The first is to attempt the hierarchical overlapping of the two pieces of absolute space at the same points, to create a polymerised socio-social relationship through warring conquest and concomitant domination, so the areas that touch each other are brought into the layers of vertical scales at the same points. This socio-spatial process polymerises into a multi-layered spatial scale through hierarchical articulation of social groups. In this case, the frontier of the superior power is extended into the previously separate piece of space that the now subordinated power occupied exclusively. The social group occupying a piece of space is conquered and its power and freedom are restricted by the dominant power that expands its own frontier. The dominant group develops into the superior power that subordinates the group with less power in the same piece of space, creating the layers of the bounded space at which a dominant/subordinate relationship develops. If a group with stronger power can push its frontier in this way, the formerly independent area will become subordinate, turning into a so-called "periphery" of the core, dominant area. Whether or not such articulation of social attributes actually occurs depends upon the relative strength of power of the two groups and the intensity of warfare between them. In short, the contradiction created by the constraints of spatial resources are transcended through the transformation of social relationships. In this case, it is important for the dominant power to keep the subordinate group dependent through various means of political suppression to avoid insurgencies. This is exactly what happened during the era of imperialism as "the distinct characteristic of this period [of imperialism] is the final division of the earth … final in the sense that the colonial policy of the capitalist countries has completed the partition of the unoccupied land on our planet…. there can only be a redivision, that is, a transfer from one 'possessor' to another" (Lenin, 1964, p. 79).

Second, if neither group in the abutting areas does not use the space so intensely, or if the group is not well integrated, then the frontier may be polymerised such that the same piece of space is jointly occupied, even if the two social groups are not explicitly articulated.

Third, however, if the integrity of the group with intense interaction exclusivity in a piece of space is to be retained and the transformation of society into that of dominant and dominated is to be avoided, the frontiers cannot extend into the other. Instead, a direct collision of the frontiers will ensue. Social interaction then becomes necessary to determine a fixed spatial boundary which divides the two adjacent pieces of absolute space under the mutual agreement of both parties. This social interaction may involve an adversarial war, followed by a peace treaty which includes clause of boundary delineation. The frontier, which had been the outer limit of the action of the social group occupying the area now disappears and transforms into a boundary; that is, a fixed line in space.

Therefore, for the exclusive and stable occupancy of a territory over a long period, the parties on both sides of the border must agree on the exact position of the boundary, and the entity occupying the territory must have strong enough power to repel intrusions into the territory. The military power of defence is an example, and its international legal backing offers the right of individual self-defence, which is legitimised by the United Nations Charter. In other cases, the residents themselves prevent others from intruding into their own residential areas by force.

Once a boundary is established, it turns to a spatially reified power and an instrument of domination and control. If people are free to move across absolute space, society may collapse, if only because the subordinated will leave society spatially to gain access to fresh ground elsewhere and obtain the status of independent and liberated persons. The dominant power therefore attempts to seal off the boundary to retain and reinforce the hierarchical social structure. In ancient Japan, for example, when the Asiatic mode of production was prevalent, the emperor's government forced the "public men" (serfs) to work in rice cultivation. These men were confined to the "public land" (state-owned paddy fields and the irrigation systems built by the emperor's government) configured in a grid-like rectangular spatial pattern called *jōri*. The serfs, not satisfied with their labour and life conditions, acted on their own to escape the public land, or the territory under the domination of the emperor, and moved to another territory, specifically the private estates of large temples. Serfdom under the Asiatic mode of production thereby collapsed.

The dominant power, therefore, needs to annihilate the free and egalitarian property of pristine absolute space. This is a *bounding* or the act of delineating a boundary around a piece of the unlimited expanse of pristine absolute space or the process of the real subsumption of absolute space. The vertical social relationship is thereby clearly secured. It is nothing but the production of "determinate and hence demarcated space" which "embraces some things and excludes others". It "negates and denies" (Lefebvre, p. 99).

Through bounding, the dominant power is now able to exercise exclusive power over a piece of absolute space. By setting up artificial boundaries across pristine space, the dominant power obtains a spatially exclusive container: *territory*. The "delimitation becomes a territory only when its *boundaries* are used to affect behaviour by controlling access" (Sack, 1986, p. 19, emphasis mine).

Territory is a piece of space produced by a person, economic entity or social group by bounding a pristine absolute space for the purpose of producing a container that helps it maintain its integrity. Sack defined territory as the area created by the act of "territoriality", which is "the attempt by an individual or group to affect, influence, or control people, phenomena, and relationships, by delimiting and asserting control over a geographic area". Through the act of producing "territoriality", the power transcends the contradiction between the homogenising nature of physical space and vertical power relation. Territory thus becomes a spatial piece in which power can exercise exclusive control. Anthony Giddens (1985, p. 120) stated that "a nation-state is … a bordered power container" within which a sovereign, or one who holds power, exercises exclusive political domination. This is the negation of the contiguity of absolute space by state power, or *the process of real subsumption of absolute space*.

Once boundaries are established, the right to occupy the territory must be maintained legitimately and the right has to be defended against the claim by or trespass of others. Boundaries will be systematically structured by the state power in the form of records in the land registry and cadastral maps, which constitute the legal system of landed property.

However, the validity of this system is recognised only among the people who are under the state power that enforces this legal system. For example, in colonial North America, the "purchases [by the European] may not have been seen as such from the Indian's perspective, settlers believed that the [bounded] territory was needed … in a form that other Europeans would recognize" (Sack, 1986, p. 143). Since the legal system of bounding is valid only among the Europeans but did not respect the indigenous rights of the Native Americans, the colonial settlers used violence to defend their "right" to space. Here, an overlapping spatial scale and the corresponding dual means in defending the existing territory emerge simultaneously: the legal system that dominates the spatial order of Europeans and the violence towards indigenous people.

Through this institutionalisation of the boundary, the economic and social group inside the bounded area acquires its own "container".

d. Effect of the physical structure of the boundary

Once the boundary is established, it stands as a new exogenous framework for individual actors and social groups, maintained by power and physical materials. "Territoriality establishes control over area as a means of controlling access to things and relationships" (Sack, 1986, p. 20).

The physical structure of the boundary reflects the various social and economic relationships of the social powers that occupy only the territories demarcated by the boundary. When members of the society on each side of the boundary need to be prevented from trespassing on the other side, a physical barrier is built along the boundary.

There are various physical forms of barriers, ranging from boundary stones that simply indicate the existence of a border and attempt to prevent movement across a border only in the social context, such as legal or moral custom, to those that use military technology, such as the border of the former East and West Germany, which made stiff attempts to prevent crossings by installing minefields, ferocious dogs and monitoring stations with armed soldiers.

The bounding of territory simultaneously enhances exclusivity and social homogeneity within a bounded territory and generates difference between the two areas. Sack drew attention to the significance of this process in cities during the advent of capitalism. In pre-capitalist European cities, "work, education, healing, and family were for the most part spatially intertwined" (Sack, 1986, p. 170); while in the capitalist era, "legal and social power must be brought to bear to exclude all other activities from a place, and to organize every last detail within it to serve the purposes of these activities." This territorial partitioning was necessary to support spatially the control of the fragmented production process by capital while "locking workers in the factory from dawn till dusk" and isolating "the worker from other workers" and preventing "him from comprehending the true relationships between labor and capital" (Sack, 1986, p. 178).

The border exists as an external hard spatial frame around the economic and social processes. Once space is bounded, resources are enclosed and individualised to each person, political power or economic entity, and each entity is responsible for managing and cultivating its own resources. The excessive utilisation and eventual depletion of resources in the bounded territory may thereby be avoided. In addition, for the sellers and buyers of goods or services being spatially enclosed, the services or goods are of no avail to those who do not pay costs. Thus, no externalities shall occur.

The production of bounded territory is therefore the spatial manifestation of the freedom in the market economy; and bounding is a market-based solution to the "tragedy of the commons". For a social group, if the space is bounded to contain the group, it is possible to prevent members from leaving or strangers from entering, and the independence and integrity of the society are firmly maintained.

In this way, parcels of space with finite extent are cut from the infinite extent of absolute space, and the parcel is used as a container to ensure the independence of a market subject or social group. Hence, each parcel of space comes to bear a specific economic and social connotation compared with others in each *territory*. Territory comes to take on the property and meaning of the entity or group contained in the territory. Once a territory is produced, the properties of pristine absolute space, such as the universal propensity for homogenisation, become operative *only within* the range of the partitioned territory.

The social groups and economic agents on both sides of a boundary can keep the integrity of the social groups or economic agents by producing territories and confining group members or economic elements within those territories. If a territory is created to contain the market entity, then the economic entity can physically secure independence and minimise the impact of externalities. Within a territory, there is strong tendency of homogenisation in contrast to other territories, and economic relations and social power can play with less interference from others.

Infinite pristine absolute space is thus transformed into a mosaic of territories, called "*collective absolute spaces*" (Harvey, 1985, p. 79). Collective absolute spaces carry within them the dialectical relationship of "separation in unity" between the contiguity of formally subsumed absolute space and artificially bounded space.

Lefebvre also pointed out (p. 193) that boundaries establish social relationships. The production of the spatial mosaic of territories is therefore also the process to etch each social structure and power relation demarcated by the boundaries onto pristine absolute space. Since the act of bounding is done through exercise of power by a class, group or individual, the territories thus produced have proprietorship. The production of space is therefore the creation of the spatial mosaic of private property.

Territory is mostly etched with the configuration for normal use. This is the spatial expanse of territory for the activities of a social group secured and controlled by the dominant social power that created the spatial configuration.

Yet, some part of the territory may be left unintegrated by the dominant social group or beyond its control due to, for example, lack of resources for spatial integration or strong opposition from dissident groups. This is the issue of "stray space", which is discussed in the Chap. 9 (p. 154ff) of this book.

3.5 Boundary Porosity

a. The porosity and creation of spatial scales

The social groups and subjects contained in a territory cannot be confined nevertheless within the prescribed "iron frame" because they need interaction across the boundary with other social groups or individuals. No territory is completely sealed off and isolated from transactions with others. If there were such a territory with absolute boundedness, it would be a contradiction, similar to the phrase "market agents without transactions" and would deny the existence of the economy and society, which is based on mutual acts with other entities and groups.

The bounding should not therefore mean an absolute ban on movement through the boundary, since "territoriality must contain a form of communication" (Sack, 1986, p. 21). Therefore, a body or group contained in a territory must "establish different degrees of access to people, things, and relationships" (Sack, 1986, p. 20) to those in other neighbouring territories. The boundary must therefore have some sort of permeability. This is the *porosity* of the boundaries between the surrounding territories that enable the interactions between subjects or groups in the adjacent territories.

There is a strong correlation between the interrelationship of the occupants of adjacent territories and the porosity of boundaries. In some cases, they come to peaceful agreement in a treaty to amicably control the porosity together; in other cases, control is carried out unilaterally in hostility. The latter especially applies to high-income states, in which state power fends off the flow of labour migration generated spontaneously through economic incentives to seek to maximise its income.

The porosity of boundaries can be manipulated. The power to manipulate porosity rests in those dominating the territory, which is normally the state apparatus. For example, to engage in foreign diplomacy, international trade, deployment of foreign labourers and global tourism, a state must allow some degree of porosity of the boundary under its control. The porosity is thus selective and manipulated. The state power allows anyone beneficial for sustaining and promoting the domination to pass through the boundary but denies anyone who is considered detrimental to itself.

To control porosity, the state power enacts various immigration and trade legislation and establishes immigration and customs and passport control posts on the border so that the persons or goods which the dominant power considers undesirable are denied entry or departure.

In short, control of the porosity of a boundary is a spatial way for the state to exercise its power over the people. In the medieval period, the spatial movement of people was checked by the state with checkpoints on major highways. In contemporary society, the borders of states are manipulated by the issuance of employment visas to create an optimal labour market within the macro-economy of a nation. Unskilled workers are selectively allowed into the macro-economy to supplement a labour shortage, while more skilled workers and managerial people can move across the global space. This control of porosity creates different extents of action space to different people, depending on the skill levels and social groups to which they belong as under the New International Division of Labour (Chap. 8). The actions endorsed by the inherent freedom and equality embedded in pristine absolute spaces are thereby negated by the dominant state power and transformed into a multi-layered spatial configuration.

Porosity can also be physical, unrelated and not controlled by the political power. Sometimes the boundaries can be physically overcome independent of the will of the state power. Boundaries drawn on a map do not automatically guarantee the independence of the entity contained within them. Due to the physical openness that results from the boundary not sufficiently rigidly constructed as a physical barrier, the autogenous porosity of the boundary occurs through spontaneous action of the people. The continuity beyond the boundary is thereby created spontaneously.

In all, porosity creates a contiguous space of action on a higher spatial scale than the existing territory. The contiguity created at a higher-order spatial scale thus annihilates or at least abates the fragmentation that has existed in the collective absolute spaces at a lower spatial scale. Then privileged people can act freely over the contiguity of this higher-order spatial scale, and there emerges a clearly layered vertical configuration of space.

This type of multi-layered scale serves the will to dominate and rule of a specific political or economic power. By adjusting porosity and controlling the expanse of the territory artificially, the dominant power creates the spatial configuration most ideal to it.

b. Weaker bounding, trespassing across borders and emergence of a higher-order scale

When the power controlling the porosity that allows crossing of the boundaries is weak for some reason, trespassing actions across boundaries will become ubiquitous, and the physical barrier of boundaries may weaken, resulting in the production of a more significant higher spatial scale. Especially when the boundary is not constructed as a physical obstacle to movement, it is impossible to contain the movements of anything across the boundary physically. A physically porous boundary may rekindle the tendency of contiguity and the egalitarian attribute of absolute space beyond the constraints of bounded spaces. It may eventually lead to the collapse of the power structure that bounded absolute space.

If the social entity at one side of the border does not recognise the existence of the boundary and attempts to alter the delineation of the boundary by force, it invades the territory and endangers the integrity of the economic and social organisation.

If the entities occupying the territories are too weak to defend the boundary, then the present configuration of the territories must be defended and legitimatised through an umbrella power at higher spatial scale, which comprehensively keeps the whole configuration of space as it is, with the judicial system set by the state power. The Registry, an institution of state power, officially records the exclusive possession of territory using real estate registries and cadastral maps. A person who trespasses across a porous border without authorisation of the umbrella power will be subject to criminal charges and arrest and prosecution by this umbrella power.

In terms of international relations, the concept of collective security, in which an invader is subjected to military sanctions by a coalition of nations, falls under this category. In these cases, the need to maintain a particular organisation of collective absolute space at a certain scale creates new instances at a higher spatial scale, such as the UN Security Council, NATO or other forms of international military coalitions. A nation that severely infringes and attempts to distort this system of collective absolute spaces composed of national territories is bound to be sanctioned by these new instances. A typical case in point is Russia invading and attempting to wrest away a part of the territory of Ukraine.

In sum, the inviolability of a territory and the integrity of the entities within them are, first, ensured by an agreement on the boundaries between the agents occupying adjacent territories or by their own force; second, if this is not sufficient, the power at higher spatial scale controls the entire configuration of the territory or the collective absolute spaces overall. If neither is sufficient, then the occupancy of the territory will always be subject to challenge from others and threats of physical aggression, and market entities or social groups will not be able to reproduce economic or social stability.

3.6 Conclusion

When absolute space is subsumed to society formally, absolute space, with the pristine property of homogenous and isotropic contiguity and expanse, comes in contradiction *an sich* with the society in which division is structurally installed.

To transcend this contradiction, the state or economic power must produce a new spatial element: a boundary or spatial division. By providing a boundary, the homogeneity of pristine absolute space is negated to the shape of the divided society and market economy. This is the process of producing territory or the real subsumption of absolute space. Absolute space now takes the *für sich* form.

The boundary circumscribing the territory contains in itself a contradiction: it has to negate penetration while also allowing it, since the society contained within the territory must interact with other societies outside the territory. The boundary must therefore be porous. Those in subservient positions can of course take advantage of this porosity to evade the grip of the state power. If only it contains this socio-spatial struggle and retains the class society, the dominant power that contains the territory must keep a tight grip on the boundary's porosity. This contradiction is nevertheless transcended through the production of a higher-order scale with contiguity, across which the power to control the porosity of all boundaries in the lower scale prevails (Fig. 3.1).

Through these dialectical socio-spatial processes, the egalitarian homogenous pristine absolute space transforms itself into a configuration that matches the structure of society and the economy: a heterogenous configuration with division, porosity and overlapping spatial scale. This would be the *an und für sich* outcome of the subsumption of absolute space.

These spatial dialectics are initiated by power over the territorial expanse. It is closely related to the struggle to contest the dominant power in the process of space production and the spatial configuration that results. More on this topic in Chap. 9.

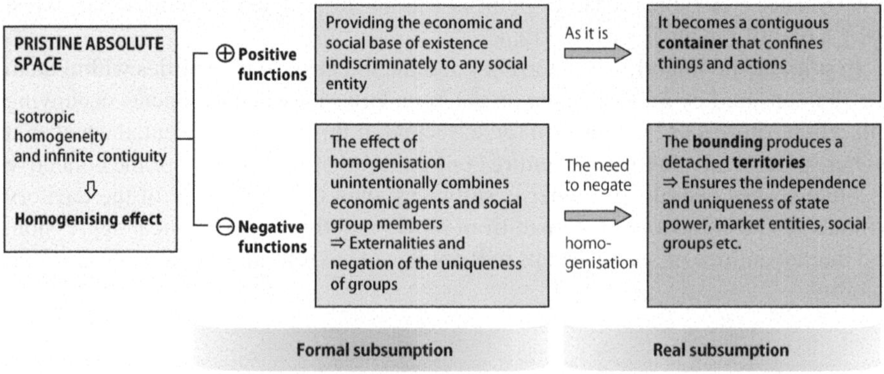

Fig. 3.1 Subsumption of absolute space. *Source* Mizuoka ed. (2002), p. 71

References

Buchanan, J. M. (1968). *The demand and supply of public goods*. Rand McNally.
Giddens, A. (1985). *Nation-state & violence*. University of California Press.
Hardin, G. (1968). The tragedy of the commons. *Science, 162*(3859).
Harvey, D. (1985). *The urbanization of capital: Studies in the history and theory of capitalist urbanization*. Johns Hopkins University Press.
Jellinek, G. (1905). *Allgemeine Staatslehre*. O. Häring.
Kristof, L. K. D. (1959). The Nature of Frontiers and Boundaries. *Annals of the Association of American Geographers, 49*(3).
Lefebvre, H. 1991 (translation). *The production of space*. Translated by Donald Nicholson-Smith, Wiley-Blackwell.
Lenin, V. I. (1964). (translation). Imperialism, the latest stage in the development of capitalism. In George Hanna (Ed.), *Lenin Collected works*(Vol. 22, pp. 185–304). Translated by Yuri Sdobnikov. Progress Publishers.
O'Brien, R. (1992). *Global financial integration: The end of geography*. Cengage Learning EMEA.
Maier, J. et al. (1977). *Sozialgeographie*. Westermann.
Marx, K. (1977). (translation). *Capital*. Vol. 1. Translated by Ben Fowkes. Vintage Books.
Mizuka, F. ed. (2002). *Keizai Shakai no Chirigaku* (*Geography of Economy and Society*). Yuhikaku.
Sack, R. (1986). *Human territoriality: Its theory and history*. Cambridge University Press.
Stiglitz, J. E. (2000). *Economics of the public sector* (3rd ed.). W. W. Norton.

Chapter 4
Relative Space

Contents

Abstract This chapter involves the dialectics of the relative space in parallel to the absolute space in Chap. 3. Pristine relative space separates substances by distance and has dividing and individualising properties. Those in power in society exploit these properties in executing power to promote discrimination and segregation in society. The divided space thus functions in contradiction to egalitarianism and fraternity. The distance property of relative space needs to be annihilated through agglomeration and spatial integration, constructing the network to transport and communicate. However, there is a paradox in that the network becomes sparser, and the spatial configuration becomes more uneven as transportation travels at higher speeds.

4.1 Properties of Relative Space and Its Dialectics

a. Introduction

The relative attribute of pristine space has properties that contrast with those of absolute space, specifically in terms of the relative spatial relation of objects with two fundamental properties: identification of the individual positions and isolation with distance between the positions. In other words, relative space works for individualisation and distantiation. Because of these properties, relative space functions as a discrete segregating and discriminatory division in society.

Society and the economy are substantiated and work properly only when every member is interconnected through communication and transactions. Once formally subsumed, relative space also functions both positively and negatively for society and the economy. Positively, relative space provides society with the spatial designator for

F. Mizuoka, *Subsumption of Space*, Contributions to Regional Science,
https://doi.org/10.1007/978-981-97-7560-6_4

the interaction of people and economic transactions. Persons cannot conduct social or economic interactions without determining a unique spatial point. Negatively, distance blocks such interaction. The distance-decay effect limits the spatial expanse of social and economic activities, making interaction difficult. Hindered by distance, agencies are fragmented and isolated from one another and society or the economy is pushed to the verge of collapse. Relative space is therefore more amenable to such concepts as differentiation, isolation and sometimes discrimination in society.

The distance-decay effect also affects political and social relations. As one moves from the core of control to the periphery, the power from the centre weakens in inverse proportion to the square of distance; whereas the social forces opposing this control may strengthen relatively on the periphery.

b. Relative space as a means of identifying positions

As every point on the Cartesian surface is uniquely defined, relative space provides the function of spatial differentiation and identification. This attribute contributes to the social property of relative space, which is the identification of the positions of things. It is essential for society to identify the location of market trade and to establish social contacts among the members of a group. Every object and subject, and various relations among them, as well as the mutual actions generated, are given separate spatial uniqueness and individuality. Economic and social processes are established and accomplished only with this property of relative space.

For example, the market economy forms a global abstract space mediated by money, which is universal and impersonal. Yet, individual transactions are carried out by independent economic agencies, with every transaction being always unique. Trade in goods takes place at discrete locations agreed by both parties. Therefore, in the global market space, a distinct location must be identified. Both parties, the sellers and buyers, must agree in advance exactly where and when to trade the goods.

The daily purchase behaviour of convenience goods by consumers and the purchase of the means of production by producers occur through a tacit agreement on the position or place at which to trade goods. For social interaction to take place, a specific position (and time) to act must be agreed between the parties involved in the activity. For example, they make a promise with their friends, saying, "5 p.m. at xx railway station, south exit".

Sometimes, the multi-layered system of territories is used to indicate uniqueness. For example, for "xx station", there is an implicit knowledge among the persons concerned about the relative position between the railway line on which the xx station is located and the city centre. Location can also be identified by a nested system of administrative divisions designated with place or street names and house numbers.

A system of relative space for the individualisation of economic and social actions is essential for the representation of "abstract metrical space" (Sack, 1986, p. 85), yet it has been created by the political power. For example, the abstract and geometrical designation of the land of the New World had the clear purpose of "conceptually and then actually clearing the land for Indians, the geometric lines of territorial authority become sweeping space-clearing and maintaining devices for territorially instituting communities" (Sack, 1986, p. 134). The passing of the prime meridian through the Greenwich Observatory in the outskirts of London, the British capital, symbolises the former global hegemony of the British Empire. The relationship between economy and society gives economic and social meaning to individual positions and their names. For example, a place name such as Beverly Hills came to represent a high-class residential area, and a street called Champs Élysées eventually implied that the shops there are of a higher class.

c. Distance

Marx explained the concepts of distance in their most pristine form as follows:

> a dimension of space, it is a certain length which may as well express the distance of two other things besides those compared... In speaking of the distance of two things, we speak of their difference in space. Thus we suppose both of them to be contained in space, to be points of space. Thus we equalise them as being both existences of space, and only after having them equalized *sub specie spatii* we distinguish them as different points of space. To belong to space is their unity (*Theories of Surplus-Value*, Part III, p. 143).

Between two different positions, there exists a distance, an attribute of relative space. Reciprocal acts are to be carried out over distances.

Interaction over the distance connecting two positions rapidly decreases, in line with the gravity model of the law of gravity in physics. In this model, the amount of reciprocity F between the two positions is

$$F_{ij} = \frac{M_i M_j}{D_{ij}^q} \cdot k. \tag{4.1}$$

This formula indicates that the amount of traffic and communication between i and j is proportional to the product M, which is the masses of the points of origin and destination, for example, the population at each position, and inversely proportional to the q power (Usually $q = 2$) of distance D between the two positions. q and k are parameters defined by factors such as the technical nature of the means of transport and the intensity of the propensity to travel. As distance increases, the economic and social interaction between i and j rapidly weakens. This is called the *distance-decay effect*.

The degree of the distance-decay effect varies according to several factors. First, the amount of information distributed per unit production cost increases as the negotiation transaction and technical information become more complicated, and even if it is the same distance, it incurs a higher cost. Thus, overcoming the distance determined by the modes of transportation also changes the extent of the distance-decay effect (Scott, 1990, pp. 48–52). The most primitive way of overcoming distance is direct physical interaction, such as personal face-to-face contact or voice communication. This leads to agglomeration, which is discussed in Sect. 3 of this chapter.

d. Position and distance used to distinguish and discriminate

All positions in relative space are separated by distance and individualised. Therefore, "distance" leads to spatial differentiation. As mentioned in the previous chapter, Buchanan tells us that goods traded need to be divisible. With distance between the masses, each good is individualised one to another. The distance that individualises the goods traded is the fundamental spatial condition for the market economy.

In a hierarchical social group, relative space is positively subsumed by those in power to distinguish and discriminate those governed. In the old Japanese family system, for example, the order of seats in the main family meeting room was determined by expressing the rank of the members in the family, using the position of the fireplace as the nodal point. In the urban segregation of North America, richer social groups prefer suburban settlements to distance themselves from poorer social groups living in the inner city for sake of proximity to jobs. The inner city is further spatially divided into those in poverty and specific ethnic settlements. Such individualisation of the living environment affects the real estate market.

e. Place

Thus, the positions of relative space have their own contextualised meanings in economic and social connotations. They offer a common understanding among the market members of the spatial position where the market transaction is to be carried out and demonstrate a common understanding of the position of the mutual actions of the social group.

The position that has thus become socially meaningful in this repeated action is called a *place*. "Places are defined by the occurrences of activities" (Sack, 1986, p. 63). "Place" can thus be defined as "a spatial position containing social or economic meaning given through repeated actions". It is different from the common use of the word, such as "The parking lot is full and there is no place to park my car."

The concept of "place" is similar to the concept of "territory" in that the attribute of pristine space comes to have the meaning of economic and social relation. However, the territory is the outcome of the negative subsumption of the contiguity of absolute space, while "place" is the outcome of the positive subsumption of the position of relative space. Therefore, place is different from territory in that it does not necessarily assume the concept of spatial expanse.

Repeated occurrences spontaneously give the place a name, which is the designator of a particular place and carries meaning. A place name sometimes manifests the history of the place and is placed in the social value spectrum ranging from prestige to stigma.

f. The relation between absolute and relative spaces

In determining the boundary and ensuring the exclusivity of territory, each point of the boundary must have a different positional identification. For the bounding of absolute space to be successful, each point of the boundary needs to have a positional property, which is a property of relative space. Thus, a territory, a product of the subsumption of absolute space, simultaneously contains the attributes of relative space. Each position of relative space with individuality is therefore a causal element of the individuality of a territory.

As discussed earlier, the infinite extent of pristine absolute space ultimately converts to the organisation of the *collective absolute spaces*, which is defined as the aggregate of the fragments of the mosaic of this region. Through the production process of this configuration of space, the homogeneity, ubiquity and isotropic nature of absolute space comes to possess the attribute of relative space.

On the other hand, spatial movements across space require certain portions of absolute space as a right of way: "the movements of peoples, goods, and ideas require society to set aside roads and the like for transportation and to disallow other activities from taking place on them" (Sack, 1986, p. 25).

Relative space also determines the inherent range that a social entity possesses in performing its action, which defines the size of the action space. Yet, as discussed in the previous chapter, political power can sometimes set a boundary to the freedom of movement, for example, using an international border control post, beyond which labour cannot move.

4.2 Annihilation of Space

By keeping physical distance, social relations can be isolated and divided, leading to their collapse. The proverb "out of sight, out of mind" expresses this ingeniously. The property of distance thus supports segregation and discrimination, or in short, division in society. To transcend the contradiction between this property and society, the distance among the social entities must be overcome. That is, this negative effect must be negated by society with produced space, through production of physical means of transportation and communication.

This is a process of the real subsumption of relative space. It is carried out through the deployment of technology and investment in transportation and communication.

a. "Annihilation of space by time"

The attempt of capitalism to subsume pristine relative space in real terms through the application of science and technology, investment and new forms of social organisation is summarised in Marx's famous phrase the "annihilation of space by time".

The process of commodity realisation, C'-M', normally takes place at a point spatially different from the location of the labour process. Space is the arena in which the private ownership of the means of production is connected with the social nature of the production activity. In this sense, space becomes involved in the capital circulation only after the commodities are ejected from the privately owned labour process. By this stage, the direct process of interaction between humans and nature, from which humans produce a commodity with use-value and capitalists exploit surplus value, is already over. Although the commodity ejected into space no longer creates fresh surplus value, the reduction of circulation time appears to the eyes of capitalists to be the original source of surplus value. This creates an incentive for capitalists to efficiently subsume space in a real manner, in this case, to annihilate space.

In the capitalist economy, even if capitalists attempt to annihilate space by the most efficient available means, they cannot do so without the people and activities which, given social demand, spread across space, even though it necessitates the means to annihilate space. This is a contradiction inherent in the subsumption of space by capitalism, of which capitalists are superficially aware. To their eyes, space is a stumbling block delaying the time when the commodity is actually sold, one that necessitates an additional expense: transport cost and cost for maintaining the continuity of production. The aim of capitalists to engage in competition to subsume space in the real manner, or to annihilate space is, therefore, to minimise the effect of this stumbling block, thus connecting the labour process with realisation processes in spatial terms as directly as possible.

Marx calls this process "annihilation of space by time". He states:

> The more production comes to rest on exchange value, hence on exchange, the more important do the physical conditions of exchange – the means of communication and transport become. Capital by its nature drives beyond every spatial barrier. Thus the creation of the physical condition of exchange – of the means of communication and transport – the *annihilation of space by time* – becomes an extraordinary necessity for it. (*Grundrisse*, p. 524, emphasis mine)

As such, "space is the envelope of time." Distance constitutes an important element of the use-value of space in the property market: "the distance from the purchaser's dwelling-place to other places, to centres of commerce, work, leisure, culture or decision". Time therefore determines the use-value of space (Lefebvre, p. 339).

Nevertheless, the above arguments of Marx suggest that the topic of the "annihilation of space" should be treated in a wider context. Space related to the circulation process of capital is a stumbling block for capitalism. Time is one means of annihilating this stumbling block; but, as the discussion of this chapter reveals, these means are not exhausted by time alone. For example, Marx himself discusses another means of annihilating the effect of space in Chapter 15 of *Capital* Volume 2: the continuity of production through spatial agglomeration. Hence, we use the more general term "annihilation of space", rather than Marx's own more restrictive phrase, "the annihilation of space by time". The "annihilation of space" is one attempt by capitalists to transcend the contradiction inherent in private production as a part of the social division of labour.

Though capitalists compete most harshly against one another using every available option, the privately owned labour process and social demand are always separated by pristine space, a physical existence which can never been annihilated altogether. The annihilation of space does not therefore mean disappearance of the physical space. Thus, the "annihilation of space" is the everlasting, yet never accomplishable imperative of capitalism. Capitalists continued, are continuing, and will continue their endless competition against one another to annihilate space, imagining that their private production is instantaneously realised as a part of the social divisions of labour.

b. Annihilation of space and acceleration of capital turnover

Under a given technology, transportation vehicles travel at a certain speed with a certain capacity across space. The potential limit of annihilating absolute space is therefore subject to the time required to connect two different points separated by a certain distance, and the volume of commodities or number of people that can be transported at one time. Thus, the attempt to annihilate space is manifested in the transport and communication technologies of a given period. For this reason, society tries hard to stretch this limit in space subsumption by improving transportation and communication.

The capitalists with more efficient means of annihilating space end up with more surplus value. They can earn extra surplus value if their efficiency is above the average. The competition for ever more efficient ways to subsume and annihilate space originates from this inter-capitalist rivalry for a larger amount of extra surplus value. The picture of this competition is similar to that for more innovative technology. If the options available for capitalists to annihilate space are finite, however, the competition for more efficient means to subsume space ends up with an equilibrated spatial configuration of capitalism.

In a capitalist economy, the higher the velocity of the turnover of capital, the more frequently the same labour process can be repeated, hence the more surplus value can be exploited. Marx states:

> the more rapid the circulation, the shorter the circulation time, the more often can the same capital repeat the production process. Hence, in a specific cycle of turnovers of capital, the sum of value created by it (hence surplus value as well, for it posits necessary labour always merely as labour necessary for surplus labour) is directly proportional to the labour time and inversely proportional to the circulation time. (*Grundrisse*, p. 627)

As circulation time grows "with the distance of the market from the point of production" (*ibid*, p. 672), capitalism must attempt to reduce this by improving technology, especially in terms of the "development of means of communication". Marx points out "the demise of old centres of production and the emergence of new ones with changes in the means of transport and communication" (*Capital*, Vol. 2, p. 327).

With this improvement, the turnover of capital accelerates, and the "commodity proceeds rapidly from one phase to another" (*Theories of Surplus-Value*, Part III, p. 285); thus, more surplus value can be exploited. The attempt of the real subsumption of space by improvements in the means of communication and transportation is, therefore, one of the crucial imperatives of capitalism, "a condition for production based on capital, and promoted by it *for that reason*" (*Grundrisse*, pp. 524–525). In other words, the means of transportation and communication are "the general conditions of the social process of production", and large-scale industry, on which the capitalist mode of production is based, necessitated "a revolution" in the means of transportation (*Capital*, Vol. 1, p. 506). Without this revolution, the attempt by capital "to tear down every spatial barrier to intercourse; that is, to exchange, and conquer the whole earth for its market" (*Grundrisse*, p. 539) is never possible. Only by improving the means of transportation and communication can capitalism annihilate space with time. Alternatively, the result is the same: capitalism can "reduce to a minimum the time spent in motion from one place to another" (*ibid*).

The means of transportation and communication with insufficient capacity, for example, those "handed down from the period of manufacture" immediately became "unbearable fetters" as soon as large-scale industry starts producing a large volume of commodities. For this reason, large-scale industry had to make these means for annihilating spac adapt "themselves to the mode of production... by means of a system of river steamers, railways, ocean steamers and telegraphs" (*Capital*, Vol. 1, p. 506).

The most common way of extending the limit of space annihilated and reducing the time allocated for the circulation process is raising the labour productivity of the transport industry by applying more innovative and efficient transportation and communication technologies. Thus, in periods of greater prosperity, capitalists put the "same passion which increased production... into the building of railways" (*Capital*, Vol. 3, p. 534).

Additionally, an increased frequency of service of the means of transportation provides another way of reducing the circulation period overall. This type of improvement in the means of transportation does not accelerate the actual speed at which a commodity travels over space. However, reducing the size of "circulation reservoirs" at a warehouse and so on helps to accelerate the velocity of the turnover of capital.

> Successive quantities of goods can now start their journey at more closely spaced intervals and thus arrive on the market one after another without accumulating in great masses as potential commodity capital until they are actually dispatched.... By this distribution of the reflux over several successive periods. The total circulation time is shortened, and hence also the turnover (*Capital,* Vol. 2, p. 328).

To stretch the limit imposed by the use-value of the commodity itself, capitalists continuously attempt to improve the means of transportation, not only in terms of its velocity, but also its quality. The invention of lorries or freight railway cars with refrigerating facilities or those that absorb excessive shocks during transportation is another outcome of the attempt of capitalism to annihilate space. Nevertheless. to the extent that these technologies have time limit to hold a commodity fresh, there is always a finite limit for capitalism in its attempt to annihilate space.

While capitalists strive hard to annihilate space, the relative differences in pristine space remain:

> improvement in the means of communication and transport shortens absolutely the period in which commodities migrate in this way, but it does not abolish the relative difference in the circulation time of different commodity capitals arising from the migration, or even that of different bits of the same commodity capital that migrate to different markets. (*ibid*, p. 327)

As long as improving transportation technology results in the accelerated velocity of capital turnover between the points connected, the relative ratios of the distances between various places do not change. However, the nature of the newly developed transportation technology may alter the relative ratios of the distances to a considerable degree.

For example, the construction of a high-speed railway (e.g. shinkansen or TGV) or motorway, which can only be accessed at designated stations or interchanges, can deprive the points along the conventional rail or road of the existing locational advantage. The introduction of the airplane totally eliminates the locational advantage arising from the proximity to land transportation lines. Hence, Marx states that "relative distance may … be displaced by the development of the means of communication and transport in a way that does not correspond to the natural distances which explains the demise of old centres of production and the emergence of new ones with changes in the means of transport and communication" *(ibid)*.

c. Contradictions in the annihilation of space

Although the capitalists attempt to annihilate space by the most efficient available means, they cannot do so without the people and activities that spread over an expanse of absolute space, providing effective demand. This is a contradiction inherent in the subsumption of space by capitalism; and capitalists are superficially aware of this. To their eyes, space is a stumbling block delaying the time at which the commodity is actually realised (sold), and necessitating an additional expense: transport cost and the cost to maintain continuous production. The aim of capitalists to engage in competition to subsume space in real terms, or to annihilate space is, therefore, to minimise the effect of this stumbling block, thus connecting the labour process with realisation processes in spatial terms as directly as possible.

The existence of physical space persists however much science and technology develop. However hard capitalism tries to annihilate space, space, which separates private production physically from social demand, still stands before it. This situation is common to every barrier to capitalism. Marx states:

> from the fact that capital posits every such limit as a barrier and hence gets *ideally* beyond it, it does not by any means follow that it has *really* overcome it, and since every such barrier contradicts its character, its production moves in contradictions which are constantly overcome but just as constantly posited. (*Grundrisse*, p. 410)

4.3 The Real Subsumption of Space by Eliminating Space Itself: Agglomeration

a. The rationale for spatial agglomeration

Alternatively, capitalism can resort to "the combination of various branches of industry, that is, the establishment of centres of production for particular industrial branches" (*Theories of Surplus-Value*, Part III, p. 285) and the consequential elimination of pristine distance itself between two points where the different stages of the metamorphosis of capital occur.

The quickest way to do this is to physically "annihilate" distance itself, to move closer to produce spatial agglomeration. The market centre in a medieval town is a typical case in point: the function of trade is made to agglomerate in a single place.

Here, the flow of information is more complete and the time in the trade of the goods can be minimised. Physical agglomeration is the geographical approximation of a one-point world in economic theory.

The agglomeration of production at one spatial point facilitates the social division of labour:

> The division of labour requires the concentration of means of subsistence and means of labour at particular points … [or] *concentration*, the gathering together of more at a given point, and of *relatively* more [means of labour] compared with the numbers of workers brought together there. (*Theories of Surplus Value*, p. 271, emphasis original)

In this respect, Marx points to the empirical fact that "in industrial areas there are machine-builders who build whole factories for the manufacturers" (*ibid*, Part II, p. 488). According to Marx, this "close succession of the production phases which the commodity itself or its ingredients have to undergo", is a typical feature of modern industries, which produce the "speed and mass-scale of reproduction" that "likewise reduce the necessity for the accumulation of commodities in the reservoirs" (*ibid*, Part III, p. 286). This gives rise to what Allen Scott (1990, pp. 36–37) found to be the "vertical disintegration" of the production process and agglomeration of the vertically disintegrated branches of manufacturing.

Marx points out "an accelerated concentration of both the centre of production and its market" due to "particular ease of commerce and the consequent acceleration in the turnover of capital" (*Capital*, Vol. 2, p. 328). For Marx, therefore, the most important cause of the spatial agglomeration of industries is the reduction of circulation time by annihilating space. The imperative of capitalism, annihilation of space, also works here, but in an inverse way: the annihilation of time by space.

In other words, the most important underlying factor for the emergence of a spatial agglomeration of industries is that two different labour processes are connected through closer proximity. Through closer locations, the commodity *C* produced by the labour process carried out by capital *A* enters the productive consumption (*mp*… *P*) of the other labour process carried out by another capital *B* without the hinderance of spatial distance. This interrelation, the most basic to the creation of a "productive centre", can be expressed in terms of the circuit of production capital:

$$P\ldots C'\text{—}M'\text{—}C\ldots P\ \textbf{[Capital } \boldsymbol{A}\textbf{]}$$

$$P\ldots C'\text{—}M'\text{—}C<^{mp}_{L}\ldots P\ \textbf{[Capital } \boldsymbol{B}\textbf{]}$$

Agglomeration annihilates distance for the "X" shaped portion of the two labour processes *P* of capitals *A* and *B*.

b. Localisation and urbanisation economies

The agglomeration densifies action space and the concomitant reduction of production cost through localisation of industries is caused by what Alfred Marshall termed the "external economy" (pp. 266 and 271–272), which has a different connotation from what we discussed earlier using the lighthouse example in Chap. 3. Scott (1983, p. 8) states:

> location theory begins with the idea that locators will always seek to mitigate the costs of distance by adopting locations that reduce linkage length as far as possible. Suppliers will want to locate close to demanders in order to maximize demand, and demanders will want to locate close to suppliers in order to minimize c.i.f. prices.

According to Edgar Hoover (1937, pp. 90–91), there are two types of cost saving through agglomeration: "localisation economy" and "urbanisation economy". The former arises from the formation of homogeneous industrial clusters in close spatial proximity to the same sector; the latter is produced by the agglomeration of different sectors. Consequently, the efficient production of infrastructure necessary for the production and distribution of goods and the management of production of non-basic goods to meet the demand within the city will be reduced. In a localisation economy, the vertical disintegration goes gradually forward due to the reduction in size of action space and easiness in the face-to-face contacts.

Conventional location theory incorporates the localisation economy. Alfred Weber noted it as "a factor of agglomeration":

> the workshops of auxiliary industries form one technical whole with the main plants for which they work. And this technical whole naturally functions best if its mutually dependent parts are locally concentrated, because then all the parts remain "in touch" with one another (Weber, 1929 edition, p. 129).

According to Weber, "an agglomerative factor" is defined as "an "advantage" or a cheapening of production or marketing which results from the fact that production is carried on to some considerable extent at one place" (*ibid*, p. 126). Thus, under Weber's understanding, through the localisation of the mutually dependent parts, production cost decreases and producers gain an "advantage". What seems to be the localisation or agglomeration of the same sector is, therefore, nothing but another type of agglomeration of various labour processes created by vertical disintegration.

The inter-capitalist competition for extra surplus value by cheapening individual values through abbreviation of the circulation time is the major driving factor for agglomeration. The social process of "cheapening of production" as the determinant of agglomeration is, in fact, similar to the process inducing technological change in capitalism.

The abbreviation of the circulation time through agglomeration is sometimes accompanied by the vertical and horizontal disintegration of the labour process, as Scott (1990, pp. 52–58) discussed in detail. A factor for more than one producer of the same sector to agglomerate at the same location is the benefits from the interlinkages between them. Seen from the scale of national economy, this process creates more heterogeneous mosaic of spatial uniquenesses.

In this sense, despite Weber's attempt to construct a "pure theory … of location" (*ibid*, p. 12) claimed to be "independent of any particular kind of economic system" (*ibid*, p. 10), Weber unconsciously introduced the social process of capitalist competition from the back door by taking "cheapening" as the crucial moment for location and agglomeration.

The urbanisation economy covers spatial agglomeration due to the benefit of "remaining in touch" in general, through attempt to annihilate pristine space directly. The shortening of circulation time leads to a higher turnover of capital, and thus more intensive use of fixed capital, which then contributes to the cheapening of cost-price.

c. The dialectics of agglomeration

The direct elimination of pristine distance, or the agglomeration of industries, always accompanies its antagonistic counterpart, the need to subsume a larger extent of pristine space in real terms, by means of transportation and communication. If agglomeration would provide capital with a cheapening of individual value to the infinite degree, the process of agglomeration would continue forever. In this case, all the social demand on the uniform plane would be supplied from a single productive centre at which all the labour processes in society are located. This is, however, not the case in reality. As capital agglomerates at a spatial point, it creates adverse effects simultaneously. Agglomeration increases the distance from the productive centre to the market, which slows down the velocity of capital turnover and increases the amount of circulating capital necessary to maintain the continuity of production. Excessive congestion of various labour processes can be more detrimental than expeditious to the "annihilation of time by space"; at a certain level of agglomeration, therefore, it gives way to dispersal. The successful annihilation of space in one form inevitably increases the necessity to annihilate more space in another. Capitalism has to negotiate this "knife's edge" of the equilibrium in annihilating space. The "capitalist optimum" of scale of production and market area is nothing but the result of capitalism's having negotiated this "knife's edge".

For instance, the localisation of the same sector at one spatial point would inevitably bring about a larger market area and a longer period of circulation. In this case, the capitalists producing a commodity in the same sector might be better off locating in a dispersed fashion, reducing the amount of space it needs to subsume and realising their product around their smaller market area in a shorter circulation period. Among these labour processes there is a relation of commodity exchange where space has been annihilated. Through this type of agglomeration, capitalism again exploits the development of the productive forces of the social division of labour.

In contrast, short distances generate the *neighbourhood effect*, and a certain social space can be established between entities located at short distances. This is the occurrence of place-based communities (*Ortsverband*).

4.4 Spatial Integration and Network

a. Spatial integration

As discussed earlier, space is annihilated, yet only virtually, through the construction and utilisation of physical means such as transportation and communication. Society must integrate and materialise a large number of entities by means of transportation and communication into action spaces. This is termed *spatial integration* (Harvey, 1982, p. 375), another process of real subsumption of relative space. With spatial integration, territories produced by the real subsumption of absolute space become more realistic.

Since spatial integration does not annihilate space physically, but it does by time, while the distance and location elements of physical space remain intact.

For the agencies of market transactions and members of social groups to act mutually in dispersed locations, resources and labour must be allocated to the production of transportation and communication to overcome distance. By overcoming isolation in this way, the isolated entities can interact with each other more efficiently in a shorter time, even with the same physical distance.

Unlike bounding, which is substantiated through the coercive power of the state apparatus, spatial integration involves the production of massive physical transport or communication lines and their subsequent maintenance mainly by the state power. For relative space, the production of the "iron frame" is accomplished with heavy public investment or private investment approved by the authority. Although the real subsumption of absolute space also needs such physical installations as demarcation stones, walls or passport control posts, the subsumption of relative space takes far heavier physical investment on the built environment.

This was a reason behind the disappearance of the great territories of the empire established by conquest. If spatial integration is not achieved, then the action space of the social group cannot be substantially formed, given the strong distance-decay effect. The inside of the territory is difficult to homogenise, and the entity in the territory cannot be consolidated. Therefore, the market and society face the failure to unify, and society would be on the verge of collapse. Relative space formally subsumed ultimately leads to the negation of society itself.

b. Integrating the two-dimensional plane with one-dimensional lines

A "flow is only effective to the extent that it enters into relationship with others" (Lefebvre, p. 347). Because pristine space is a plane with a two-dimensional width, mere assemblage of separate flows is not sufficient to establish relationships. The connection of a mere two points by means of transportation and communication is insufficient.

To integrate the area realistically and make it into a real action space, with the exception of wireless communications, a *network* has to be created. In this context, Lefebvre did not forget to list "junction points" as an element of the spatial mosaic. Without it, the social groups in the produced space cannot engage in the social interactions which support the consolidation of society. These junction points are a form of agglomeration, which are mostly prepared and managed by those with state or economic power. However, oppressed people may create and manage some other points in secrecy.

In the network, multiple one-dimensional segments are intertwined like a web, creating a fictitious "one-point world", despite the area being a two-dimensional plane. Thus, the means of transportation and communication must be produced as a web-like configuration, or a network.

Historically, networks were created in Medieval Europe as "a space of exchange and communications" (Lefebvre, p. 266): a "network of overland routes: those of traders, pilgrims and crusaders", as well as "hydraulic … ports and seaboard cities" and "inland water transport".

The cities emerged out of the nodal points of the network, or "a unified entity—and as a *subject*" (*ibid*, p. 271). Towards the end of the Middle Ages, the royal power made up "towns and urban systems" or the secularised urban network (*ibid*, p. 378). In the contemporary urban space, a city, the nodal point of the network ensures "links are properly maintained between various flows involved: flows of energy and labour, of commodities and capital" (*ibid*, p. 347).

c. Spatial dialectics of the network

The main dialectics of the network are embedded in its geometry. One-dimensional segments need to be used to integrate a two-dimensional territory. Each position on the plane has an unequal distance between transport lines or agglomeration points. The distance-decay effect in a network is therefore not proportional to the physical distance. The isotropic property of absolute space is thereby negated.

A denser network or more rapid means of transport might seem to be a solution in transcending this dialectic towards the perfect space integration. However, these approaches confront the network with another round of dialectics.

First, consider the possibility of making the network infinitely dense. As the density of networks increases, there will certainly be economies of scope at first, and the individual lines of the network will be more efficiently utilised. Compare the efficiency of the facility between a local ski area with only one lift and a run and large ski resort with a network of many lifts and runs.

However, as the network becomes denser, the individual lines that make up the network become more redundant. The traffic demand for each section (a line segment) constituting the network decreases and the management of each network component becomes less profitable. The extent of the economies of scope is determined at the point where the marginal increase in revenue due to user growth resulting from denser networks comes at par with the marginal increase in cost due to the construction of an additional line.

Denser traffic networks also face physical challenges. A dense network requires more space for rights of way for transportation and communication and reduces the area that can be used for the real payload function. The higher the density of the action space, the smaller the space to be allocated for the real function becomes, is another paradox in network construction, which becomes an acute problem of a limit to high-rise buildings, because the space of the lift hall increases as the building becomes taller.

Due to these paradoxes, the socio-spatial process of spatial integration cannot fully recover the perfectly uniform isotropic planes as in the original absolute space. A spatially integrated territory is thus not perfectly homogenised.

The locational advantage is greater when a point is connected by multiple transport lines. In this case, nodes or junctions of the transportation lines may be created, and these nodes provide a particular potential advantage for the new location of the labour process. Every node of a transportation route does not always experience the agglomeration of economic functions.

These nodes can offer a favourable locational condition. The node becomes "a locus of action", which will grow into a point of agglomeration around which the social and economic activities are organised. It "replaces the notion of totality" and develops into a spatial "centre and "decentring" " of society (Lefebvre, p. 399).

d. The two types of network and power

The network has two types: *nodal* and *homogeneous.* They are closely related to the class nature of the network.

The power and class are clearly etched into the spatial configuration of a network. The pattern of the network is planned and produced to facilitate the power domination, capital accumulation or military deployment. The resulting configuration is a typical *représentation de l'espace,* where the vertical power structures are clearly embedded and the subordinated people must follow.

The dominant power prefers a nodal pattern, centring its power at the node of the highest order. To facilitate domination, the power creates a hierarchical nodal system of space consisting of the highest-order core, secondary nodal points and so on, and a more marginalised periphery. These hierarchical points of agglomeration are connected by a transportation and communication network built through public investment by the political power. The nationwide spines of railways and highways, with the centre of administration occupying the most important agglomeration point of the network, reinforce the nodal space.

In colonies, the network is configured in the interest of the colonial power, typically to connect the peripheral areas with the major port that connects the suzerain. It was by no means built in the interests of the indigenous people. The indigenous people would need a more homogenous network for their spatial mobility and communication to the benefit of everyone; yet it was largely neglected. The spatial mobility of people is thus canalised into the hierarchical configuration where the suzerain power dominates. The growth of an urban system also tends to follow this spatial spine, which indigenous or traditional urban systems are forced to follow.

e. Increased velocity aggravates spatial unevenness

There is an inherent paradox of spatial integration in networks consisting of lines and nodes. This paradox manifests itself more clearly as more efficient means of transportation travelling at higher speed or carrying larger volumes are put into use. Faster means of transportation cost more per kilometre to build and operate. Therefore, such networks become inevitably sparser than the conventional ones, aggravating spatial unevenness and generating a spatial configuration with a "hub-and-spoke" structure.

Therefore, in the market economy, it is not economically feasible to construct a dense and homogeneous network of transport lines capable of operating vehicles at such high-speed. This is clear when considering the difference in the density of the network between the conventional and high-speed rails, or the difference in the density of the network between a conventional road and motorway.

Therefore, the high-speed transportation system indispensable for supporting the globalisation is bound to be organised in a sparser network, and more and more places are separated from the wayside. Additionally, even for a place is along the line, isolation increases in the areas which do not have high-speed rail stations or motorway interchanges. In this way, the spatial unevenness aggravates and pristine distance revives its power as transportation speeds increase.

In Japan, after the opening of the Shinkansen, although it certainly became faster and easier to reach Morioka, a major city in Tohoku (northeastern Honshu), from Tokyo along the direct Shinkansen line, the city of Akita on the Sea of Japan coast once served by a direct conventional train service from Tokyo can now only be reached via Morioka, and for Aizu Wakamatsu, an inland city on a branch line that also had direct service, the passengers now need to transfer from the Shinkansen to conventional lines at an intermediate station. A large disparity in transportation services began to arise among cities in the Tohoku region, which had been essentially equal until the advent of the Shinkansen.

Furthermore, pressure from a political guru tends to influence the decision on the routes and stations of high-speed transportation. Even an international travel guidebook (Lonely Planet, 1991, p. 129) states:

> The Joetsu [shinkansen] Line is frequently held up as a prime example of Japanese political corruption. Niigata [a city on the Sea of Japan coast with population of 0.8 million] is not really of sufficient importance to require a Shinkansen railway line, so passenger usage has relatively been low. To make matters worse, the route had to tunnel straight through the mountainous spine of Honshu, which made it a very expensive project. So why did it get built? Because Niigata was the hometown of Prime Minister Kakuei Tanaka, whose political activities also included taking a couple million US dollars in bribe money from Lockheed Aircraft!

Generally, the neo-liberalist deregulation policies freed the operators of public transportation from maintaining a more homogenous network of transportation services overall and including the sectors in underpopulated areas that were kept running through internal subsidies. These operators resorted to concentrating on services in densely populated areas where demand is higher and more profit is expected. They thus switched to a strategy of cream skimming, which is necessary for maintaining the profitability of their business but does not entertain the money-losing sectors.

Thus, the configuration of national space becomes increasingly uneven along with the development of higher-velocity means of transportation. The distance-decay effect thus does not completely disappear despite the speeding-up of the means of transportation, but it even enhances the barrier of pristine distance in the sparser transportation network.

In sum, the increasing velocity and volume of transportation aiming at further efficiency in annihilation of space makes spatial configuration more uneven. Even if the transport lines that form the axes of the national land is maintained, it does not guarantee a homogenous national space. To maintain efficiency, the spatial configuration inevitably shifts to more nodal structure, constituting of "core" and "peripheral (surrounding) area".

f. Emergence of "hub-and-spoke" space under neo-liberalism

Now that air and marine container transportation have become the global standard, the spatial configuration has increasingly become more nodal. Major airline companies established a hub-and-spoke configuration, in which large international airports are set as a base called "hubs" where trunk lines between hubs are efficiently connected by large aircraft, and branch lines connecting hubs to small cities around hubs are connected by small ones. In Southeast and East Asia, only a few airports, such as Singapore, Incheon (Seoul), Bangkok and Hong Kong, function as hubs. In marine container transportation, physical distribution occurs from the hub ports of Hong Kong, Singapore and Busan. Cargo is transported by small vessels or lorries to these large container terminals, where it is transhipped to large mainline marine container ships and transported to Europe and North America.

Hub-and-spoke spatial structure is a neo-liberalist product of the pursuit of efficient spatial integration that seeks economies of scale on trunk lines by consolidating traffic flows into few larger traffic arteries, and uses smaller and cost-effective transportation to meet demand in peripheral areas along branch lines.

Under neo-liberalism, the principle of cross-subsidy that supported the homogeneity of spatial configuration has been criticised and scrapped. The production of homogenous spatial configuration networks through channel of public finance and cross-subsidy has been reduced due to national and local fiscal crises. Hence, it is impossible to run a loss-generating sector in the transport network.

New low-cost air carriers (LCC) enter only in the sectors where high passenger demand is expected. In this cream-skimming strategy, some fare reduction is made in the trunk line section, but in the spoke sectors, the service thins out in exchange for enhanced monopoly, where the users are forced to patronise inferior services at higher fares.

In recent years, the pursuit of profit under the principle of self-support deteriorated public transport in rural areas, where cream-skimming operators are not attracted to invest and operate. Thus, these sectors can be managed as a form of social capital by a public and private partnerships. However, as neo-liberalism dominates even in the public sector, demanding the social capital be managed under the market principle, the service of unprofitable sectors in the rural district was forcefully abandoned. The public transport system itself is disappearing from rural areas, with residents left to personal automobiles, and the traffic right of the people who cannot drive or own a car; that is, the right to the action space, is deprived, while urban agglomerations with transit hubs or trunk terminals in which economies of scale operate have a competitive advantage in the potential for further growth.

This leads to more intense inter-city competition to attract hubs to its own city. Only the "Greater Metropolis" that wins this competition will be eligible to claim the title of "world city" in the global neo-liberal competition. Thus, the spatial configuration under neo-liberalism greatly changed from the dense homogeneous space network attained through cross-subsidy to a hub-spoke nodal space with the agglomeration of metropolitan areas as the core and traffic flow concentrated, while rural areas are deserted. Thus, the process of the annihilation of space under neo-liberalism creates a more uneven landscape.

g. The paradox of the network and Internet

The Internet seems to have transcended this contradiction of spatial integration for communication. No matter where the user is, information flows around globally at the click of a mouse. The Internet, which combines maximum speed and network density, seems to have perfected spatial integration, making global convergence a reality.

Infinitely perfect spatial integration is a situation in which any quality and quantity of interaction is carried out anywhere regardless of time and location, with transportation and communication costs being kept minimal, regardless of the distance. On the Internet, since the spatial conditions on the access to the information are supposedly ubiquitous, there seems hardly be any need for agglomeration, creating the situation where "location is mobile", as in Alfred Weber's industrial location theory (1929, p. 62).

In the background of the virtual homogeneity of the Internet, however, there is a physical network of optical fibre, which is highly nodal. This extreme contrast between the virtual and the real is a significant contrast of the spatial configuration of the Internet.

While the homogeneity and temporal immediacy of the organisation of cyberspace give the Internet an almost complete physical form of the "annihilation of space by time", the fibre-optic and other networks through which actual information flows form highly nodal spaces centred in the United States and with a few large cities around the world as secondary hubs. Drawing upon Lefebvre's example, computer science "can dominate space in such a fashion that a computer…can assemble an intermediate mass of information relating to a given physical or social space and process it at a single location" (p. 355).

Information on the Internet is transmitted by dividing it into small "packets". Data indicating the destination of information is attached to each packet, and many information packets flow simultaneously on the same line, like cars on a road. Unlike a telephone call, where a pair of users occupy one line exclusively, the line does not become "engaged". However, if a large amount of packets flow through the small bandwidth simultaneously, "traffic congestion" occurs, just like when many cars rush onto a narrow road, making information transfer slower. It is this time when the user who goes to the personal computer is irritated and realises the materiality of cyber space.

Conversely, to obtain customer satisfaction and overcome competition in the e-commerce industry, servers must be installed in the nodal cities where lines with sufficiently large bandwidth converge so that packet congestion does not occur on the servers hosting e-commerce programmes and data. The agglomeration of the e-commerce businesses in these hub cities is also necessary to arrange the system where huge amount of goods are stocked and dispatched quickly to the consumers.

The demand space of e-commerce is expanding globally, supported by the immediacy and homogeneity of cyberspace. Therefore, the spatial configuration of e-commerce creates the contrasting landscape of strong nodes consisting of extreme business agglomeration versus vast and flat demand space.

This gives cities with Internet hubs the potential for agglomeration through strong clustering of e-commerce business. To win the competition between cities and to attain the status of a world city, it is desirable to lay high-bandwidth Internet cables at the centre of the city in a nodal manner, together with large airports and marine container terminals. The city successful in winning will have a competitive advantage as a global node.

Another factor that shatters the illusion of homogenous space created by the Internet is the paradox inherent in the nature of information itself. It makes no sense to compete for ubiquitous information available to everyone. For example, websites and search engines on the Internet are very useful for widely disseminating and obtaining universal information; but they are not suitable for delicate negotiations or a competitive collection of confidential information. What is important for competition is personalised and restricted information that can be monopolised by only a few members of the group. A market economy generally cannot offer this sort of information through an impersonal relationship mediated by money, but it takes a special personal relationship to obtain it.

This type of personalised information also includes the assurances of quality, delivery dates and business integrity essential to support the market itself. Moreover, information that can only be transmitted through personal relationships includes information about new technologies and new markets, which positively contributes to the competitive advantage of individual market players. This creates incentives for them to make locational decisions with a view of increasing their competitive advantage by physically annihilating the space for face-to-face contact and skilfully collecting information that exists only in the agglomerated points.

Thus, while the information space aims to create a ubiquitous absolute space mediated by the Internet, the limit of physical bandwidth is producing the individualisation and unevenness of space through the production of spatial agglomerations.

4.5 Conclusion

Pristine relative space has the properties of determining a position and distance between the positions. Society uses these properties to identify the spatial location of actions. They are also amenable to the class society to differentiate between those in power and various subservient classes.

However, the property of distance has a negative effect to society in that it fragments its members. Therefore, relative space has to be negated. This is the real subsumption of relative space, which can be expressed in well-known term "annihilation of space" put forward by Marx in his *Grundrisse*.

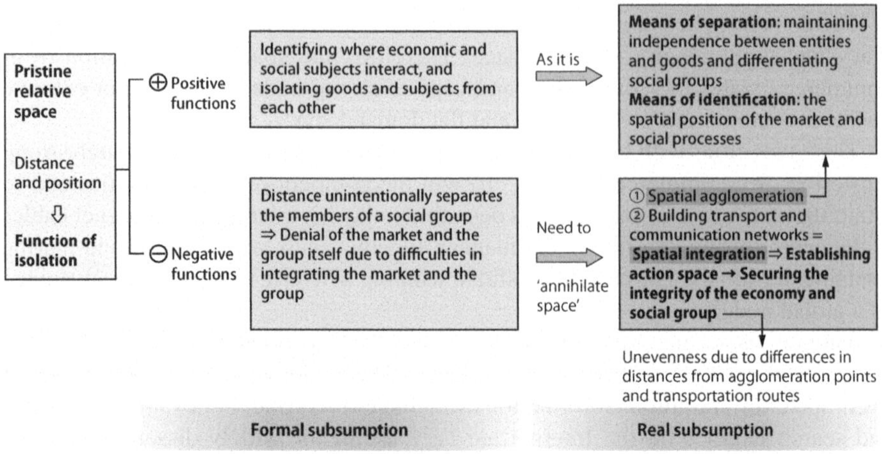

Fig. 4.1 Subsumption of relative space. *Source* Mizuoka ed. (2002), p. 91.

The annihilation of space is normally carried out either virtually by time, that is, spatial integration through the means of transport and communication, or directly, as in agglomeration. Agglomeration is triggered by the drive of the capitalists to reduce turnover time. Furthermore, localisation economy, a version of agglomeration, brings about the vertical disintegration of labour processes at a locality and concomitant reduction of cost-price. The limit of agglomeration is set through the increasing cost to cover wider action space for realisation of the commodity produced there.

On the other hand, spatial integration has inherent geometrical dialectics, since the means of transport and communication are one-dimensional lines, whereas the space to be annihilated is two-dimensional plane. To transcend this paradox, a network has to be constructed. The network consists of the nodes, which often grow into a centre of agglomeration and the transport lines that connect them. It thereby creates spatial unevenness, since its line segments cannot be made infinitely dense. Introduction of means of transportation travelling at higher speed which is more expensive per kilometre makes the network even sparser. Therefore, in the neo-liberal era, the network comes to take the hub-and-spoke configuration to provide maximum efficiency from the capitalist perspective (Fig. 4.1).

The process of the real subsumption of relative space thus creates a more uneven produced space and spatial discrimination.

References

Harvey, D. (1982). *The limits to capital*. University of Chicago Press.

Hoover, E. M. (1937). *Location theory and the shoe and leather industries*. Harvard University Press.

Lonely Planet. (1991). *Japan: A travel Survival Kit*. Lonely Planet.

Marx, K. (1971) (translation). *Theories of Surplus-Value. Part III*. translated by Jack Cohen and S. W. Ryazanskaya. Progress Publishers.

Marx, K. (1973). (translation). *Grundrisse*. Translated by Martin Nicolaus. Vintage Books.

Marx, K. (1977 and 1981) (translation). *Capital*. Vols. 1 and 3. Translated by Ben Fowkes. New York : Vintage Books.

Mizuoka, F. ed. (2002). *Keizai Shakai no Chirigaku (Geography of Economy and Society)*. Yuhikaku.

Sack, R. (1986). *Human territoriality: Its theory and history*. Cambridge University Press.

Scott, A. (1990). *Metropolis: From the division of labor to urban form*. University of California Press.

Scott, A. (1983). Location and linkage systems: A survey and reassessment. *Annals of Regional Science, 17*(1).

Weber, A. (1929) (translation). *Alfred Weber's theory of the location of industries*. Translated by Carl Joachim Friedrich. University of Chicago Press.

Chapter 5
Relational Space

Contents

Abstract From the subsumption of space, the logical scene turns to the absolute and relative attributes of pristine space together with the elements of produced and pristine spaces. They are combined to form *relational space*, of which fundamental dialectical dichotomy is contiguity and separation. Power strives to place the entire system of relational space under its domination and control. The relational space is subsumed into society through two processes: vertically as territorial integration, in a logic akin to Christaller's central-place theory, and horizontally as land-use coordination, akin to that of von Thünen. This chapter offers a Marxist reappraisal and reformulation of these conventional theories of economic geography to incorporate them into Marxist geography.

5.1 Components of Subsumed and Produced Space

I have so far explained the subsumption of space separately by each attribute of pristine space. These two attributes of space as well as pristine and produced space co-exist and interrelate to form a system of spatial configurations.

In the simplest contradiction, "space 'is' whole and broken, global and fractured at one and the same time" (Lefebvre, p. 356). Taking the example of the shepherd's space, Lefebvre (p. 193) demonstrates the configurations more in detail:

1. Accessible space for normal use: routes followed by riders or flocks, way leading to fields, and so on. Such use is governed prescriptively—by established rules and practical procedures.

F. Mizuoka, *Subsumption of Space*, Contributions to Regional Science,
https://doi.org/10.1007/978-981-97-7560-6_5

2. Boundaries and forbidden territories—spaces to which access is prohibited either relatively (neighbours and friends) or absolutely (neighbours and enemies).
3. Places of abode, whether permanent or temporary.
4. Junction points: these are often places of passage and encounter; often, too, access to them is forbidden except on certain occasions of ritual import—declarations of war or peace, for example.

As described here, the spatial outcomes of the real subsumption of both absolute and relative space are now scattered across the produced space. The outcome is the "oddness of … space", which is "at once homogenous and compartmentalized" (Lefebvre, p. 310).

Lefebvre then questions himself: "how does this space … as at once homogenous and broken up, maintain itself in view of the formal irreconcilability of these two characters?" (p. 320). Indeed, "everything that is dispersed and fragmented retains its unity … within the homogeneity of power's space" (p. 365). The hegemony of the ruling class functions as "the organization of space, the regularization of its flows, and the control of its networks" (p. 383). Yet, how can this "unity" be achieved and the space organised by political and economic power?

This chapter analyses this "oddness" and how it could be reconciled through the power of the state and economy in a dialectical way.

5.2 Multiple Layers of Space Superimposed upon Each Other

The subsumption of space creates not only one but multiple social spaces, which are superimposed upon and penetrate each other through networks. Lefebvre states:

> We are confronted not by one social space but by many – indeed, by an unlimited multiplicity or uncountable set of social spaces which we refer to generically as "social space"… As concrete abstractions, however, they attain "real" existence by virtue of bunches or clusters of relationships. Instances of this are the worldwide networks of communication, exchange and information… Thus social space … emerged in all its diversity – and with a structure far more reminiscent of flaky *mille-feuille* pastry than of the homogenous and isotropic space of classical (Euclidean/Cartesian) mathematics. (Lefebvre, p. 86)

However, the spatial *mille-feuille,* originally the word for a French gateau with many layers, thus produced does not guarantee that it is compatible with the sustenance and needs of the dominating power. The task of the dominant political and economic power is therefore to subsume and reconfigure this spatial *mille-feuille* overall so that it supports and sustains the power structure that dominates space.

a. Subsuming the contiguity and separation by the power

Let us look back on the properties of pristine space and the process of their subsumption into the economy and society as discussed in Chaps. 3 and 4.

Pristine absolute space has the property of contiguity, which has the propensity to homogenise the substances and relations contained in it. On the other hand, when relative space is subsumed into the economy and society, contiguity is artificially produced by spatial integration using networks. Thus, there is a common property of *contiguity* both in pristine absolute space and produced space derived from the subsumption of relative space.

In contrast, pristine relative space originally has the propensity to separate with distance and to individualise through the identification of positions. On the other hand, when absolute space is subsumed into the economy and society, it is fragmented into a mosaic through the act of bounding and becomes territories with unique connotations, where the separation is artificially produced. In this way, there is a common property called *separation* between the pristine property of relative space and the property of produced space derived from the real subsumption of absolute space.

Then, an intriguing dialectic appears from the combination of "homogenous and broken up" (Lefebvre, p. 317). "Separation" artificially produced by bounding as the result of real subsumption of absolute space was originally the attribute of distance, or the property of pristine relative space. On the other hand, "contiguity" artificially created by spatial integration, which is the process of real subsumption of relative space, is a property originally possessed by pristine absolute space. Thus, in the process of the real subsumption of space, the properties of the pristine absolute and relative spaces are subsumed separately into the economy and society, and the properties of pristine space, which are the antitheses of themselves, are artificially produced: the real subsumption of absolute space artificially produces the property of relative space; and the subsumption of relative space artificially produces the property of absolute space.

Lefebvre (pp. 355–356) identifies "the binary relationship" of the "homogenous/fractured character of space" and these two aspects contradict one another. Space is "whole and broken, global and fractured at one and the same time". The contradiction that Lefebvre thus identified suggests that the subsumption of space is not completed only by the spatial social process which subsumes each of the two attributes of the space separately.

In this context, the binary properties "absolute and relative" of pristine space are transformed into the other binary properties of "*contiguity and separation*". The ensemble of pristine and produced absolute spaces and the pristine and produced relative space create this new binary attribute. This is what is called *relational space*. Relational space is one in which the absolute and relative spaces are inter-correlated, and at the same time, pristine space and produced space are also inter-correlated though the operation of the socio-economic power to exert its "repressiveness" (Lefebvre, p. 318).

Relational space is to be subsumed into the economy and society as it is. Its subsumption process is to "organise its own component factors" (Lefebvre, p. 317) to the dictates of the dominating socio-economic power. Any economic or social relationship must have the configuration of space that best supports those in power, for sustenance of the domination and for the dominating process to proceed. This configuration of space combines contiguity and separation in its own unique way. When contiguity or separation in the original relational space supports those in power, it can remain as it is; whereas if it is contradictory, the original elements are to be negated and transformed by the power. Further reconfiguration of relational space will then ensue.

The *subsumption of relational space* is a socio-spatial process that aims at the real subsumption of the contiguity and separation created through subsumption of pristine space. The problem here is whether a particular spatial configuration presents a combination of contiguity and separation appropriate for those in power in the particular economic and social relation. If it is not appropriate, but ridden with contradictions, then the dialectics of the relational space must be transcended. The ultimate aim of the subsumption of relational space by the market or state power is to make the configuration of space compatible with the dictates of power, by sealing off and getting rid of any elements of separation or contiguity that remain uncontrolled by the dominating power.

b. Two forms of the subsumption of relational space

There are two rationales for real subsumption.

First, the bounding of pristine absolute space is imperfect. The boundary is always porous and those in power cannot necessarily control it perfectly. Some porosity of the border is always left uncontrolled, and the contiguity in the higher order which cannot be really subsumed is left unbounded. In addition, spatial integration does not yield a perfect homogeneous plane. In a network consisting of an unequal set of transport networks and nodal points, the actual configuration of spatial integration may be left somewhat uncontrolled, leaving pristine elements of distance and position virtually unsubsumed.

Second, the element of contiguity that remains unsubsumed in real terms, as well as the element of separation caused by distance that is also likely to be left unsubsumed, creates various obstacles to those in power constantly. Therefore, to produce the spatial configuration as an optimal organisation for those in power in the dominant mode of production, the relational space cannot simply be left as a mere jumble of absolute and relative spaces subsumed independently.

Both have to be coordinated by the dominant economic and social power, as Fig. 5.1 shows.

Thus, the formally subsumed relational space must face anew the process of producing the ensemble of optimally correlated contiguity and separation through the dictate of those in power. This is the process of the real subsumption of relational space.

There are two forms of real subsumption of relational space. This reflects two spatial attributes, absolute space and relative space, which constitute relational space and reflects the subsumption process peculiar to each attribute.

The *first form* is the process to coordinate the *vertical* overlapping of spatial scales. Neil Brenner (2004, pp. 9–11), by putting together the past arguments on the concepts of spatial scale, defines the scale as "'vertical ordering' of social formations", assimilating it to a *mille-feuille*. Those in power control the entire ensemble

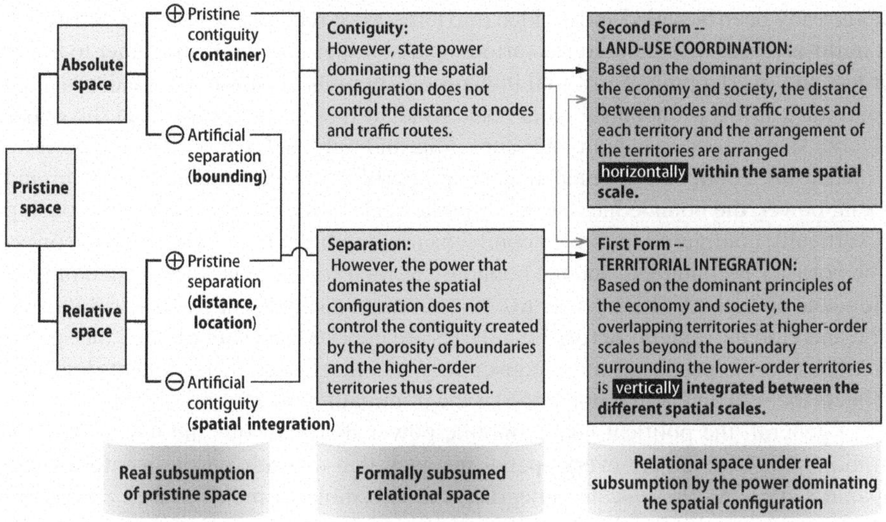

Fig. 5.1 Subsumption of relational space. *Source* Mizuoka (2002), p. 158

of multiple spatial scales through appropriate bounding, and gives spatial order to the spatial system as a whole that suits the exercise of the dominant power. This should be called *territorial integration*.

The *second form* is the *horizontal* coordination. It controls the positioning of territories from the agglomeration point or nodes of network that cannot be subsumed by spatial integration, and to give order to the collective absolute spaces so that it forms coordinated mosaics for those in power in the economic and social system to dominate the full ensemble of the territories. This should be called *land-use coordination.*

Through these two forms of the real subsumption of relational space, those in dominant power could put stray and uncontrolled contiguity and separation under their own control. It thereby produces the whole spatial configurations that best support the dominating power, through which the original economic and social system and the exertion of power is restored. By this socio-spatial process, the separation and contiguity are coordinated, creating a skilful combination of the coordinated multi-layered mosaic of territories. This relational space subsumed in real terms makes the exercise of economic and social power most comprehensive and efficient. The economic and social power thus produces the space in its own image.

5.3 The First Form: Territorial Integration

a. Introduction

Territorial integration differs from the notion of spatial integration dealt with in Chap. 4 (p. 58ff). The territorial integration is, first, the integration of space which has already been bounded and divided into territories; second, the set of the territories is multi-layered, with porosity, in various spatial scales ranging from higher to lower orders and overlapping. Territorial integration attempts to subsume in real terms the contiguity still left uncontrolled at each scale so that all the porosity in the entire layered spatial system is put under conscious and purposeful control of the power.

Once the contiguity of each scale is properly controlled by the economic and social power, the boundedness at each spatial scale in the multi-layered relationship is vertically configured in a form commensurate with the domination of the power. The porosity is contained, and the boundary at each scale can be surmounted only to the social entities who have power to enjoy access to the higher scale space arbitrarily. The anarchic movements across boundaries are checked and shut off, and the spatial configuration is produced more consciously as one stiff multi-layered system that reflects the will and actual operation of the dominant power.

In general, the political and economic power that performs the territorial integration should dominate every spatial instance that controls all the territories and spatial scales. As these scales integrate, the ensemble of multi-layered configuration of territories and scales represents the power of the dominant class, while the stiff configuration itself imposes the iron frame of their actions on the subordinated people.

b. Christaller's central-place system revisited

A good example of the territorial integration is readily available in economic geography in Walter Christaller's central-place theory, which explains the process of coordinating vertically-overlapped layers of territories constituting multi-layered spatial configuration. Central-place theory is one of the origins of spatial and urban economics and now widely adopted in standard textbooks of neo-classical regional and urban economics.

However, Christaller had firm socialist ideals. After studying economics at the University of Heidelberg, he completed his thesis *the Central Places in Southern Germany* (Christaller, 1966 edition), with which he obtained his doctorate at the University of Erlangen, Bavaria. Unfortunately, his work was not appreciated among the conservative German geographers in academia, where descriptive chorography persistently dominated the mainstream. Not only did he never get a permanent job at a university, he was suspected of being a GDR (German Democratic Republic, East Germany) agent by the government of West Germany, where he lived. His academic achievement was first accepted by geographers of the US in the context of the quantitative revolution, in an era when McCarthyism was rife. As an alleged communist, he was refused an entry visa to the US and was unable to travel to deliver an invited lecture at Harvard University. Just before he passed away in 1969, he received an award from the president of West Germany and honorary doctorate from the University of Lund, Sweden; thus his honour was finally restored (Hottes, 1983).

Attested by this career, Christaller's ideal, which is quite contrary to that of neo-liberalists, is clear in his central-place model, as demonstrated below.

The central places supply goods to the inhabitants who live evenly in their surroundings. This demand space for suppliers, called "*complementary region*", has two properties for its radius: range (upper limit) and threshold (lower limit).

Assuming that each resident in a complementary region has the same income regardless of their place of residence, and that the variety of goods in their basket for consumption is identical, the cost and time required for "annihilating space" to acquire goods increases with the distance from the central place. At the endpoint, consumers cannot spend any money on goods themselves. This point, called the upper limit of the range, or simply *range,* is defined by Christaller as "the farthest distance from the central place from which it can be obtained from this central place" (p. 54).

Christaller himself defined the *threshold* (lower limit of the range) as "determined by the minimum amount of consumption of this central good needed to pay for its production or offering of the central good" (p. 54). If the threshold is in same size in area as complementary region, then "the income will just cover expenditures, and there will be no profits" (p. 55). It is the demand existing between the range and threshold that gives profit to the supplier.

Christaller built his central-place system based only on range. He also stated that when the threshold is below the standard, there may be a lack of supply of certain kinds of goods, and thus the central places may not develop much. What is suggested here is that by accounting for the threshold, the variety of goods supplied at each central place can be different from the system based on the range. As this has an important implication for the struggles over space, it will be discussed in further detail in Chap. 9 (p. 159ff).

In understanding how the hierarchical central-place system is built, it would be convenient at the beginning to take out from the network of the central places an equilateral triangle that is a part of a hexagonal market area (Fig. 5.2). In the equilateral triangle of the central places of equal order B_1 B_2 and B_3, with the distance b between the central places for each side, a circle (the thin line in the figure) is drawn with a radius k such that three circles surrounding the points B_1, B_2 and B_3 overlap at the central place of order K. Between b and K, a relationship

$$b = k\sqrt{3} \tag{5.1}$$

shall be established by the theorem of three squares.

Goods with range of k (which is called "central good Number k") are supplied from points B, which is arranged in a honeycomb-shaped consumption area. As is clear from Fig. 5.2, the whole plane in question is receiving the supply of this commodity without fail.

Next, consider the central good k-Δ. The radius of the range is defined as the distance k-Δ, where Δ is a positive number infinitesimally greater than 0. Due to a condition set by Christaller to minimise the number of central places, the central good k-Δ is included in the set of goods supplied from central places of rank B as before. As is clear from Fig. 5.2, the point where the goods cannot be supplied, indicated by the dotted shade in the figure, appears on the plane.

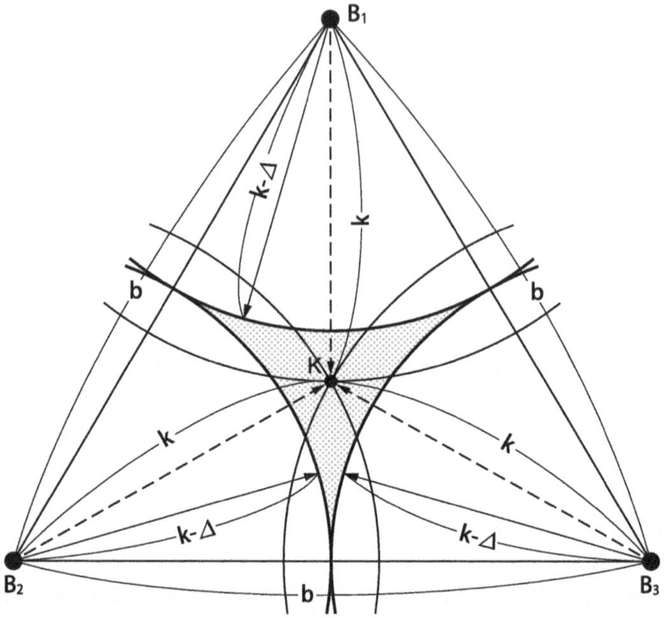

Fig. 5.2 Establishment of a lower-order centre. (*Source* Heinritz, 1979, p. 29 (edited by the author))

Christaller established an *egalitarian condition* that every good needs to be supplied to the consumers regardless of the places where they live in constructing his central-place system. Therefore, a new, lower order of central place, named *K*, shall be established at the centre of the dotted shade.

At point *K*, where the central goods *k*-Δ are supplied, the number of goods supplied is limited to a smaller range, and therefore the variety of goods supplied there is also small, and thus point *K* is a lower-order centre than point *B*. As can be seen from Fig. 3.7, the shortest distance between the points to which the central goods *k*-Δ are supplied, that is, points *B* and *K* together, is *K*.

Point *K* is the lowest of the following points, unless the situation in which the dotted portion shown in Fig. 3.7 occurs again for goods in the less accessible sector. A series of goods smaller than the central good *k*-Δ satisfy the condition that the supply of these goods becomes ubiquitous thanks to the emergence of this point *K*. However, if the range becomes too small and a part like the dotted shade is generated again, a centre at an even lower order (called point *A*) needs to be established. The shortest distance between the points *A* and the points *B* and *K* combined, as shown in the figure and in Eq. (5.1), is:

$$a = \frac{k}{\sqrt{3}} \tag{5.2}$$

Now, conversely, look at the formation of a centre higher than point *B*.

If the product of a good whose range is *b* in radius (good *b*), as shown in Fig. 5.3, point B_2 may be supplied by the points of the same order; that is, B_1, B_8 and B_9, and point B_3 by the points of the same order B_1, B_8 and B_{10}. Thus, these two points are no longer necessary for the supply of goods of the sector with goods number *b* and higher. Similarly, all points *B* above the hexagon shown by the thick line in the figure become unnecessary. Therefore, for the hexagon $B_{2\sim7}$, only B_8, which is not on the hexagon of the thick line, is required to satisfy the requirement for the "poor people's optimum" (Peet 1972, p. 3). However, of these 7 points of *B*, 6 ($B_{2\sim7}$) are shared by 3 "complementary regions" including 2 adjacent ones, meaning only 1/3 of one "complementary region" as a whole.

Thus,

$$6(\text{the number of points that becomes unnecessary}) \times 1/3 = 2 \qquad (5.3)$$

is no longer needed, and one of the centres remains as the higher-order central place.

In sum, the central-place system by Christaller was established with egalitarian assumption that every person, no matter where he or she lives, must be supplied with goods of all the existing varieties.

c. The successful territorial integration in Christaller's model

Since, by assumption, consumers obtain goods from the nearest centre of the same order, there is no action space stretching beyond the boundaries between complementary regions of the same order. Therefore, the complementary regions of the

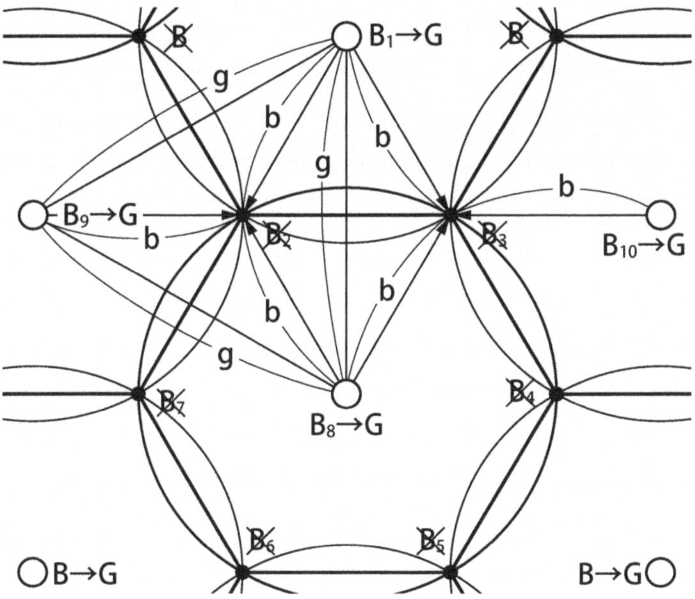

Fig. 5.3 Establishment of a higher-order centre

same order are completely separated from each other, with respect to the purchase of the goods supplied from the same order. The territory of demand space at each centre is integrated by the dominating norm, which is, in Christaller, the egalitarian socialist ideal. The complementary regions are coordinated to satisfy it; that is, to have egalitarian access to services no matter where he or she lives, without need of crossing boundaries unnecessarily towards neighbouring territories.

This principle applies to all the multi-layered configurations of Christaller's nodal territories. Thus, all the moments for contiguity and separation of this relational space are subsumed and controlled in the real terms.

d. The central-place system under the principles of market economy

As demonstrated above, the market economy has a built-in mechanism for territorial integration for hierarchically organising the ensemble of the multi-scaled territories as well.

Brian Berry and William Garrison (1958) attempted to rebuild Cristaller's central-place system based on the threshold of goods. Their assumptions are the same as those of Christaller, except that the system is arranged in order of their threshold; that is, the minimum extent of the demand space in which the capital supplying the goods of the sector can earn at least "ordinary profit". Suppose *n* kinds of good are supplied in a plane, and name them *n, n-1, … n-i, … n-j, …k, …,* 1 in descending order of the size of the threshold. Various supplying capital are distributed to compete with each other spatially and secure its surroundings as its own demand space most efficiently. In this case, the demand space imputed to each supplying capital should be large enough for the supplying capitalists to obtain "normal profit". The location of the capital supplying good *n* is called the "A-centre". The supply of goods with threshold is less than goods *n*, namely goods *n*-1, *n*-2, are located in the centre of *A* in the same way because of the "advantages from association with other establishments providing central goods" (Berry and Garrison, p. 112). In this case, for goods *n*-1, *n*-2, …, the demand space defined by goods *n* is bigger than the extent of threshold, thus, "excess profit" accrues to the capital supplying these goods.

The smaller the threshold of goods, the larger the interstitial purchasing power in the area which is not covered by the demand space for the good centred at *A* centres (shown in the upward oblique line in Fig. 5.4). If the area of the interstitial area for good *n-i* is of the same area as the demand spaces centred at points *A*, then a new supply centre for the good *n-i* becomes economically feasible. The good that gives rise to a new lower-order centre is called the *hierarchical marginal good*. It is to be located at the centre of the interstitial purchasing power, together with the existing centres *A*. The new centre may be called the *B*-centre, which supplies goods of which threshold is *n-i* and smaller.

Then, by the same token, as the threshold gets smaller, the *C, D, E* … and finally the *M* centres shall emerge. At the *M* centre, goods with the minimum threshold 1 are supplied, and a centre of lower order than this will not emerge. The final outcome is shown in Table 5.1. Although this table does not show the spatial relationships between the centres, as that in Christaller's work, it is the extension of what is partially as shown in Fig. 5.4. The condition for the territorial integration is also met in Berry

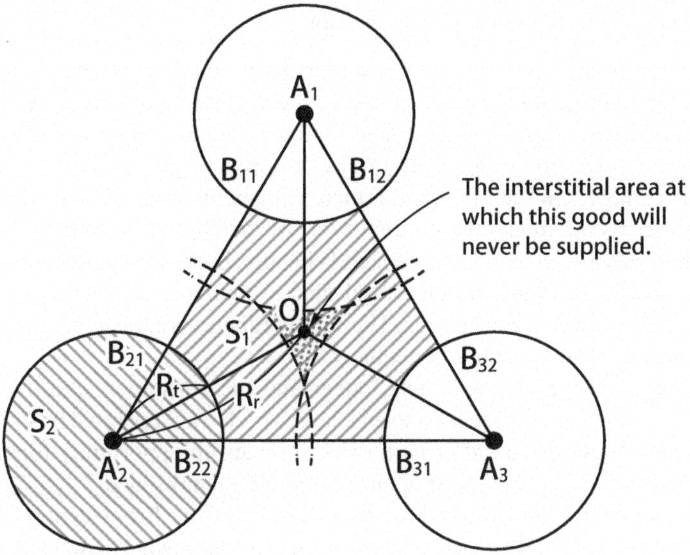

Fig. 5.4 Relation of the complementary regions *B* to the *A*-centres

and Garrison's system of central places, since it is assumed that the consumers move only to the nearest centres without crossing the boundary to neighbouring complementary regions.

Now we have two central-place systems based on different social norms: the egalitarian, socialist principle and the capitalist, profit-making principle. How are they different in terms of the goods supplied from each order of centres and what is the implication of the difference from the viewpoint of the spatial struggle and alternative configuration of space? This point is analysed in Sect. 6 of Chap. 9 (p.159ff).

Table 5.1 Berryand Garrison's central-place system. *Source* Berry and Garrison (1958, p. 113)

Centres	Goods				
	$n^*,n\text{-}1,\ldots$	$(n\text{-}i)^*,n\text{-}(i+1),\ldots$	$(n\text{-}j)^*,n\text{-}(j+1),\ldots$	...	$k^*,(k\text{-}1),\ldots,2,1$
A	*x*	*x*	*x*	...	*x*
B		*x*	*x*	...	*x*
C			*x*	...	*x*
.				...	...
.				...	...
.				...	...
M				...	*x*

* indicates hierarchical marginal goods, *x* indicates the set of goods supplied by the centres

e. The dynamism in the territorial integration

Transformation in the economy, society and technological development are driving forces to change the configuration of hierarchical systems of space. As technologies for spatial integration and investment in transport and communication facilities develop, the accessibility to the central places improves, each commodity comes to have a longer range. On the other hand, increasing economies of scale due to technological progress augments the optimal scale of the capital investment for supply and concomitantly the demand space extends its threshold. These processes shift the goods from lower- to higher-order central places, thus a lesser variety of goods is supplied from the lower-order centres. The supply function of the lower-order centres shall be contracted, and eventually declines.

As the spatial range of goods gets longer and the consumers can travel faster, thanks to, for example, a bridge built to an island which was separated by the sea from the mainland or high-speed rail or motorway, it opens up opportunity for capitalists to seek scale economies because it opens up more demand space.

This may also simultaneously lead to a decline of the lower centres, which is called the "straw effect". When once self-sufficient, closed and fragmented economic territories are swallowed into the expanding frontier of higher-order territory and is included in the national or global market, these former central places lose autonomous centrality and becomes peripheral. The higher centres thus prevail and more people would get supply from the higher-order centres.

Having the central-place system thus defined, the political power tends to superimpose its hierarchical organisations of administrative and judicial functions over this system. If the dominant power manages to control the ensemble of hierarchical spatial system as a whole, the attempt of the subservient people to undermine the dominant structure through simple escape can be checked and blocked. Boundaries arising out of economic rationality can transform itself into the boundary of prohibitive spatial restriction. This countermeasure of the authority was well manifested in the early Christian Church history to prevent illegal escape of the church officials to resist the authority: "to have larger territorial authorities enforce prohibitions against such movements and coordinate the activities of smaller territories" (Sack, 1986, p. 112). Consequently, the central-place system can become a means of spatial domination for those in power and the spatial fetter for the people.

5.4 The Second Form: Land-Use Coordination

a. Introduction

The second form of the real subsumption of the relational space is the process to configure the ensemble of territories *horizontally* in a single spatial scale to create separation through distance and make them adhere to the norm of the dominant economic or political power.

Once an economic entity of the society produces an exclusive territory, others can no longer occupy it legitimately. The most primitive way to determine which entity occupies a piece of absolute space as *Wirkungsraum* is *the principle of occupation of terra nullius* in international law, as explained in Chap. 2. In this principle, the first stable inhabitation of an uninhabited space acquires the exclusive right of occupation.

After state power begins to intervene and dominate the ensemble or territories, landed property becomes a concept legitimised by a state at a higher spatial scale and regarded as inviolable, except in pursuance to the prescribed economic transactions and legal procedures set by the state power. This is the process of *land-use coordination*.

An intriguing case is a seated wedding reception in Japan. The reception hall is a nodal space where the relative honorary order of the seating is determined by the distance from the seat of the bride and groom, who sit at the centre of the reception room. It is physically impossible to seat all the guests in the "seat of honour", which is close to the bride and groom. If seats are unreserved and the participants can take seats on a first-come-first-served basis, then honoured guests who come late may be forced to have seats at the periphery of the reception room. Since this is not morally appropriate, the host of the wedding ceremony, who has the power to control and dominate the whole reception proceedings, designates the seats such that the distance and the importance in social relations to the couple are inversely proportional. The host forcibly makes all guests sit in positions based on this principle of controlling spatial order. This is one of the processes of land-use coordination.

As the scarcity in *Wirkungsraum* arises in a particular spatial scale, competition for space sets in. Since the relative superiority of positions differ at every point, especially depending on the distance from the node, the competition for relatively superior position needs to be controlled through some principles. The competition is governed by the power under a single principle which covers across that particular scale. In this sense, land-use coordination assumes two scales in the ensemble of the spatial configuration: the upper scale with the controlling power with the principle of landed property, and the lower scale, where actual activities take place. Thus, the configuration of horizontal mosaic of the lower-scale collective absolute space is rearranged according to the principle dominating in the upper scale.

The most common model of land-use coordination is that of von Thünen; that is, a socio-spatial process in which the power at higher-order scale reconfigures the ensemble of territories at the lower-order scale with one node at the core and the concentric territories surrounding according to relative distances from the node. Even if the entire expanse of the lower-order scale is not fully subsumed in this socio-spatial relation, the process of land-use coordination will occur, but partially.

From the standpoint of Marxist geography, this process must be explained based on the ground-rent theory in *Capital* Volume 3, which requires development to handle multiple land uses cases.

b. The ground-rent theory of Marx revisited

In the circulation of production capital,

$$P \ldots C' - M' - C < \begin{matrix} mp \\ L \end{matrix} \cdots L,$$

we find two processes of capitalist competition. One is the threefold competition for the realization of the product (C'-M'); the other is M'-$C(mp)$, to obtain the means of production that enable capitalists to produce the same product at the lowest individual value.

Once market value has been established through the first process of capitalist competition, the way left to capitalists to earn extra surplus value is to produce the same amount of the commodity at a lower individual value by applying a superior condition of production. If this condition of production is reproducible, all capital will eventually adopt it; and thus, market value itself shall fall and extra surplus value disappear. However, if this superior condition of production cannot be reproduced and can be monopolised, the second process of capitalist competition comes to the fore: the creation of differential rent.

Differential rent is not the only form of rent that landed property creates: *monopoly rent* is another. Marx himself questions "if landed property gives the power to sell the product above its cost-price, at its value, why does it not equally well give the power to sell the product above its value, at an arbitrary monopoly price?" (*Theories of Surplus-Value*, Part II, p. 332).

Indeed, landed property occasionally has such power, especially in urban areas, to extract another form of rent, "monopoly rent". Marx states that a characteristic of the rent of buildings is "the prevalence of monopoly prices" (*Capital*, Vol. 3, p. 908). Harvey (1974, pp. 241–242) states that "class-power" to achieve "monopoly rent", or in his terminology, "class-monopoly rent", indeed exists, partly because the landlords, often belonging to a class of speculator developers, individually "can survive quite well without releasing all of the resource units under their command". This corresponds to Marx's statement that in all modern societies, "a relatively significant portion of the land always remains uncultivated" (*Capital*, Vol. 3, p. 891). This type of monopoly rent, which accrues when the product of land is "sold not only above its price of production but also above its value, as a result of the barrier that landed property opposes against the rent-free investment of capital on untilled land" (*ibid*, p. 910), is one of the two types of monopoly rent, the other being the case where "the monopoly price (independent of rent) creates the rent".

Differential rent is concerned with "unequal products of equal amounts of capital applied to different lands of the same area" which is "independent of capital" (*ibid*, p. 789). Two general causes for this inequality are "fertility" and the "location of land", although their theoretical natures are in principle the same. As our point of departure is pristine space without any difference in terms of physical geography, this "condition of production" is assumed to be related only to distance. Distance constitutes an important element of use-value of space, especially in the property market: "the distance from the purchaser's dwelling-place to other places, to centres of commerce, work, leisure, culture or decision" (Lefebvre, p. 339). This partly reflects the fact that "in case of the ground-rent of houses, situation constitutes just as decisive a factor for the differential rent, as fertility (and situation) in the case of agricultural rent" (*Theories of Surplus-Value*, Part II, p. 365).

To analyse the social process which gives rise to the formation of differential rent, we thus assume that there is land with different qualities in terms of location, or different proximities to the productive and distributive centres. We further assume that the extent of land with such a superior location is physically limited and cannot be reproduced.

Capitalists compete in the process of *M-C(mp)* for a plot with a more advantageous location. In this context, Michael Chisholm's (1968, pp. 21–24) explanation of the process of competition based on the Ricardian model is of importance. As the basic conception of Marx's "first form of differential rent is … in principle, no different from that which Ricardo advanced …" (Harvey, 1982, p. 354), we first take up Chisholm's explanation to examine the social process of competition among the economic subjects that takes place in *M-C*(*mp*) for the creation of the first form of differential rent, or differential rent *I* (*Capital*, Vol. 3, p. 788).

Chisholm assumes an imaginary case with two different land fertilities, one yielding 2 tons of wheat per annum and the other 1½ tons with the same technology. The cultivation of both qualities of land is assumed to be necessary to fill the demand in a town. All land is assumed to be owned by one landlord. Chisholm's explanation goes as follows:

> the situation in which farmers occupying grade A land get a 1/2 ton of wheat more than their neighbours on each hectare they farm, and for no greater outlay. Now it would be worth the while of a farmer on grade B land to offer a farmer on grade A soil anything up to a 1/2 ton of wheat a year for the right to cultivate a hectare of this better land. This 1/2 ton represents the "surplus" which the farmer operating the better land obtains through applying his labour there rather than on the poorer land... In this case farmer Y on the B quality land may go to [the landlord] offering to pay 1/4 ton a hectare for the land currently farmed by X on the better land. At the time Y goes to the landlord, nobody pays him anything for the use of the land they cultivate. If the landlord accepts the offer, will now obtain 2 ton from each hectare but will have the additional expense of the 1/4 ton given to the landlord; this will leave him better off by as much as a 1/4 ton. On the other hand, farmer X will now have to cultivate some of the poorer soil, from which he will be worse off by 1/2 a ton. It would therefore be to the advantage of farmer X to offer the landlord somewhat more than a 1/4 ton to retain the use of his A quality land. If farmer Y offered more, it would be worth the while of X to raise his own bid as high as a 1/2 ton, which is the highest figure to which Y could go. At this figure, both farmers would be getting the same return and the "surplus" which accrues to the better land would be taken by the landlord…[Here e]conomic rent is a 1/2 ton a hectare on the better land and nothing on the poorer. It is equivalent to the surplus production that can be obtained from the use of the better soil above the return which could be obtained by applying the same resources of labour etc. to the poorer land. (pp. 21–22)

"Surplus" of land *A* over *B*, in Chisholm's terminology, is in wheat. It transforms itself into "economic rent" when the market value is regulated by the individual value of the poorest land. This principle of determining market value in the case of the product of land is called the marginal principle, which creates a knotty problem related to a "false social value" (*Capital*, Vol. 3, p. 799). I elaborated on this topic in a separate article (Mizuoka, 1979). In Chisholm's statement above, one point should be made clear: if we reformulate the "surplus" in Chisholm's terminology in terms of the amount of capital invested for a certain amount of wheat, then what seems to be "surplus" becomes only a savings or reduction of individual value of the labour process on the superior land over the inferior one.

In short, differential rent ultimately boils down to the principle of capitalist competition aiming at production at a lower individual value. The only difference between the products of land and other products is whether the source of such savings is limited and can be monopolized or not. Thus, in the latter case, the "saving" is the source of extra surplus value going to the pocket of the capitalist, while in the former case, savings become fixed and transforms into differential rent.

The above explanation of competition by Chisholm can therefore be interpreted as the process by which the savings in individual value at superior land plots transforms itself into ground-rent.

c. The conditions for land-use coordination in the market

Nevertheless, Chisholm's explanation needs to be expanded to include more than one economic sector under the market principle. This amounts to land-use coordination under the market principle.

Ground-rent is created from the social process of subsuming space. Nevertheless, ground-rent is not merely the final result of an attempt by capitalism to subsume space. On the contrary, ground-rent, the result of the subsumption of space, can emerge as a positive producer of spatial configuration.

Harvey (1982, p. 368) pointed out, "by perpetually striving to put land to its 'highest and best use', landowners crate a *sorting device* which shifts land uses and forces allocations of capital and labour that might not otherwise occur" (emphasis mine).

Marx states:

> rent – as the price of land – determines the method of production, whether a large amount of capital is concentrated on a small area of land, or a small amount of capital is spread over a large area of land, and whether this or that type of product is produced – e.g. cattle or corn – the market price of which covers the rent most effectively. (*Theories of Surplus-Value*, Part III, p. 515)

In short, ground-rent has a dual role in a market economy: the source of income for the landowner and the allocator of the land use across the space. In line with the dichotomy of formal/real subsumption of space, the latter role of ground-rent as the "sorting devise" of land use or as a producer of the spatial configuration of capitalism is analysed here. It is indeed another form of the real subsumption of space.

Here, what matters is the *inter*-sectoral competition of more than one system of ground rents created through various inter-sectoral competitions. Marx further elaborates the above point:

> in stock-raising and in the general average of all capital invested on the land that does not go into the production of the major staples, such as corn for example, the determination of price is completely different. Price here is determined by the fact that the price of the product of land which is used, say, as an artificial pasture for cattle, but which could equally well be turned into arable land of a certain quality, has to rise high enough to yield the same rent as equally good arable land; in this case, therefore, *the rent of the corn-growing land is a*

> *determining factor in the price of cattle, so that ... the price of cattle is artificially raised by rent. by the economic expression of landed property. and thus by landed property itself.* (*Capital*, Vol. 3, p. 902, emphasis mine)

Here the point is that, because of inter-sectoral land-use competition, the price of a product of Sector *A*, which has to compete against Sector *B* for use of land, must pay the rent of the competitors (i.e. sector *B*) as well, to win the land-use competition over Sector *B*. Consequently, the price of the product of Sector *A* is artificially raised under a new demand/supply relationship. Categorically, this rent obviously belongs to monopoly rent, where rent creates the monopoly price in Sector *A* "as a result of the barrier that landed property opposes" the investment (*ibid*, p. 910).

These conditions are my point of departure in analysing the multi-sector land-use model.

d. Ground rent theory as a base of the Marxist theory of location: inter-sectoral land-use competition

Let us start from the "Thünen ring" as modified by August Lösch (1954, Fig. 3b on p. 37) and see how it is adjusted in the Marxian context. Assume two sectors, more intensive Sector *A* and less intensive Sector *B*, run by multiple farmers.

In general, the more intensive the land use is, the more crops per hectare are harvested from the land, so the transportation cost per hectare to bring the harvest to the agricultural market at the centre is higher. The higher the transportation cost per hectare, the greater the decrease in the absolute transportation cost (which means savings to the farmer) that occurs when moving by 1 km to the centre. This saving amount per hectare when moving one kilometre has been called the *index of land rent* (*Grundrentenindex*) by German agricultural economist Theodor Brinkmann (1935, pp. 87–90). Savings over distance as compared to the most inferior plot, or the rents as defined by Chisholm in the quotation above, is expressed with the function line in downward slope from the central agricultural market shown in Fig. 5.5. The function line touches the x-axis at the poorest plots assumed necessary to fill the social demand. No untilled plots are assumed to exist within area towards the market centre. The ground-rent of the plots inside the poorest land comes from savings in individual value arising from the cost of transport in comparison to the poorest plot, after the principle of Marxian theory of ground-rent.

The larger the index of ground-rent, the steeper the slope of the rent function. The slope becomes the coordinator in the market of land-use adjustment, based on the twofold competition among the farmers themselves and between the farmers and landlords. Generally, a sector that attempts to evict the competing other sectors from a plot of land must pay more rent than Sector *B* for the same plot, in addition to the differential rent proper to that sector, to win the competition to obtain the lease of land from the landlord.

Assume that Sector *A* has a higher land index of ground-rent (i.e. a steeper rent function) and Sector *B* has lower land index of ground-rent (i.e. a gentler rent function), both of which have production fields located in a concentric circle around a single market where the demand for their products exists. Since Sector *A* saves more

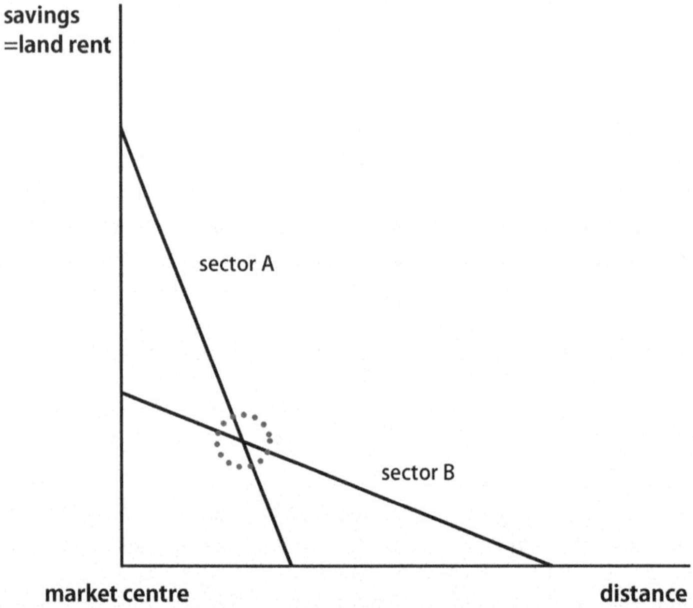

Fig. 5.5 Ground-rent functions of Sectors *A* and *B* in a concentric spatial arrangement

money when it moves one kilometre inwards than Sector *B*, it can use this saving as a source to bid for more rent to the landlords. Landlords let their land to the farmers in the economic sector offering the highest bid, so the farmers in Sector *A*, whose index of ground-rent is higher, (steeper rent function slope), acquire the land closer to the centre.

The detail of the competition process is explained in Fig. 5.6. The portion surrounded by a ○ is enlarged (the aspect ratio is altered to make it easier to see). The transportation cost per hectare is determined by the distance from the market centre and is equal both for Sectors *A* and *B* at the cultivation area of ◆ (called the "equilibrium point"). The vertical bars with arrows on each side indicate the amount of savings or losses (increase in production costs) per hectare in comparison with cultivated land of the equilibrium point:

 indicates either marginal savings or loss for Sector *A* in each area compared to the equilibrium point;

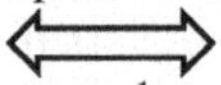 indicates either marginal savings or loss for Sector *B* in each area compared to the equilibrium point. These differences in rent are generated by the difference in transportation costs per kilometre from the market centre;

 indicates the marginal difference in cost savings between Sectors *A* and *B* caused by the relocation inwards from the equilibrium point. Using this saving, Sector *A* outbids Sector *B* for each plot to secure a plot closer to the market for cultivation. This competition pushes Sector *B* out to a doughnut-shaped area that surrounds the territory of Sector *A*.

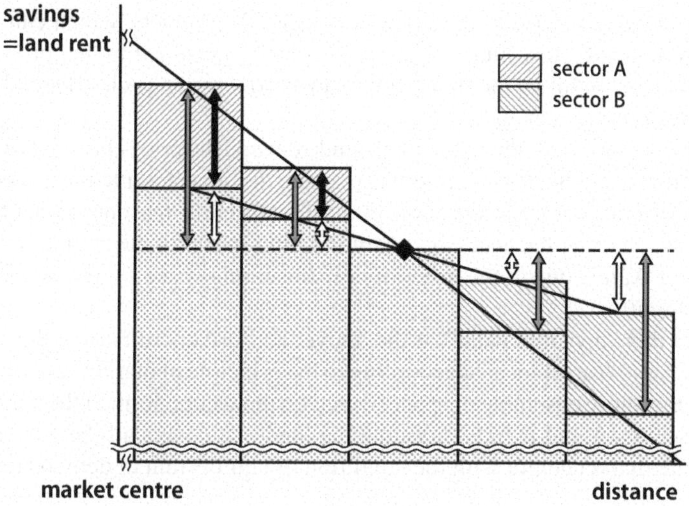

Fig. 5.6 Bidding of ground-rent between two sectors with different indices of land rent. *Source* Mizuoka et al. (2002), p. 181

At the end of this competition, Sector *A* cannot expand its territory beyond the equilibrium point using differential rent only; thus, the *Wirkungsraum* of Sector *A* can no longer be expanded. This is because Sector *B* has an advantage over Sector *A* in its funds for bidding on the plot, as Fig. 5.6 suggests.

However, note that each of the sectors is evicting its competitor from the plot, leading to an insufficient supply of the products of both sectors due to decreased acreage. The insufficient supply pushes up the prices of both Sectors *A* and *B* at the centre. The supply of Sector *A* goods is less than the social demand because Sector *B* now intrudes into the territory of Sector *A* and occupies the outskirt of the farmland of Sector *A*. Consequently, the price of the product of Sector *A* rises, as dictated by the price elasticity of demand.

This increase in price is used to outbid Sector *B* as the monopoly rent to the landowner. Therefore, the amount of monopoly rent that "artificially raises" the price of the product of Sector *A* depends on the price elasticity of demand on the product of Sector *A* at the market centre. If the consumers are willing to pay whatever the amount Sector *A* will charge for its product, then the monopoly rent will go up to the maximum limit which keeps the space originally subsumed for Sector *A*'s production the same as that before Sector B entered the competition; for example, there is no reduction in the volume of potatoes produced. Thereby Sector *A* secures more plots in an area closer to the market centre. By contrast, if the consumers are so vulnerable to the price increase, the demand on the product of Sector *A* will shrink, which would reduce the territory for Sector *A*'s production. At any rate, Sector *B* will be pushed outward as a consequence. As the production area occupied of Sector *B* is pushed outwards, which forces Sector B farmers to pay more transport costs to the market centre. This leads to a rise in the price of Sector *B*'s products, which can lead to a decrease in demand. How much of the area actually occupied by the production of Sector *B* and the width of the doughnut-shaped concentric circles depends also on the price elasticity of demand.

In short, two variables, the index of ground-rent and the price elasticity of demand, determine how much Sector *A* can actually secure the area closer to the market centre. The prices of both corn and potatoes go up for different reasons: in Sector *B*, the price increase is due to the necessity of annihilating space for the circulation process, and in Sector A, it is due to the necessity of subsuming space for the labour process (*Wirkungsraum*).

Through this "invisible hand" of the above land-use coordination, the territories for Sectors *A* and *B* are allocated according to the principle of market economy, which dominates the entire ensemble of space. Based on the second form of the subsumption of space, Sectors *A* and *B* fully subsume the land that covers all the available plots closest to the market centre with the condition of equilibrium in demand and supply satisfied.

The outcome of the competition is shown in Fig. 5.7. The Sector *B* farmers are pushed outwards by the amount of land necessary to fill the demand for the product of Sector *A* at the market centre under the new supply/demand condition created through the incursion of monopoly rent. Sector *B* can occupy the space depending on the amount of transport cost that Sector *B* farmers can afford based again on the elasticity of demand.

5.5 Conclusion

The conventional locational models are thus reinterpreted and transformed into socialist or Marxist contexts in analysing the two forms of the real subsumption of space. The anarchical contiguity and separation in the economic space are thus duly subsumed into the theoretical framework of Marxist economics.

Physical space is an objective entity filled with dialectics. The contradictions are subsumed into the economy and society, and a fresh stage of dialectics in the subsumption develops and manifests itself in the socio-spatial process under the dictates of the modes of the economic and power structure. The production of a new configuration of economic and social space transcends this contradiction and annihilates the obstacle that pristine space created, and facilitates the operation of the economy and society again.

The economy and society thus return to the original process under the virtual "one-point world", with the political and economic power retained. Through production of the spatial configuration, therefore, the contradiction between the attributes of pristine space and the power of aspatial economy and society is externalised and transcended.

In reality, however, the subsumption is normally not perfect, and some elements of pristine space are left unsubsumed. There are always "loopholes" in subsumption,

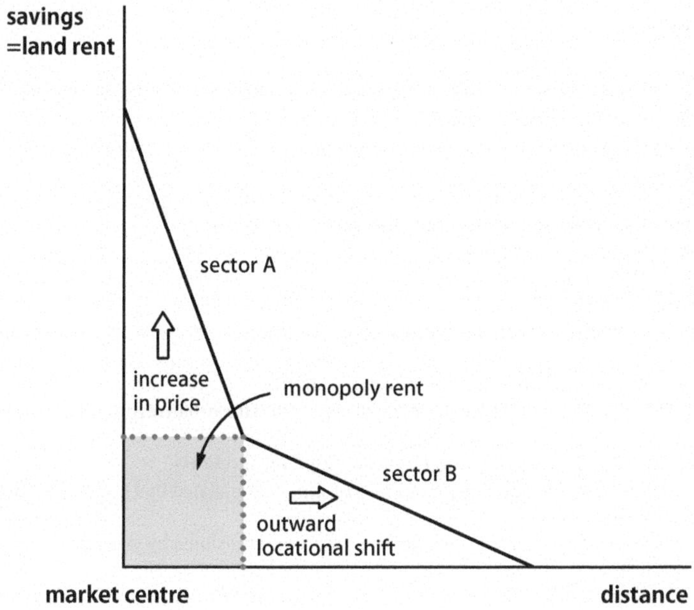

Fig. 5.7 The outcome of the land-use coordination in the market. *Source* Mizuoka et al. (2002), p. 182

which those contesting the power can deploy in the social struggles. Those who face the struggle against the power in the real economy and society, which still could not bring space to the stage of ultimate subsumption, are given the opportunity to deploy the space left unsubsumed to wage another struggle or at least to seek a quick refuge to protect themselves from arbitrary infliction of power.

Imperfect subsumption means that human society or some classes or groups consisting of it face negative moments of the space, thus the exertion of power of the dominant class gets stranded, may face the challenge from the subservient people or run into crisis of collapse in the worst case.

Therefore, the social struggle in many cases involves spatial struggle, or struggle deploying space as the crucial element. The struggle thus becomes socio-spatial. Although the ultimate attainment of the complete real subsumption of the relational space has been sought by those in power, the subservient people seek to scrape up the unsubsumed elements of space to create their own alternative configuration of space. This is the social struggle in the realm of the real subsumption of space. The production of space is therefore inevitably infested with struggles and offers various vents for them. More on this point in Chap. 9.

Until relational space is fully subsumed and the adverse elements of space have all been annihilated, utopians, visionary socialists, futurists, city planners and science fiction writers will depict the ultimately subsumed space under their own dictates, which are largely devoid of classes or conflicts.

References

Berry, B. J. L., & Garrison, W. L. (1958). Recent developments of central place theory. *Papers and Proceedings of the Regional Science Association, 4*.
Brenner, N. (2004). *New state spaces: Urban governance and the rescaling of statehood*. Oxford Univ. Press.
Brinkmann, T. (1935). (translation). *Theodor Brinkmann's economics of the farm business*. Elisabeth T. Benedict et. al. (Ed.), University of California Press.
Chisholm, M. (1962). *Rural settlement and land use*. Hutchinson University Library.
Christaller, W. (1966) (translation). *Central places in southern Germany*. Translated by Carlisle W. Baskin. Prentice-Hall.
Hottes, R. (1983). Walter Christaller. *Annals of the Association of American Geographers, 73*(1), 51–54.
Heinritz, G. (1979). *Zentralität und zentrale Orte*. Teubner.
Harvey, D. (1974). Class-monopoly rent, financial capital and the urban revolution. *Regional Studies*, 8.
Harvey, D. (1982). *The limits to capital*. University of Chicago Press.
Lefebvre, H. (1991) (translation). *The production of space*. Translated by Donald Nicholson-Smith. Wiley-Blackwell.
Lösch, A. (1954) (translation). *The Economics of location*. Translated by William H. Woglom. Yale University Press.
Marx, K. (1971) (translation). *Theories of Surplus-Value. Part III*. translated by Jack Cohen and S. W. Ryazanskaya. Progress Publishers.
Marx, K. (1973). (translation). *Grundrisse*. Translated by Martin Nicolaus. Vintage Books.
Marx, K. (1977 and 1981) (translation). *Capital*. Vols. 1 and 3. Translated by Ben Fowkes. New York : Vintage Books.
Mizuoka, F. ed. (2002). *Keizai Shakai no Chirigaku* (*Geography of Economy and Society*). Yuhikaku.
Mizuoka, F. (1979). On the source of 'false social value.' *Hitotsubashi Journal of Social Sciences, 3*(4), 94–112.
Peet, R. (1972). Some issues in the social geography of American poverty. R. Peet ed. *Geographical Perspectives on American Poverty*, pp. 1–4. Antipode.
Sack, R. (1986). *Human territoriality: Its theory and history*. Cambridge University Press.

Chapter 6
The Built Environment

Contents

Abstract The configuration of relational space is etched onto the land surface and the human mind. The former is the built environment, the physical materialisation of relational space, thus made tangible and visible. The huge cost of producing the built environment induces the state power to create space. As the built environment is a part of the material space, it can change its shape only when certain economic conditions are met. It, therefore, forms a fetter for society in its development and functions to curb the movement of the oppressed to achieve their autonomy and freedom. Sect. 4 offers a long digression on the 'relocation rule' of the built environment, which constitutes a theoretical clue for analysing the capitalist space in dynamism in Chap. 8.

6.1 The Nature of the Built Environment

a. Relational space engraved onto the land surface

The configuration of relational space is inscribed on the land in the form of physical objects. Once the relational space has been carved into the land, it is no longer a social relationship, but becomes a fixed and physical entity with its location and shape cannot easily be changed. Relational space thus assumes the objective and tangible form as *the built environment*, which is the physical expression of socio-spatial relations, or the social relation engraved onto the land's surface.

The built environment is an ensemble of material components that incorporate the configuration of contiguity and separation appropriate for the economic and social relationships that produced them.

F. Mizuoka, *Subsumption of Space*, Contributions to Regional Science,
https://doi.org/10.1007/978-981-97-7560-6_6

It is an artificial, as opposed to pristine, space which embodies the subsumption of relational space. It is composed of the assembly of buildings and other artefacts which form the parts and parcels of relational space. It is a systematised ensemble of human labour in which various elements such as buildings and traffic routes are organically integrated.

Since it must function as a collection, in many cases which the useful effect does not materialise unless all components are completed. This is the lump-sum property of the built environment. For example, a tunnel dug halfway only up to the middle of mountain is completely useless for the purpose of transportation.

Because of the exclusive nature of territory, only one element of the built environment can occupy a specific position. However, a certain kind of built environment may be jointly utilised by all people and groups with different class positions in society.

The origin of the concept of the built environment goes back to the landscape theory (*Landschaftskunde*) put forward at the beginning of the twentieth century by German geographer Otto Schlüter (1906). He set the aim of geography to overcome time in comparison with history, which considers events in a time axis. Although Schlüter spent his final decade in the GDR (East Germany), Marxist influence is hardly found in his academic works. According to Schlüter, landscape (*Landschaft*) is a form of a group of visible and immobile artefacts and natural landforms rooted on the ground surface, similar to the built environment concept with visible features of artefacts rooted on the land.

b. The built environment for domination of power

"Arrangement and classification" of the built environment is carried out by the political authority in power (Lefebvre, p. 375). The built environment as a processed and artificialised pristine space has multi-layered artificially produced contiguity and separation, together with various properties of expanse and distance found in pristine space. It provides the political power with a material basis of container and transportation and communication, or contiguity and separation, to achieve domination.

Thus, the built environment has inevitably been infused with the dictate of state power. Lefebvre states (p. 378), "the state and its bureaucratic and political apparatuses intervene continually in space, and make use of space in its instrumental aspect in order to intervene at all levels and through every agency of economic realm". It is modelled after "private enterprise, private property" (p. 376).

Lefebvre also gave an example of the built environment produced by the ancient Greek state:

> A space in which each focal point, whether that of each house or that of the polis as a whole, was ideally placed upon a well-chosen, well-situated eminence, sunlit and close to an abundant source of water. The Greek city, as a spatial and social hierarchy, utilized its meticulously defined space to bring dames, aristocratic clans, villages, and groups of craftsmen and traders together into the unity of the polis. (p. 249)

The configuration of the built environment produced by those in power, which has money and labour at its disposal, is carried out such that the hierarchies of society and space correspond to one another.

In modern society, the configuring the built environment is a major means of leverage of the state power. It "often seeks to reorganize urban infrastructure and urban life with an eye to the control of resistive populations" (Harvey, 2012, p. 117). An example that Harvey drew upon is Haussmann's planning of Paris, and planning of the same nature exists also in the Hong Kong Mass Transit Railway (MTR) project under British colonial domination (Mizuoka, 2018, Chap. 6). The MTR was planned to run under Nathan Road, the sole urban artery of Kowloon Peninsula, to counter and contain possible insurgencies of local Chinese, like the anti-British Chinese uprisings in 1967, using mountain tunnelling in the heart of urban Kowloon instead of open-cut methods common for urban underground railway construction, which is vulnerable to blasting. The MTR thus offered a redundancy in urban transport network for secure and quick deployment of the colonial police and armed forces in case a similar violent struggle by the insurgent Chinese would take place there in the years to come.

The physical configuration of the existing built environment has power to coerce a particular mode of human action and lifestyle, normally purposefully designed by those in power. For example, in Los Angeles, where the current urban built environment has been constructed, after the complete demise of the once efficient Pacific Electric inter-urban railway network by the automobile monopolies, upon the premise of automobile traffic, the citizens have to use automobiles every day, no matter their awareness of environmental protection. Nevertheless, some citizens opposed the construction of motorways in Los Angeles, which is the most visible manifestation of motorisation. The movement against the construction of motorways to protect the environment won a victory, reducing the number of lanes and constructing a light-rail line in the median strip. However, even radical activists of this movement who do not own or use cars manufactured by the automobile capitalists would be dropped from normal economic and social life in Los Angeles. The urban built environment of Los Angeles therefore has power to coerce citizens to own and drive cars.

In addition, the built environment has a symbolic meaning for the social integration as it is visible and planted on the land, giving potential for symbolism, yet again this symbolic nature is infested with class interest, thus can cause conflicts and struggles between social classes regarding its implication for the heritages of different classes and groups. The built environment thus has in this sense "*reifying* power" (Sack, 1986, p. 32).

The built environment thus serves the role of physical platform for social integration on the one hand, though it can sometimes serve as the arena for social struggles between classes and groups on the other. The built environment is therefore artificial physical space fixed in a specific position, reifying the economy and society which produced it and reinforces the territory and network.

Through production of the artificial physical space in the form of the built environment, which is unevenly scattered across space, society virtually restores the original one-point world.

6.2 The Subsumption of the Built Environment

a. The past power relation projected into the present

Lefebvre states, "every society … produces a space, its own space" (p. 31). In the transition of the modes of production, "the shift from one mode to another must entail the production of a new space.... a fresh space is indeed generated during such changes" of transition (p. 46).

The built environment is not a unilateral reflection of economic and social relations. When the physical form of the built environment produced in the past regime is subsumed into the existing economic and social relations, the particular configuration of contiguity and separation can adversely affect the functioning of existing relations. The physical configuration of separation and contiguity embedded in the built environment produced in the past regime can create obstacles. The configuration of the built environment produced by the previous power comes into contradiction with the new power regime. Furthermore, even under the same political power regime, the configuration of the optimum built environment is different in relation to the position of the class or group in the society.

The dominant economic and social relations may have been given a meaning as a specific symbol in their elements for the purpose of their long-term stable existence, and they were positively utilised. The glittering "capital city" planning and construction was a typical example of this. All of these have now to be transformed to fit the current power regime.

Therefore, its physical form needs to be altered if the existing built environment is to support the current relations of the economy and society. This is the subsumption of the built environment into the economy and society, or the subsumption of the past into the present.

The built environment produced in the past is not elastic, as with social relations. Thus, the configuration produced with the physical object does not change fluidly, unless it is physically destroyed by war, for example, or it is exposed to weather, time and concomitant decay. Although it is different from what the current economic and social relation itself needs, when power shifts, the new power regime must subsume the configuration of the built environment produced in the past.

First, when the past embodied in the built environment would create obstacles, the most radical way would be to construct a completely new configuration of contiguity and separation in the built environment commensurate with the new economic and social relations in the original space that has been destroyed, cleared and reclaimed.

Nevertheless, both the destruction and production of a new built environment require a significant allocation of resources and labour. If such allocation is not sufficiently made, the economic and social organisations would face difficulties through the obstacles created by the existing built environment, as the current society must put up with the configuration of the *Wirkungsraum* and action space designed in the past.

The configuration of contiguity and separation as well as the image attached to the built environment in the past, the symbolism attached to it remain and the past is projected into the present, producing the complicated relation with the current economic and social relation.

b. Opposition and struggle around the built environment

The people must essentially subsume the produced built environment as the physical frame of daily life.

The Panopticon-like contiguity of the built environment can be a facile platform for a surveillance society with undesirable connection to the people. The separation created by the built environment unilaterally deteriorates the social relations and solidarity necessary to support daily life. With the development of the economy and society, the capacity of the means of spatial integration in the past can become insufficient, and even if it functions normally, social relations and solidarity are paralysed.

From this, the people who are under the domination of power and constrained to a specific part of space struggle to find and expand the opportunity to contiguity, while those under surveillance in the Panopticon-like contiguity struggle against interference by the state power using space.

In short, there is struggle in the configuration of contiguity and separation between those in power and those dominated. The dominant power has financial resources to create the built environment, which forces those dominated to create their own configuration of contiguity and separation, using loopholes in the existing built environment.

This is a form of spatial practice from those being dominated. More in general terms on the issue of this spatial struggle in Chap. 9.

6.3 The Built Environment in Capitalism

a. The two categories of the built environment

According to Harvey (1982, pp. 232–238), the built environment in capitalism is divided into two categories: *fixed capital,* related to production of material goods, and *consumption fund,* related to consumptions of the general public such as the reproduction of the labour force and families.

As production further expands across space, fixed capital comes to "cover investment in space, such as highways or airports, as well as all sorts of infrastructural elements" (Lefebvre, p. 345). Lefebvre lists "multifarious establishments" of a town, namely, post offices, railway stations, storehouses and transportation systems as fixed capital (p. 347).

The consumption fund is the element of space "simply consumed (in such forms as travel, tourism, or leisure activities) as a vast commodity" (p. 349). Fixed capital and consumption fund may be separate entities. A factory is fixed capital and a house is consumption fund. One cannot live in a factory, and one cannot produce anything for markets at home.

b. The collective nature leads to social integration

However, some physical entities often serve for both categories. For example, a lorry carrying car parts and cars that families drive for the resort run on the same motorway. The entities of the built environment being often shared by the production of capital and the livelihoods of the public, a significant component of the built environment functions as commons in the action spaces of same society, regardless of the class or group. Thus, the urban built environment becomes a means of "*collective consumption*" (Castells, 1978, pp. 15–36).

The collective nature of the built environment creates social integration. Many people share a common interest in the production and use of one and the same built environment, and class relations, which are at odds as economic relations, are locally concealed and relaxed, forming the *local class alliance*. From this, the concepts of communities (*Gemeinschaft*) and *residents* arise and strengthen as territorial groups of people share a common interest in a local matter.

c. "Social Capital": Intervention of state power to rectify insufficient supply of "meta-commodity"

It is normally difficult for the "invisible hand" of the market mechanism alone to produce and coordinate the elements and produce the whole ensemble of the perfectly functioning built environment, if not some elements of it.

This is because the "invisible hand" of the market mechanism is to produce the whole ensemble of the built environment effectively, if only the following three conditions are met:

1. Given the lump-sum property of the built environment, funds to create the entire built environment are provided all at once and produced as a system simultaneously.
2. When this is difficult, each component of the built environment, which is fixed in physical form, must immediately respond to market adjustments.
3. The externalities arising from the "indivisibility" of goods and the services they provide do not lead to market failure.

As explained earlier, the fixed physical properties of the built environment make these conditions hard to fulfil. Therefore, at least some elements of the built environment have to be produced and supplied and the entire ensemble coordinated by the "visible hand", which is the dominant state power, through urban planning and national land planning. Individual elements of the built environment may also be provided publicly through taxes.

When a large number of members of a group are within reach, the entire group may be considered as beneficiaries of the element of the built environment. For the elements of a privately owned built environment, the costs associated with their production and destruction are to be paid privately by the owner or manager, and each economic entity must cover these costs with its revenue. If externalities cannot be fully internalised, the amount of income for individual economic entities will be less than the benefit of the whole group enjoying the utility of the built environment.

Consequently, the private entities cannot fully recover the cost of producing the elements of this built environment, resulting in the under-provision of a service, as in the lighthouse example discussed in Chap. 3 (pp. 29–30). Thus, under the market economy based on the principle of private ownership, it becomes difficult to produce the built environment as a networked system functioning smoothly as a whole. Thus, the built environment comes under the control and management of nation or local states in a form of "*social capital*".

The state power is forced to provide elements of the built environment as social capital when they belong to the category of commodity, which would be called "*meta-commodity*", or a general necessary condition for the market to transcend the negative aspect caused by pristine space to subsume pristine space thus to recover the spaceless "one-point world". Meta-commodities can become social capital if it belongs to the means for the market to subsume pristine space in real terms (Mizuoka 1989, p. 194). Ken-ichi Miyamoto (1976, p. 26) claims, for example, that "the bourgeois nations come to control bourgeois society itself by building and managing the universal instruments of labour, which are the general and mutual social conditions of capitalist production."

Nevertheless, this does not mean all the meta-commodities are provided publicly. The state plays a role in providing the prerequisite "social capital" for capitalist production and exchange only in so far as "no individual capitalist would find it possible to provide [the "social capital"] at a profit" (Harvey, 1976, p. 184).

Many elements of the built environment are, in fact, built and managed privately for profit, which is made possible by the formation of the joint-stock company, even though it is categorically a "meta-commodity". In the annihilation of space, many means of transportation and communication are provided by private companies. Railways in nineteenth-century England, telecommunication services, airlines and freight railway traffic in the contemporary US and extensive networks of private commuter railway and bus lines in the Osaka and Tokyo metropolitan area of Japan are only a few examples.

For road construction, Marx positively admits the possibility that, in a developed capitalist society, roads can be built and sold profitably by private capitalists:

> all general conditions of production, such as roads, canals, etc., whether they facilitate circulation or even make it possible at all, or whether they increase the force of production... presuppose, in order to be undertaken by capital instead of by the government which represents the community as such, the highest development of production founded on capital. (*Grundrisse*, p. 530-1)

> capital must be able to sell the road ... in such a way that both the necessary and the surplus labour are realized, or in such a way that it obtains out of the general fund of profits – of surplus values – a sufficiently large share to make it the same as if it had created surplus value .... for capital,... if it is to undertake the building of the road, it must be presupposed that not only the necessary labour time but also the surplus labour time worked by the worker can be paid for – this is where his profit comes from. (*ibid*, p. 532-3)

Marx believed that "the separation of public works from the state, and their migration into the domain of the works undertaken by capital itself, indicates the degree to which the real community has constituted itself in the form of capital" (*ibid*, p. 531);

and it is society, which constitutes "itself in the form of capital", that we are now analysing.

Whether the state manages the built environment as "social capital" or not is primarily dependent on the most basic capitalist criteria: the possibility of earning a sufficient profit. State management of the built environment becomes necessary only when it is unprofitable from the individual capitalists' point of view.

d. "Social capital" and crisis: the secondary circuit of capital

For individual capital "to undertake the building of the road, it must be presupposed that not only the *necessary labour time* but also the *surplus labour time* worked by the worker can be paid for—this is where his profit comes from" (*Grundrisse*, p. 532). If building and managing a road accrue surplus value, then the road will indeed be constructed and managed by private capital.

However, even when "the value of the road is not valorized ...it is built only because it is a necessary use value for the commune, because the commune requires it at any price" (p. 526). The built environment belonging to the category of meta-commodity which does not valorise is thus produced through taxes by the "commune", or in the capitalist mode of production, by the states. However, during the period of primitive accumulation of capitalism, the situation was quite different. In this period, the state has not accumulated sufficient fund to accomplish the production of "meta-commodity". In the absence of sufficient savings in the macro-economy, its elements were instead produced by forced mobilisation by resource and labour power.

For example, in Hokkaido, Japan's northernmost island developed over the living space of indigenous Ainus in the late nineteenth century, for example, most of the means of spatial integration necessary for its colonisation were constructed by prison labour or the transportation of workers brought from the former colonies on the Korean peninsula. The spatial integration of national land space was carried out through this sort of state power. Capitalism needs the most fundamental elements of social capital at any rate as social capital, even if it does not accrue profit.

Harvey (1978, p. 220) summarises this relation as follows:

> failure to invest in those elements in the built environment which contribute to accumulation is no different in principle than the failure of entrepreneurs to invest and reinvest in fixed capital equipment. The problem with the built environment is that much of it functions as *collective* fixed capital (transport, sewage and disposal systems, etc.). Some way has to be found, therefore, to ensure that individual investment decisions are coordinated in both time and space so that the aggregative needs of capitalist producers are met. By the same token, failure to invest in the means of consumption for labor may raise the wage rate, generate civil strife or (in the worst kind of eventuality) physically diminish the supply of labor. In both cases failure to invest in the right quantities, at the right times and in the right places can be a progenitor of a crisis of accumulation and growth.

For these reasons, Harvey claims that "state intervention is an omnipresent feature in the production, maintenance and management of the built environment" (*ibid*, p. 221).

In a crisis, of which spatial import will be discussed in detail in Chap. 8, the capitalist state intervenes to drain away plethora of capital, which can be detrimental to the capitalist mode of production itself. The involvement of the state in the affairs of the built environment is closely related to staving off the crisis tendency of capitalism.

Here, the investment in social capital is an ideal means to stave off crisis. The state is properly termed the "crisis-manager" (Harvey, 1978, p. 222). The integration of the states as the "executive committee of the bourgeoisie" (Harvey, 1982, p. 322) and the financial oligarchy further facilitate this function.

During the considerable gestation period required to construct an element of the built environment, it keeps unilaterally absorbing resources and labour, without emitting any economic benefit.

The funding is met by excess capital existing in society. Excess capital is directed to producing the building environment as social capital through the state power engaging in the process Harvey called *the secondary circuit of capital*. The state issues high-quality public bonds backed by its power to collect taxes. The secondary circuit of capital absorbs excess capital and thus shuns overproduction and economic crises. The production of the built environment contributes to the stability of the capitalist society by removing excess capital and bringing about social integration through the provision of the common infrastructure of the built environment.

e. Neo-liberalism and class struggle in the provision of the built environment

The state often builds and manages the built environment which has the functions of both fixed capital and consumption fund simultaneously as social capital. The composite nature of the built environment comes in part from the physical nature of the use-value of a particular element of the built environment, as explained earlier. For example, a telecommunication system, often built by the state power, can be used by both capitalists for business communications and labourers for personal calls alike.

When the nation or the local states manage a built environment having both functions simultaneously, the state does so by "taking advantage of the nature of the each means and its composite characteristics, to the advantage of the capital" (Miyamoto, 1976, p. 43). For instance, the toll on a turnpike is often cheaper for a lorry than a passenger car if compared in terms of the weight of the vehicles.

The neo-liberalist state intervenes in the process with the "cost–benefit principle" to avoid further financial burdens and to offer the big businesses clearer benefit in the operation of social capital. The state thus begins to contemplate the provision of "meta-commodity" more prudently, and avoid providing services that do not really belong to this category. A typical example is local railway lines, which no longer function as the nation- or region-wide network of spatial integration. The state then deploys the principle to persuade the people for poor service to stave off the struggle around the construction and use of built environment put for collective consumption of the people.

The ultimate picture of the "cost–benefit principle" in the social capital provision in the era of neo-liberalism would be the withdrawal of the state from the construction and management of the built environment itself, or the introduction of "more competitive" self-supporting accounting systems. The ever-increasing magnitude of fixed capital will be operated by private capital under the name of deregulation.

However, this shift could merely aggravate the poor provision of "meta-commodity", which can trigger the rupture of social integration, and hinders the maintenance of the current mode of production, or causes the collapse of appeasement in strife-ridden class relations. This can sometimes be detrimental to the maintenance of functions more innate to the capitalist state, such as monetary, military, police, education and other oppressive and disciplining institutions, and detrimental for the capitalists in that it pushes their rate of profit down further, as the financial burden would call for a higher tax rate.

Thus, the capitalist state can come back to the provision of consumption fund in their guise of benefiting people, as a countermeasure to fend off class and ethnic struggles to the degree of the need for co-opting subservient classes or ethnic groups. Inwardly however, the capitalist state takes the initiative in building and maintaining the means of collective consumption for labourers, in order to guarantee the capitalists and the vested interest groups a higher rate of profit or more benefits.

For example, "capitalists may themselves seek to provide cheap housing ... or they may even side with the demands of labour for cheap, subsidized housing, under public ownership, provided that this permits the payment of lower wages" (Harvey, 1976, p. 274). Massive public housing of poor quality built in the 1950s by the Hong Kong British colonial government for the Chinese "refugees" from the People's Republic of China, who had the potential to be the source of cheap labour, is typical to this case (Mizuoka, 2018, Chap. 4). The child guidance centre and other related "social care" establishments are a good example of how to nourish the vested interests of the national and local states and other "welfare" agencies under the guise of "protecting the rights of the child" (see Chap. 9, p.169ff).

6.4 Digression: The Relocation of the Elements of the Built Environment in the Market Economy

a. Introduction

Since the built environment is fixed to the land in the form of physical form, there arises another problem: it is impossible to change the physical form instantaneously as other economic variables to meet the fluctuation of price and demand, and enormous cost and time is required for the renewal or reform of it, if only because those who own the built environment often cannot sufficiently pay this cost.

As the privately created built environment is bound to suffer devaluation according to the whims of changing relative position in the configuration of relational space, the market entities may attempt, to some extent, to modify existing built environments that create impediments to capital accumulation and social development. This shall be carried out, however, *only if* the income generated by the newly created built environment exceeds the income generated by continuing to use the old construction environment, and in the meantime, this excess of the income can cover the costs of demolishing the old built environment and producing the new built environment. Needless to say, this condition is not always satisfied.

Thus, the supply and renewal of the built environment can be difficult if it is left to the decision-making based on the private cost and benefit relations in the market economy. Hence, the whole built environment does not function properly as a system. Thus, there is always a disparity between the actual physical organisation of the built environment and the market economy or social power that seeks to produce a particular configuration relational space in its physical form.

Although the built environment is fixed spatially, economic development and social change sometimes call for its relocation. Yet, the property of the built environment fixed in space as a physical form is often generalised empirically as "geographical inertia". This does not mean, however, that the spatial configuration thus created is eternally immobile. Harvey (1982, p. 394) puts forward a "rational re-location rule": the production capital fixed to the land is to have "the gain in surplus value from the move outweigh the devaluation incurred". Harvey is indeed right that the "devaluation" is the key in understanding relocation of the elements of the built environment. The case of the built environment falls on the concept of the place-specific devaluations.

This digression examines economic relations by drawing upon Marx's own arguments to prepare the theoretical basis for the analysis in Chap. 8 on space in the business cycle.

b. Place-specific devaluation

The devaluation of capital and "loss" is distributed unevenly among individual capitalists. Marx states:

> the distribution being decided instead by a competitive struggle in which the loss is divided very unevenly and in very different forms according to the particular advantages or positions that have already been won, in such a way that one capital lies idle, another is destroyed, a third experiences only a relative loss or simply a temporary devaluation and so on. (*Capital*, Vol. 3, p. 362)

Thus, the devaluation of capital is not distributed evenly across geographical space. Instead "devaluation, arising for whatever reason, is always particular to a place, is always location specific" (Harvey, 1982, p. 378). This brings about the necessity of scrutinising the process of "*place-specific devaluation*" before examining the "relocation rule".

As in the discussion of land-use coordination in the last chapter, capitalism creates an economic landscape through its attempt to balance sectoral and spatial differences in the rates of profit. In terms of the actual spatial distribution of economic functions, the physiognomy of the resulting hierarchical spatial system indeed looks uneven, yet in terms of the rate of profit, which is the object that capitalists pursue, the landscape attains the capitalist egality of the average rate of profit over the space.

Nevertheless, as this capitalist egality over space presupposes a free spatial movement of capital, it exists only in a relatively longer time span. In the short run, as production capital is fixed to a particular place, capital cannot relocate rapidly enough to facilitate this capitalist egality. Immobile capital fixed at a particular location now turns out to be the factor hindering capitalism from achieving the capitalist egality, or an equal rate of profit across space. Capital located at an unfavourable location accrues a lower rate of profit than that at a more favourable location, and this difference cannot be averaged out in the short run due to the existence of immobile fixed capital, or an element of the built environment.

The following example can be presented. If capital of $1,500 invested at location *A* earns only the same amount of profit, $100, as capital of $1,000 invested elsewhere (at location *B*) for a place-specific reason, then the additional amount of capital $500 invested at location *A*, as compared to that of location *B*, fails to produce the corresponding amount of surplus value, and is thus reduced to useless as capital, or self-valorising value. The $1,500 of capital invested at location *A* functions only as $1,000 of capital invested at location *B*. From the position of location *B*, capital at location *A* is devalued to $1,000; or, taking the same amount of capital at both locations *A* and *B*, the capital of $1,000 at location A is now devalued to $666 $\frac{2}{3}$.

In this context, we can interpret the spatial difference in the rates of profit arising from the existence of immobile fixed capital as a case of capital devaluation. A part of the capital invested at an unfavourable location can be regarded as less fertile, which would reduce the profit level of the capital at location *B* to a lower level. Thus "place-specific devaluation" is an outcome of the short-run spatial differences in rates of profit. This difference cannot be averaged out for some time, as the time available for relocation is too short.

It is not averaged out by the appropriation of ground-rent by landlords either, as there is still open and untilled space for the direct valorisation process of non-agricultural capital in the vicinity of the locations *A* and *B*. The relocation takes place only when there is no way for capital to resolve this "place-specific devaluation" by choosing a better location to create a more efficient hierarchical spatial configuration in the longer run.

In sum, the need capitalists feel for relocation comes from the unevenness in the place-specific differences in the rate of profit, and relocation is the way to resolve the short run "place-specific devaluation" that the capitalists are suffering.

c. Relocation of immobile fixed capital

When technological innovation and development and, consequentially, capital accumulation proceed in the existing built environment without relocation, the spatial disparity of the rates of profit comes to be aggravated. "Place-specific devaluation" hits capitalists at different locations to different degrees according to the relative position of a place across whole spatial configuration with its differences in the rate of profit created due to technological development. There can be a considerably wide spectrum of spatial differences in the profit rate and "place-specific devaluations". If capital overproduction caused by technological innovation is quite severe, the capital located at unfavourable place-specific conditions comes to accrue absolutely no profit, or absolute capital devaluation occurs, while other capital at more favourable conditions can accrue some profit.

Nevertheless, capital can overcome the obstacle of being immobile capital fixed to land by taking two actions simultaneously to alleviate this "place-specific devaluation": to abandon or to sell a portion of the immobile fixed capital at the location suffering "place-specific devaluation" and invest in fresh immobile fixed capital at a new location. If this process brings about a higher rate of profit than before, then relocation should take place.

However, all that concerns the capitalists is the rate of profit accrued and the remaining value in their account book with no devaluation considered. In the eyes of a capitalist, the loss in existing capital investment which needs abandoning for relocation is the remaining value of immobile fixed capital yet to be depreciated less the value recovered through such sales in the second-hand market. If there is no second-hand market, or the capitalist can find no one willing to purchase the existing immobile fixed capital, then the capitalist can do nothing but abandon it. The value recovered is zero in this case.

Capitalists do not take the value corresponding to the portion of fixed capital that has already depreciated and transferred to the product into account as a loss when they consider relocation. This portion is already incorporated into commodity capital and has been realised or will eventually be realised and returned to the capitalist as money capital under normal market conditions.

The real concern for the capitalists facing to consider relocation is therefore abandoning the full or partial value of the existing capital yet to be depreciated, which forms a part of the cost of relocation to the capitalist. If construction of new immobile fixed capital can only be done with the closure of the existing premises, then the abandonment of fixed capital constitutes a part of the cost to construct new premises, and should serve as a base for computing the profit rate.

Nevertheless, when computing the rate of profit, the depreciated portion not included in the cost also plays a role. The "rate of surplus value, *as measured against the total capital*, is known as the rate of profit" (*Capital*, Vol. 3, pp. 133–4, emphasis mine). This "total capital" includes the depreciated portion of the production capital which remains in the capitalists" hand as a fund for future replacement of the fixed capital.

The cost required to move, especially for the transportation of commodity capital and maintaining the continuity of production, is also involved in the process.

However, as mentioned above, there is space left to be annihilated between the existing and new prospective locations; therefore, the difference between the two locations with respect to costs required to annihilate space does not transform itself into ground-rent. In addition, although this cost constitutes a part of the money capital required to maintain the circulation of capital, this portion of money capital is not directly related to the labour process, hence is not deployed in the production process for the exploitation of surplus-value.

To summarise the above argument in mathematical terms, the condition for the relocation to take place is as follows (for simplification, circulating capital as well as the cost for its transportation from the old to the new location is abstracted away):

$$\frac{C_{do}}{C_{ao} + E} < \frac{C_b}{C_b + (C_{ar} - C_s)}, \qquad (6.1)$$

where C is the value of immobile fixed capital, which is further defined by subscripts: a is the value at the existing location before devaluation, d that after devaluation and b that at a new location; r is the remaining value after depreciation, o the full value before depreciation, and s the value obtained by selling the existing immobile fixed capital in the second-hand market. E is the additional amount of money capital necessary for moving at the old location relative to the new location.

The numerators of the formula are the actual values of currently functioning capital. Note that the rate of profit comes to the numerator, yet as it is assumed that it is the same for both terms; it mutually cancels out and does not appear in the formula. The amount of money capital necessary for moving, or to annihilate space E appearing in the denominators of left terms does not appear in the numerators, since it is annihilated through relocation and therefore does not transform into ground-rent. E is merely a burden on individual capital which cannot be realised in the social division of labour.

The smaller the left term of the above formula relative to the right, the higher the probability for a relocation of capital. For example, if capital devaluation is quite severe, as in case of crisis, the incentive for relocation is also substantial, as the numerator on the left side of the inequality is likely to be quite small or even zero.

If C_{do} is zero, or the capital at an existing location is totally devalued, then it is absolutely imperative for capital to relocate, or the capital will vanish. On the other hand, if there is little difference in "place-specific devaluation" over space, then there will not be much spatial movement of immobile fixed capital, because the numerators on both sides of the inequality are similar, due to the similarities between the values of C_{do} and C_b and the smaller value of E. Additionally, the denominator of the right term is larger than that of the left, due to the inclusion of C_{ar} in the right term and again the similarity between the values of C_{ao} and C_b. Nevertheless, this relation can be modified according to the condition of the second-hand market for existing capital. The more favourable are the conditions in which the existing capital can be sold, the higher the probability for relocation. Furthermore, regardless of the severeness of devaluation, the more the fixed capital of immobile kind is depreciated, the larger is the probability for relocation, since C_{ar} decreases along with the process of depreciation. Therefore, a place where the immobile fixed capital of an older vintage is located can more easily be abandoned by capital than that of a newer vintage.

This suggests that Harvey's claim quoted earlier, "the gain in surplus value from the move [must] outweigh the *devaluation incurred*" for relocation to be facilitated is misleading (Harvey, 1982, p. 394, emphasis mine). Capitalists do not, and cannot, care about the portion of capital that has already devalued and went missing, but do care about the portion that *remains at hand* as self-valorising value.

Of course, a capitalist need not close or sell the existing immobile fixed capital to create a new one elsewhere, unless the devaluation of fixed capital at the existing location is so substantial that the operation of the existing capital itself incurs a loss to the capitalist. The establishment of new premises, while keeping the existing one remain open, belongs essentially to the case of expanded reproduction. If we take expanded reproduction into account, as soon as the capital accumulated at a capitalist's hand reaches the "normal minimum of capital investment below which the business in question will cease to be competitive" (*Capital*, Vol. 2, p. 335), a new set of plants or facilities for circulation will be created at the location where the current and future potential for location-specific devaluation is least. This is not "*re*location" in its strict sense, but an entirely new location of plants and other immobile fixed capitals.

d. The relocation of the consumption fund

The relocation of the consumption fund that has already dropped out of capital circulation follows a rule different from that we have discussed. As this type of consumption fund is not for capitalist production, hence does not accrue profit, the above formula does not apply.

A labourer is spatially bound to the location of capital by "invisible threads" and has to live within the radius of the "commutable space" to earn the cost of reproducing labour power. If a labourer remains at the existing location after capital is relocated beyond the radius of commutable space, his/her labour power cannot be sold to a capitalist, which makes the labourer feel "a cruel nature-imposed necessity that his capacity for labour has required for its production a definite quantity of the means of subsistence, and will continue to require this for its reproduction" (*Capital*, Vol. 1, p. 277).

To relocate, a labourer must sell the consumption fund under his or her ownership (for example, a house) at the existing location; and the money obtained from this sale is applied to the purchase of a new consumption fund at the new location. The labourer becomes better off by relocation if

$$F_s > F_b, \tag{6.2}$$

where F is the price of the consumption funds, s the sale at the existing location and b the purchase at the new location.

However, unlike the case of the relocation of capital, this inequality does *not* mean that the labourer will not relocate unless the condition is met. Even in the opposite direction of inequality, the labourer must relocate if the job opportunity exists only at the new location b. In this case, the labourer has to cope with this situation by "moral degradation" in his/her living standard, to bring the two values in the above inequality closer. A labourer who used to live in a detached house may now have to put up with a one-bedroom studio at the new location, for example.

As the relocation of labour is determined by the relocation of capital that has suffered from "location-specific devaluation", the price of the existing consumption fund located at a place abandoned by capital is likely to decline. In this case, the "moral degradation" of consumption can be even more severe.

If even the severest sort of "moral degradation" cannot make the relocation of labour power feasible, labourers at a place being abandoned by capital are forced to become the "stagnant relative surplus population" and "paupers", which offer the capitalists "a broad foundation for special branches of capitalist exploitation" (*Capital*, Vol. 1, p. 796). The lower the price F_s, the smaller is the room for further "moral degradation", thus the smaller the probability for the relocation of the labourer. The poor who do not have a sufficient consumption fund at the existing location to sell are therefore most likely to suffer from "'location-specific' devaluation" of capital and likely to be driven to dead pauperism. The regional unemployment problem of the pool thus emerges and increases.

References

Castells, M. (1978). Collective Consumption and Urban Contradiction in Advanced Capitalism. *City, Class and Power*, pp. 15–36. Translated by Elizabeth Lebas. St. Martins.

Harvey, D. (1976). Labor, capital, and class struggle around the built environment in advanced capitalist societies. *Politics & Society*, *6*(3).

Harvey, D. (1978). On planning the Ideology of planning. In Robert W.Burchell, George Sternlieb (Eds.), *Planning Theory of 1980* (pp. 213–233). The Center for Urban Policy Research, Rutgers University.

Harvey, D. (1982). *The limits to capital*. University of Chicago Press.

Harvey, D. (2012). *Rebel cities: From the right to the city to the urban revolution*. Verso.

Lefebvre, H. (1991) (translation). *The production of space*. Translated by Donald Nicholson-Smith. Wiley-Blackwell.

Marx, K. (1973) (translation). *Grundrisse*. Translated by Martin Nicolaus. Vintage Books.

Marx, K. (1977) (translation). *Capital*. Vol. 1. Translated by Ben Fowkes. New York: Vintage Books.

Mizuoka, F. (2018). *Contrived Laissez-faireism*. Springer

Miyamoto, K. (1976). *Shakai Shihonron (Studies of Social Overhead Capital)*. Revised ed. Yuhikaku.

Sack, R. (1986). *Human territoriality: Its theory and history*. Cambridge University Press.

Schlüter, O. (1906). *Die Ziele der Geographie des Menschen*. R. Oldenbourg.

Chapter 7
The Autogenous Bond of Space and Body

Contents

Abstract This chapter covers the native and contrived bond of body and mind with space, termed the "autogenous bond of space and body". The configuration of relative space becomes a part of the native human mind and body in various ways autogenously through the quotidian contact of the human with space. However, as Ueno points out in the case of Minamata disease, the state and capitalist power destroy the environment and alienate this intimate autogenous bond. Power artificially attempts to contrive this bond, as demonstrated in the construction of the Catholic Church as the "spiritual centre" in Hanoi by France as a past colonial power and Disneyland in the contemporary world.

This book has thus far discussed the production of physical space.

It in part constitutes the forces of production, "a role originally played by nature, which [the social space] displaced and supplanted" (Lefebvre, p. 349). Another aspect of nature that constitutes space is the human body and its mind. In fact, the "whole of (social) space proceeds from the body, even though it so metamorphoses the body that it may forget it altogether—even though it may separate itself so radically from the body as to kill it" (p. 405). The particular economic and social relationships embodied in the elements of the built environment pierce through time, as landscape theory posits, where the power structure of the past is frozen and preserved in the bodies of the subservient people, projecting the past power into the future.

This chapter analyses how the body, which is "along with space" and "in space" (p. 407) as well as nature by default, is alienated and removed from it.

F. Mizuoka, *Subsumption of Space*, Contributions to Regional Science,
https://doi.org/10.1007/978-981-97-7560-6_7

7.1 Spatial Configuration and Lived Space Carved into the Body

a. The autogenous bond of space and body

The spatial configuration is engraved not only as a physical form on the ground surface as the built environment but also in the mental aspect of the human body of the labourers and subservient people.

The landscape consists of the built environment and physical nature, topography and flora, which is the property of physical geography, and takes a configuration similar to the Gestalt of psychology as a whole, and the common signs of the place are engraved in the body of the subservient people who were born and raised in the same place, or those who lived there in the past for a long time. Even after the state power has come into control of space as the society transforms itself into an agricultural one, to a household of peasants, "the land he works and the village in which he lives may still seem to him as a natural entity, as the place to which he belongs emotionally and spiritually." The peasants thus have a "sense of belonging to a place" (Sack, 1986, p. 74).

Sack (p. 64) points out that in primitive society, "space … and experience are so intimately interrelated." Lefebvre identified spatiality as "the perceived, the conceived, and the lived; representations of space and representational spaces; the spaces proper to each faculty, from the sense of smell to speech; the gestural and symbolic". The whole body is thus integrated into social space, especially when the cognition is more primitive, as in one's childhood or in pre-modern society. The process of integration emerges through the autogenous process, just as a baby learns to acquire its native language through exchange with other humans, especially with its parents.

Lefebvre further points out (p. 240), "it is indeed a space, at once and indistinguishably mental and social, which *comprehends* the entire existence of the group concerned" (italics original). I would call it the *autogenous bond of space and body*. Here, "space" includes not only pristine space, but also produced space as an outcome of space subsumption and physical nature.

The autogenous bond is a notion of space that we often hold in our intellectual development from infancy to adulthood, and especially in the early stages of human development from primitive to increasingly advanced civilisation. The most primitive and fundamental aspect of the relationship between the body and its outer space, the autogenous combination of space and the body, is thus created and persists. In the same way that infants acquire native language, they acquire the property of space surrounding their bodies to create the innate bond of space and their own body.

Spatial awareness in childhood remains self-centred and subjective. It is known that when a child is asked to draw a cognitive map, he or she draws a place strongly related to himself or herself or a place which gives him or her a comfortable feeling more conspicuous and larger than other places. Furthermore, the infant has no awareness of the property relations of space independent of its material property. A child tries to attach his or her own cognition of "ownership" to various elements of space through his or her own subjective judgement, without being able to judge sufficiently whether the particular spatial element is actually under their own exclusive control or ownership, under control or ownership of others, or is used as non-exclusive commons.

The place where people have been living in a certain social space from their childhood is embedded within the mentality of the subject and becomes a innate part of his or her body. As a field of the autogenous binding of space and body, words such as *furusato* in Japanese or *Heimat* and *Heimlich* in German represent a territory or place supported by real economic and social experiences of a body.

This phenomenon also manifests itself in a group, for example, the people living in the same city or territory for a considerable period. However, in general, the recognition of the social property of the space matures as the subject grows and independent personality is established, and the right to the space of the self and the respect of other persons to it as well as the cooperativity in the group related to the social space grows among the members of the group.

At the same time, the range of perceived space also expands, and the recognition of the multi-layered spatial configuration in which the lower spatial scale becomes nested into the layers of higher spatial scale is formed in the body. The cognitive map of a child becomes gradually more objective and the reference frame comes closer to the surveyed maps. In this way, the recognition of space matures and becomes more objective. Yet, it does not completely become identical with the contiguity and separation drawn in a surveyed map. Even the everyday spatial cognition of adults living in a civilised society is developed to a considerable extent based on a relative framework consisting of a set of meanings and values of places given to space. The intensity and contrast of the meanings is often associated with the pristine or artificial separation or contiguity. When the spatial mobility of an individual or a social group is restricted, distorted spatial images and values are more likely to result. As the child comes of age, he or she is likely to begin experiencing this alienation from once intimate space.

b. Inscription of pristine and subsumed space in the mentality

A body as a biological substance bound in space becomes an integral part of relative space. The body determines direction of left, right, top and bottom as well as distance, all of which are the properties of relative space. Lefebvre points out (p. 226), "the level of singularities stretches outwards around bodies." The units of measurement of distance, such as feet and inches, were derived from the size of parts of the body. A part of a body is also used to describe the built form in physical space, as for example "phallic verticality" (Lefebvre, p. 36).

The relational space inscribed in the body as a "mental map" or mental map components attaches positive or negative value to the components in the relational space and becomes the norm or a guideline of the behaviour of a person.

The interconnectedness of spatial elements such as the built environment and physical landforms carved in the brain is reflection of the objective network of spatial configuration. This cognitive space is not necessarily an exact reflection of the pristine and built relational space, topography or vegetation. A person tends to remember strongly what he or she cares most about, what he or she enjoys, or what he or she often experiences. Yet the feature is distorted with loaded values for each individual.

If a believer in a religion has a common representation of a topographic feature and recognises that "God" exists in it, then the topographic feature is understood as if it contains supernatural forces. In geography, the individual points within pristine space that has been established with certain relationships with others in social mutual understanding are called *place*, and when the place is reified as having a certain power in society, they are called *spatial fetish.* A sense of spiritual belonging to a place of origin is constantly created and enhanced through daily life experience.

It is a derivative of the common homing instinct found other creatures. The autogenous bound of space and subject persists in consciousness of the subject, the children and adults alike, as the most innate spiritual base of a person, as the association with the biological parents or the native language.

This spiritual sense of belonging to the features of relational space triggers and motivates religious or social actions based on one's faith. In this sense, a spatial fetish is an objective factual aspect in the sense that there is a fact that space is inscribed in the human body, rather than a complete falsehood or empty subjectivity.

When many people share a particular understanding or value of a place, it can become a "place of hope" or "place of stigma". In this way, the system of relational space receives the mental image of groups, which in turn creates their own map of relational space in the mind of each person.

Such relational space coloured with the common imagery of living space strengthens the sense of community as "local class alliances" (Harvey, 1985, pp. 148–152) and the concept of the local inhabitants or simply the locals. It can affect the industrial location as the tendency of a family-owned company to set up its manufacturing plant in its hometown, as the proverb "return to one's hometown loaded with honours" aptly expresses.

c. Past discussions on this topic by Marxist and humanistic geographers

However, this inscription is never harmonious or stable in the class society under private ownership.

Noboru Ueno, the prominent Marxist geographer in Japan, points this out in relation to the alienation of the body of the working class from his or her space as follows:

> The biggest victims of the alienation from material-nature are mainly the working class. They are swayed by the illusion of quantitative contrasts while contemplating that they stand on the basis of their intrinsic use value and direct social relations. It is only when he or she overcomes the illusion and gain a position of direct use value, that is, when the land itself is restored to its original form, he or she would find peace of mind as a common human being. This amounts to grabbing back of the ensemble of space-body, which has been transformed into a fantasy, to his or her innate property. (Ueno, 1972, p. 204)

Here, Ueno focuses on the alienation and destruction of the autogenous bond of space and body under private ownership. In formulating this tenet, Ueno was inspired by the following statement of Marx in the first manuscript of *Economic and Philosophic Manuscripts of 1844* (1977 edition, p. 74, as well as Ueno, 1972, p. 109):

> It is just in his work upon the objective world, therefore, that man really proves himself to be a *species-being*. This production is his active species-life. Through this production, nature appears as *his* work and his reality. The object of labour is, therefore, the *objectification of man's species-life*.... In tearing away from man the object of his production, therefore, estranged labour tears from him his *species-life*, his real objectivity as a member of the species, and transforms his advantage over animals into the disadvantage that his inorganic body, nature, is taken away from him.

In fact, Ueno showed interest in a humanistic interpretation of Marxism in geography in as early as 1972, much earlier than when humanistic geography gained momentum in English-speaking countries.

A similar point was developed by humanistic geographers in subjective idealism into one of the main streams of modern geography with the understanding of intersubjectivity and "lived space". In Kant's conception, the object of recognition was space itself, but phenomenological geography emphasises the intuitive recognition based on a subjective perception of heterogeneous space filled with materials.

The primary point in phenomenological geography is that we live in a world composed of perceptions of the environment that surrounds a body. The space which surrounds us is "the lived space" (*espace vécu*), and it is called the "life world" (Buttimer, 1976) of the subject or "climate".

However, humanistic geography fails to recognise that the "lived space" is alienating, and does not see inherent conflict and struggle within it. Whereas Ueno (p. 204) states:

> The ultimate purpose of [Marxist] chorography is to critically analyse the reality in which the ensemble of space-body, which is the foundation of human existence, is transformed into an illusory objectivity and alienates local human groups under the private ownership system. Moreover, on the basis of this critical analysis, the [Marxist] chorography proposes praxis to be carried out against the environment where local human groups are transformed into illusory objects.

Indigenous people legitimately claim an "indigenous conception of 'the rights of mother nature'" (Harvey, 2012, p. 142), together with alienation from it, which is often used as leverage in social struggles for more rights and independence of indigenous people.

When it relates to something in the past, it is called "collective memories". The collective memories can also develop into the driving force for struggles against those who have attempted to destroy the physical source of memories due to profit motives. It can become "the key element" in the political strategy of the oppositional groups, especially when it is "so special as to be very hard to trade upon" (Harvey, 2012, pp. 108 and 112). Also, it can sometimes be incorporated into commercialisation by global or local capital in a contrived manner.

7.2 The Manipulation and Alienation of the Autogenous Bond by State and Economic Powers

a. Uprooting of the autogenous bond by state power

After agriculture became the mainstay of economic activity, people found and spontaneously occupied space and cultivated it into farmland for production as well as residential areas for their rural communities. As long as agriculture is self-sufficient in the community, the occupation of space by the body would have been a form of spontaneous occupation of *terra nullius* based on the principle of equality and agreement among community members. At this stage, the autogenous bond of the body of the subject and space has not been uprooted.

Once private property and a class society are established, the ruling class emerges as the ultimate power in ruling the configuration of space. Class society is a regime based on the possession of surplus by the ruling class, and in the pre-capitalistic society, the surplus taking the form of agricultural products is produced by the production space of agriculture that spread across the territory under its domination. The power of the institution and violence of a state "grind down and crash everything before them, with space performing the function of a plane, a bulldozer or a tank" (Lefebvre, p. 285). The original autogenous bond is thus brutally uprooted.

In the ancient Asiatic mode of production, the state power exercised the direct possession and control of the agricultural production space itself, including its associated irrigation facilities produced by the state power. The state appropriated all production space from individuals and then coordinated the land-use. The state power "partitions its empire and people territorially, classifying and controlling groups, both large and small, through the control of the area" (Sack, 1986, p. 74), to appropriate surplus product from the peasants.

A good large-scale example is the *jori* system based on the *handen shuju* system in Japan. The entire production space is subdivided, and the subjects were allocated by the state power as the serfs to one of the subdivided plots for the farm production. In this configuration of production space, the autogenous process of binding one's body to space was distorted and broken by the state power. A similar alienation from the autogenous bond between body and space can be found in the enclosure movement by the owners owner of the surplus in the United Kingdom. This process led former farmers to migrate to the city and the concomitant creation of proletariats in large cities, where the autogenous bond with space had been broken. The artificially superimposed boundaries in Africa and other colonised areas cut through the ethnic space, also leading to migration, which alienates people from the autogenous bond with space.

On the other hand, in the process of farmer liberation in France and Germany from the end of the eighteenth century to the beginning of the nineteenth century, free ownership and sale of land were admitted to farmers and citizens. The people appeared as the principal subject of space ownership and the ultimate agent of land use coordination, free from any forms of slavery. They can thus build a fresh autogenous bond with the space that they themselves own.

b. Relational space contrived and monetised to coerce people

The state intervention and monetisation of property relation dissociated the body from space. The entire spatial configuration was subordinated "to the unifying but abstract principle of property", which is "external, and supposedly superior, to "lived experience" " (Lefebvre, p. 252). The state authority instead attempted to deploy its power to contrive a bond of body with space.

In urbanising Medieval Europe "a social and a mental space" emerged. According to Lefebvre (p. 261), the façade in the built environment assumed the role of "trumpet[ing] the associated authorities of Church, King and city to the crowds flocking to the porch". The geometry and logic of relational space colluded with authority. The wrapper of the relational space, or façade, is given a coercive symbolic meaning by the authority to oppress people psychologically. The cities with such façades are alienating places, dissociated from their own rural *Heimat*, where the people could still have enjoyed an autogenous bond.

The mentality to respect authority is sometimes formed through the creation of a mystical imaginary configuration of space, artificially created by the state power. In the pre-modern era, for example, the autogenous bond with space was often displaced using rituals. Space is mystically infused, for example, in case of the "Chinese four quarters", which "was conceived of as the mirror of cosmic order" (Sack, 1986, p. 77), where the people are alienated and relegated to a mere component of it. This is a geographical variant of the organistic theory of society.

In some cases, the state power intentionally induces its people to have a bond of body with national land, often instigated by an imperialist motive. For example, in the earlier period of the US, there was "concerted efforts to keep the relationships between people and place intimate; to create a sense of community… Late eighteenth- and early nineteenth-century American life was full of national patriotism and love of land". It eventually developed into "manifest destiny", calling for conquering as far as the Pacific coast (Sack, 1986, p. 153). State power also takes advantage of the innate bond to "divide and fragment the consciousness of the working class", since the labourers "may form allegiances to their neighbourhoods and districts, rather than to their class" (Sack, 1986, p. 164).

Once the market economy managed to commodify space, the property market in general became the organiser of space as it entitles full private ownership of space under proprietary individualism. Space thus becomes "the recipient of an accumulation of riches" (Lefebvre, p. 264). That is, in carrying out their own production activities and selling their products in the market at their own responsibility, the subjects occupying the space of action as a general condition for production and life, are freed from their subordinate relationships in terms of the possession of the space they occupy, and each subject has the right to exclusively own a space with its right of free disposal.

In this context, the right of the body to bond with space is interrupted by economic power exercising the market process of the second form of subsuming relational space. The state can normally no longer unilaterally abolish or alter the ownership of space by the individual subjects. Proprietary individualism in the occupation of space is established through the legal apparatus of the nation-state appearing to support and administer the mosaic of collective absolute spaces deploying its state power. The protection of the exclusivity of bounded space, and the protection of the land market that creates the configurations of collective absolute spaces, are all possible only through the unitary transposition of power to the scale of the bourgeois state apparatus. Here, an unequal economic and society structure leads to differences in the ability to pay for property, which disrupts the bond of body with space.

Nevertheless, this power structure has also attempted to confiscate *terra nullius* and the customary commons with ambiguous exclusive ownership of space was transformed by state power into state ownership. The bond of space and body was thus disrupted and displaced by the state power.

7.3 Manipulation of Cognitive Space by State and Economic Power

a. The role of monuments

The state can also contrive to enhance its power in the process of generating the bond between body and space. A typical case in point is the production of monuments by the state power. Monuments "constitute the strong points, nexuses or anchors" of the web of the configuration of space (Lefebvre, p. 222). A monument, which tends to assume the nodal position in the network of relational space, displaces the autogenous bond of space towards placing something created by the power as an object for the bond. Those in power can thus manipulate the function of these objects to produce the guise of an autogenous bond of the people with the authority; "reification and displacement make places themselves appear to have power" (Sack, 1986, p. 114) and induce those being dominated into accepting the power autogenously and spontaneously by way of the monuments.

The various facilities representing the state power, such as the palace of a king or government or court buildings that control society, and that sit in a higher-order nodal point can also function as monuments. As Lefebvre (p. 220) states, "monumental space offered each member of a society an image of that membership, and image of his or her social visage." A monument in space intrudes on and bonds with a body, and the state power represented by the monument becomes embedded as an essential part of the body. The "imperishability" of "the will to power" (p. 221) is thus implanted to each member of the society. The monument in space thus "effected "consensus", and this in the strongest sense of the term" (p. 220).

These monuments can be incorporated in the process of urban development such that the palace was placed in the splendid place in the city centre, and "the symbol of the spiritual integration" such as a temple or church, was also placed adjacent to them to raise the prestige and legitimacy of the ruling class. France as the colonial suzerain built catholic Cathédrale Saint-Joseph in Hanoi right upon the site of the former Vietnamese spiritual symbol of Buddhist pagoda. In this city as a stronghold of power, the political rulers of society were those who had the legal right and financial means to plan and redevelop the city which they ruled, taking this as the basis to systematically direct the configuration of the collective absolute spaces of the city as needed. The subordinated subjects were thus alienated from their city, divided and allocated only unilaterally to the urban districts as determined by those in power.

When a large number of people share a single and common cognitive map admitting in the monument prestigious value and spiritual sense of belonging to the monument at the spatial node, the intersubjectivity of the "living space" in the mind of the subjects may direct the behaviour of the subjects to sustain the social system dominated by the power as well as on the process of producing objective spatial configuration.

However, such an attempt to eternalise power with a monument rests in fact merely upon the ephemerality of the political power. Time shall eventually come when "a monument loses its prestige or can only retain it by means of admitted oppression and repression". It is the time when "space as a whole becomes prone to sudden eruptions of violence" (Lefebvre, p. 223), since the monument loses the contrived prestige to keep the nodal position in the configuration of the cognitive map.

To take examples of urban imagery, the building of the former headquarters of the Japanese colonial government in the former colonial capital of Gyeongseong (Keijo)/ Seoul was the place where establishment of the Republic of Korea was proclaimed in August 1948, and subsequently served as the parliament building of the independent Republic of Korea, representing the change of power from the Japanese colonial administration to Korean autonomy. Yet this site of such historical value to Korean history was later dismantled since it was considered to be a symbol representing the domination of the former colonial power. The former East German government destroyed the Prussian Palace in East Berlin, as it was considered a symbol of aristocratic power in the past, and built the socialist GDR parliament building there; yet after reunification, the German government decided to destroy the former GDR parliament building and to revive the Prussian Palace, suggesting that the socialist past in the Eastern part of Germany should not be regarded as an authentic and legitimate part of German history. These two episodes suggest that the built form of a society is always conflict-prone according to the economic and social organisation and power relations. From this, the opposition and strife around the built environment comes about.

b. Manipulation of cognitive space by capitalist power

Capitalist power, especially property developers, also manipulate cognitive relative space to maximise profits. Subjective evaluations made for different residential districts occur in a manner disproportionate to geometrical relative space. The subjective evaluation of properties may have negative or positive impacts on real estate values, which promotes or discourages urban residential developments. If a developer succeeds in creating an image that a commercial agglomeration is more attractive than others, people will have a cognitive map accordingly in their mind, and their purchasing behaviour would be based on this cognitive map. On the other hand, if there is psychological barrier or boundedness in their mind regarded as difficult to overcome, even if it is not in reality, their action space for purchasing behaviour can be restricted. The neatly nested hexagonal system of the outcome of the first form of relational space subsumption is thereby distorted by the profit motive.

Thus, property developers and commercial capital seek to transform the value of the cognitive relational space in the mind of the people and to redraw their map to enhance their opportunity for profit. They may resort to economic incentives or an aesthetic sense, both of which may differ from the real utility or value.

Gentrification is a typical case in point. It has often been associated with commercial development. When various redevelopment projects are implemented concurrently, the cognitive maps of the people are reconfigured through their strong impact. If a property developer successfully manages to redraw by this means the cognitive maps of the subjects within the action space of the gentrified place, profit will accrue to the developers from the "rent gap" (Smith, 1987, p. 464). This will encourage further commercial development and agglomeration.

c. Production of non-quotidian space as compensation for alienation

As discussed earlier, space with autogenous bonds with the body is constantly alienated by the state and economic power. It is full of "force and repression, of manipulation and co-optation" (Lefebvre, p. 354). Here, the body seeks to engage in an illusory bond with the space in which the body is situated. Lefebvre points out (p. 353) concerning the "areas set aside for leisure": "the body regains a certain right to use, a right which is half imaginary and half real, and which does not go beyond an illusory 'culture of the body', an imitation of natural life". In short, the alienation from the autogenous bond with space is compensated by the bond with the capitalist space of leisure which is claimed to be rich in natural environment or historical heritage.

Tourism is a typical case in point. It is an act of "a reinstatement of the body's rights that remains unfulfilled" to call for space with "a corresponding restoration of desire and pleasure"; for example, "a beach, a place of festivity, the space of the dream" (Lefebvre, p. 353) and illusory emancipation. The meaning of the space of leisure to the body is therefore the displacement "from the quotidian to the non-quotidian through festival ... or again from labour to non-labour through putting into brackets and into question of toil" (Lefebvre, p. 354). In this sense, tourism is a capitalist pursuit to have the people seek a contrived emancipation, or ephemeral bond with non-quotidian space. The people spontaneously pay for the cost of transportation and accommodations by themselves for this type of tourist action.

A typical example of this behaviour to save themselves from alienating quotidian space is the space of Disneyland. Disneyland is a typical non-quotidian festival space where the real question of real toil is set aside, while it also tacitly functions as an ideological device. Originally built in Anaheim near Los Angeles in 1955, copies popped up in Japan, France and China.

Disneyland is not just an amusement park for children. It has its own ideology of society and history, and embodies the ideals of frontier expansionism of civilised society to overcome the territories of indigenous people, which Disney regarded as the bastion of savagery and barbarism. The struggle with real toil is evaporated and replaced with the possibility of infinite expansion of the frontier, or spatial fix.

Take the example of Tokyo Disneyland. After entering the main gate, turn left at the World Bazaar, an early American style shopping arcade, and tour the themed areas clockwise. The first is Adventureland, which contains Africa (Jungle Cruise), and Asia ("Chiba Traders" which the prefectural government requested when Disney planned to construct Disneyland in Chiba Prefecture where it is actually situated).

There are the ideas of "savage and barbarism" represented in non-European and indigenous American worlds such as Latin America. The Pirates of the Caribbean, who commit atrocities, are not the Taliban, but they do represent "barbarism", which needs to be overcome. Next comes "Westernland", where the images of mining railways in the West and the Mississippi river boats are represented, in which civilisation and enlightenment gradually spread through the frontier of the US expanding to the west. The contemporary economy and society as the outcome of the frontier expansion to the whole world is symbolised by "Fantasyland". The contemporary world rife with struggles and wars is best concealed by the attractions relocated from the World Exposition of New York in 1964: "the happiest cruise in the world", in which all ethnic peoples in the world sing and dance to a song called "It's a small world" made in the US. Visitors would innocently believe that the integration of the world's territories, with the US at the core, brings happiness and harmony to the peoples of the world without any sort of struggle. Finally, in "Tomorrowland", symbolised by the space technology developed by the US, an infinite future appearing "geographically as a dynamic [and progressive] relationship between people and events on the one hand and territorial molds on the other" (Sack, 1986, p. 78).

As such, in Disneyland, all the socio-economic conflicts and contradictions at home are put into bracket, concealed from the cognition of visitors and replaced it with the illusory emancipation outward into infinitely open space, while the US-centred "harmony" created through overcoming "barbarism" is celebrated at home. By spending non-quotidian leisure time, visitors are tacitly indoctrinated in the global ideology that the state power of the US expects everyone in the world to have generally, and Walt Disney Productions profits from it. Through this cultural device, leisure thus "actually encourages that enemy, actually helps to revive it" (Lefebvre, p. 354).

Naturally, those oppressed also have a right to create a non-quotidian configuration of space. The most typical of all is the Occupy Movement. It ingeniously created a virtual bond with public space. Those activists claiming to represent 99% of people occupy the public space, showing their way of producing an autogenous bond with what the authority claims is "public". To demonstrate "the collective power of bodies in public space is still the most effective instrument of opposition" (Harvey, 2012, pp. 161–162).

Chapter 9 of this book discusses more issues related to alternative space.

References

Buttimer, A. (1976). Grasping dynamism of life-world. *Annals of the Association of American Geographers, 66*(2).

Harvey. (1985). *The urbanization of capital: studies in the history and theory of capitalist urbanization.* Johns Hopkins University Press.

Harvey, D. (2012). *Rebel Cities: From the Right to the City to the Urban Revolution.* Verso.

Lefebvre, H. (1991). (translation). *The production of space.* Translated by Donald Nicholson-Smith. Wiley-Blackwell.

Marx, K. (1977) (translation). *Capital.* Vol. 1. Translated by Ben Fowkes. New York: Vintage Books.

Sack, R. (1986). *Human territoriality: Its theory and history.* Cambridge University Press.

Smith, N. (1987). Gentrification and the rent gap. *Annals of the Association of American Geographers, 77*(3).

Ueno, N. (1972). *Chishigaku no Genten (The Ultimate Origin of Chorography).* Taimeido.

Chapter 8
Business Cycles, Falling Rates of Profit and the Dynamism of Capitalist Space

Contents

Abstract This chapter returns to the capitalist space, this time in its dynamism. The capitalist spatial configuration is always subject to the crisis, analysed in Sects. 2–4 in consecutive order of the business cycle, incorporating space as the theoretical element. The business cycle culminates in crisis and, in the long run, into the tendential fall in the rate of profit, which has triggered global capitalism to mobilise countervailing forces to overcome the profit squeeze. This leads to the shift of capitalist regimes from Fordism to neo-liberalism. Its spatial manifestation is the new global configuration of economic space, most notably the New International Division of Labour, to exploit the global pool of cheap labour to the advantage of multinational capital.

8.1 Introduction

This book now turns back to the theoretical domain of Marxist economics in space.

Analysis in this book thus far has been based on the static structure of capitalism. The crisis-prone dynamism of capitalism, including expanded reproduction of the capitalist economy, concomitant financialisation and neo-liberalisation have not been analysed.

This chapter introduces the concepts of expanded reproduction, business cycles, crisis and devaluation in order to explain the uneven development of the capitalist space in its dynamism. Works about uneven spatial development are legion, for the "law of unevenness of growth and development … is becoming worldwide in

F. Mizuoka, *Subsumption of Space*, Contributions to Regional Science,
https://doi.org/10.1007/978-981-97-7560-6_8

its application—or, more precisely, is presiding over the globalization of a world market" (Lefebvre, p. 335). However, unless the social process that creates uneven spatial development is explained with real categories of Marxist economics, "the law of unevenness" is just an empty phrase. It is therefore important to analyse the real and tangible economic processes of capitalist dynamism within the spatial context in Marxist terms.

In the quotidian operation of capitalism, the capitalist dynamic takes the form of periodical business cycles, which is a corollary of crisis theory. The capitalist business cycle consists of several phases, each of which creates a distinct pattern of geographical unevenness. Michael Webber (1982, p. 7) states:

> just as accumulation proceeds in phases separated by periodic depressions because accumulation contains contradictions, so each phases establishes its own distinct geography of production.

Marxist theory of the business cycle thus forms an important theoretical base in explaining the unequal spatial development of capitalism.

Several authors have attempted to construct a theory of capitalist business cycles, including Ernest Mandel (1968 edition, pp. 345–57), Harvey (1982, pp. 300–5) and Japanese Marxist economist Ryozo Tomizuka (1975, pp. 176–228). Their modes of explanation vary slightly, but are not mutually exclusive. They share the common view that a cycle passes through four distinct stages: stagnation, moderate activity (recovery), overexcitement and crisis (crash) (*Capital*, Vol. 2, p. 264); and an explanation for the cycle has been given by various moments, especially fluctuations in the rate of profit, credit and interest rates, and interdepartmental relations in capital investment.

In this chapter, I first analyse the process of the dynamism of spatial configuration by following the consecutive order of the four different stages of the capitalist business cycles. Then, in Sects. 5 and 6, the perspective shifts to the longer trend, where the falling rate of profit, monopolisation of capital, New International Division of Labour and the globalising neo-liberalism play a significant role.

8.2 Stage 1: Stagnation and Recovery

a. Technological innovation and new investment

After an outburst of crisis, in which the absolute overproduction of capital manifests itself, the industrial cycle enters "the depressed period that opens the new business cycle" (*Capital*, Vol. 2, p. 358). The balance of the economy is gradually restored through a temporary suspension of the labour process, or destruction of production capital.

Marx states:

> the balance will be restored by capital's lying idle or even by its destruction, to a greater or lesser extent. This will also extend in part to the material substance of capital; i.e. part of the

> means of production, fixed and circulating capital, will not function and operate as capital, and a part of the productive effort that was begun will come to a halt... what we have here is a far more intense actual destruction of means of production ae the result of a stagnation in their function. (*Capital*, Vol. 3, p. 362)

Both the fixed capital owned privately by an individual capitalist and that shared by a multiple capitalists are affected by the process of underuse and destruction. This devaluation comes along with a severe reduction in production activity and low prices, hence a low rate of profit. Harvey (1982, p. 301) explains as follows:

> prices are forced downwards as producers dispose of surplus inventories at less than their process of production. Unemployment is widespread and wages typically adjusts downwards. The rate of interest is low, the plethora of loanable money capital produced out of overaccumulation is now in evidence.

Another "starting-point of new investment" (*Capital*, Vol. 2, p. 264) is prepared under these circumstances. The low rate of profit and lower market prices compel capitalists to apply more efficient, improved technology if they want to survive. The replacement of the technologies used in the labour process as well as in the built environment for collective use are facilitated by low interest rates thanks to the "plethora of loanable money capital", a low price of the means of production due to the producers and commercial capital's disposal of surplus inventories for hard cash. Due to the devaluation suffered by the existing labour process with old technology, fixed capital invested "to last out for a definite average lifespan", which otherwise forms an obstacle to the rapid general introduction of improved means of labour, now gives way to competition that compels premature renewals "before their natural demise" (*ibid*, p. 250). The aftermath of crises thus encourages capitalists to invest in a new, more efficient technology, which puts capital "on seven-league boots, in order to reach a development of the productive forces which could only be achieved very slowly within its own limits" (*Theories of Surplus-Value*, Part III, p. 122). The coercive laws of technological development are most prevalent in this period.

This process is in the meantime the process of "expropriation of capitalist by capitalists, transformation of many small into few large capitals" (*Capital*, Vol. 1, p. 777), or that of the concentration and centralisation of capital. Capitalists capable of introducing an innovative technology tend to be those of large scale. This is because the new technology that replaces the old has an increased productivity, which generally involves a "rising minimum amount of capital needed for the successful pursuit of an independent industrial business", and "once the new and more expensive equipment has been generally introduced, smaller capitals are in the future excluded from this line of business" (*Capital*, Vol. 3, p. 371).

Nevertheless, this does not mean a lack of role for small capital. In the course of concentration, "offshoots split off from the original capitals and start to function as new and independent capitals" (*Capital*, Vol 1, p. 776). This smaller capital crowds into the spheres of production which large-scale industry has taken control of only sporadically or incompletely (*ibid*, p. 777). The sectors that attract the mass of smaller capital are likely to be where "mechanical invention is...are in their infancy" (*Capital*, Vol. 3, p. 371) and still in the stage of research and development. Competition among these small capitalists crowding together in the new developing sectors rages "in direct proportion to the number" of such capitals (*Capital*, Vol. 1, p. 777), and is usually extremely fierce.

In short, technological innovation during this period of depression is twofold. One is the further increase in the scale of production, using an existing technology, accompanied by the concentration and centralisation of capital. The other is the emergence of new research and development in technology not completely controlled by large-scale industry.

b. The creation of the new configuration of space

"The general devaluation" that liberated capital "to establish new technologies" functions simultaneously to establish "new spatial structures" (Harvey, 1982, p. 394). The main features of the structural change are the creation of a new agglomeration of production capital producing new use-values that innovative technologies require, and a widened spatial sphere of capital circulation which connects the new agglomeration centres and the existing productive centres which support the new technologies and investments.

In this case, the use-value produced at the existing productive centres becomes obsolete, "place-specific devaluation" and the consequential demise of productive centres and general restructuring of the locations due to the introduction of new technology and use-values occur simultaneously. Especially when the introduction of innovative technology accompanies resynthesis of the labour process, older productive centres once created to perform a fragmented part of the vertically disintegrated labour process are abandoned. As Webber (1982, p. 8) pointed out,

> the obsolescence [of shared aids to production and consumption and the established relations of production] gradually develops but is most rapidly developed during the period of most rapid and most fundamental change – during the transition from one phase of accumulation to another. The region becomes obsolete as a production unit.

The capital which suffered "place-specific devaluation" but is still capable of bearing the cost of relocation will relocate to a region which provides capital with a stronger competitive power. The actual relocation is indeed easiest in this period since the value of C_{do} in Eq. 6.1 of Chap. 6 is relatively small due to forced devaluation in the crisis; consequently, the left term of the inequality is much smaller than that of the right. The smaller "offshoots" of capital engaging in the research and development are compelled to adopt rigorous criteria in the annihilation of space to survive the fierce competition. They may have to put a greater priority on agglomerating closer to the source of scientific information to develop a new technology than to secure a sufficient spatial sphere for capital circulation, which is still uncertain.

These structural changes are supported by the gradual resumption of the construction of the means of transportation and communication lines crucial to the further expanded reproduction of capital, which may have been originally planned during the period of past speculative fever. The creation of the built environment with innovative technology also supports this.

In an existing urban area, the structural change of the capitalist spatial configuration at a nationwide scale necessitates a new pattern of land use. The devaluation and consequential underuse or abandonment of the urban built environment make the creation of new patterns of urban land use especially easy. The landlords who let their urban land out for the construction of the obsolete or now abandoned built environment could attract new tenants by forgoing some of the monopoly rent they used to appropriate; so, competition around landed property is more favourable to the capitalists than to the landlords.

In a freshly emerging urban centre with a new prospect, land is still relatively abundant and there is little pre-existing built environment. Therefore, urban land-use patterns can be created almost from scratch, with little constraint imposed by landed property and the existing built environment. The social process of inter-capitalist competition to create a pattern of land-use coordination in the cities, works best in this phase of the business cycle.

By contrast, the lines of transportation and communication that are now obsolete or unnecessary from the capitalists" point of view are gradually abandoned by this stage. For these reasons, "the validity of bourgeois location theories at best restricted to this period of somewhat idyllic expansion when those of feuding brothers who survived have returned home, and are again a cosy fraternity" (Smith, 1984, p. 129). In the atmosphere of "a cosy fraternity", capitalists again seek capitalist egality across space.

Of course, in some cases, the existing built environment may promote the development of current economy and society. That is, the past built environment and the current regime may not be in contradiction against one another. For example, even if a railway line was built by speculation before the economic crisis and the owner-operator of the line went bankrupt, the railway remains engraved on the land. The line is utilised for the economic development in the recovery period, which would be facilitated by the railway through promoting the exchange of the commodities and persons. A good example is Hanwa Railway Co., Ltd. in Osaka, Japan, which was fully opened in 1930 amidst the Great Depression, and the company was liquidated in 1940, probably because its affiliate company, Keihan, faced financial difficulties. Yet the line was nationalised in 1944 and now functions as a busy inter-urban Japan Railways (JR) West line in Osaka. The same relation can be seen in the transportation routes and the built environments left by colonial rulers which are now used for economic development and reconstruction in the countries after independence.

Because of this restructuring of the spatial configuration, the labour class suffers considerably. The general law of capitalist accumulation

> within the capitalist system all methods for raising the social productivity of labour are put into effect at the cost of the individual worker ... in proportion as capital accumulates, the situation of worker, be his payment high or low, must grow worse. (*Capital*, Vol. 1, p. 799)

applies to the spatial context as well. The capitalist mode of production endogenously creates "a disposable industrial reserve army", which is "a mass of human material always ready for exploitation by capital in the interests of capital's own changing valorization requirements" (*ibid*, p. 784). In the aftermath of the crisis, especially the reservoir of "the surplus population" (*ibid*, p. 785) is filled. Capital, with improved technology requiring fewer labourers due to its increased organic composition, has little difficulty in finding labourers at the new location. Labourers have to give up some of their rights won through class struggle in the previous business cycle, otherwise they will likely be left without jobs. In newly emerging urban area, organised labour is hardly formed yet, and labourers are virtually forced to submit themselves to the domination of capital.

Labourers living in places where jobs are no longer available after the crisis must, in order to continue to survive, relocate to join the competition for jobs at one of the new places thriving in the current business cycle. A great number of labourers who lose their jobs, or are laid off, migrate to the higher-order agglomeration centres where large capital locates itself, as well as to newly emerging urban centres. This creates more competition for residential space in these thriving centres; and once again a possibility for landlords to milk monopoly rent from their property. This process incurs a considerable "moral degeneration" or impoverishment with respect to housing standards.

8.3 Stage 2: The Amassing of Contradictions During the Period of "Moderate Activity"

a. Capital accumulation in a newly structured spatial configuration

In the pursuit of capitalist egality across space, the seeds for further uneven spatial development are prepared. The process of creating spatial egality is, in the meantime, a process whereby value created in the centre with industries of low organic composition of capital flows into the agglomeration centre with industries of which the organic composition of capital is high. As mentioned, this is not a direct cause of uneven development, but the formation of an average rate of profit with high organic composition on a par with that of low organic composition. In this manner, value transfer provides only a seed, but an important seed, without which spatial unevenness might not be created.

In this newly restructured spatial configuration, the mass of new investment in more efficient technology with a higher organic composition of capital and the emergence of new small industries dealing with the development of more innovative technology set the path for new economic growth. The new investment creates demand on the means of both production and consumption through revived employment of a part of the industrial reserve army. The increased demand raises prices and restores the rate of profit.

The newly created fixed capital now working in the labour process is hardly depreciated yet, not to mention devalued. The values of C_{do} and C_{ar} in Eq. 6.1 of Chap. 6 are high, and, as the spatial configuration has now just been restructured, the value of E is reduced to a minimum. These conditions make the difference between the left and right terms of the inequality small or even zero. The probability of relocation is therefore least; the accumulation of capital proceeds at the existing agglomerations where investments have been made in immobile fixed capital.

Nevertheless, the newly restructured spatial configuration supporting capitalist egality creates the conditions for new uneven spatial development. The lower spatial mobility of capital during this period inhibits the averaging of the rate of profit across space and sectors; and the difference in the rate of profit that gradually emerges, due to the difference in industrial structure by regions, can hardly be balanced out. The process of expanded capital reproduction is led by autonomous capital accumulation in the sector producing the means of production, whereas the sector producing the means of consumption is always dependent upon it. Thus, in the territory in which the sectors producing the means of production are located, agglomeration takes the lead in the capital accumulation, leaving other territories behind. Money capital needed for accumulation is often supplied through interregional transfers. It is at this stage of the business cycle that spatial difference in industrial structure immediately affects unequal spatial development.

However, although uneven regional capital accumulation comes to be gradually apparent by this time, the spatial situation may not be so serious to the capitalists. Space for capital circulation is virtually annihilated by existing and new means of transportation and communication completed by now, and their constraint has not yet emerged; competition for landed property is relatively low, as the built environment currently in use has already been created by now.

b. The gradual emergence and amassing of contradictions

As the accumulation of capital proceeds, the demand for labour power and landed property rises. The labour demand will be met by further absorption of the industrial reserve army, especially the latent surplus labour in the territories catering for agriculture, through encouraging the spatial mobility of labour. This mobility abates otherwise consequential wage increases so they do not erode profit, nor lead to that fatal consequence of the absolute overproduction of capital. By contrast, capitalists cannot control the gradual rise of monopoly rent in the growing urban regions due to the increased demand for landed property, since, unlike the commodity labour power, absolute space is not mobile. Additional production and/or commodity capital created through capital accumulation gradually overflows the existing size of the plot of land that the labour process is currently occupying. However, the urban built environment, renewed or created afresh during the period of stagnation and recovery, cannot be altered easily, as it is little devalued yet. This confines the urban activities into a restricted spatial area; the built environment thus puts a constraint on the ever-increasing demand for new urban space arising from capital accumulation in the urban area. The outcome of the conflict between the increasing demand for urban space and the constraint of the existing urban land use is a growing amount of monopoly rent appropriated by the class of urban landlords. Capitalists accumulating at a rapid pace are forced to spare a part of the extra surplus-value exploitation to bid away competing tenants and secure a superior or "prestigious" urban space, which slows down the rate of profit and capital accumulation. Space to be subsumed thus emerges as a constraint for further capital accumulation, and landed property gradually gains strength.

By this time, therefore, constraints are felt by many capitalists in growing urban areas. Even real wage rates, as well as the additional cost of maintaining the continuity of production starts to rise. If the amount of additional capital is above the "normal minimum" of capital investment required in the sector concerned and there is a prospect of securing a market (at the period of business prosperity indeed there is), capital is likely to place the additional immobile fixed capital at a new location. Capitalists thus carefully and quietly attempt to transfer the inner contradiction elsewhere in space. Such an "outer transformation" is likely also because one of the aims of expanding production at this stage is to secure and possibly increase market share under the seller's market situation with a part of demand kept unfilled. Capitalists hope that the "outer transformation" may help them secure a market in the immediate surroundings of the new location of capital. The processes of "socio-spatial dialectics" thus proceed.

The constraint of space also creates problems for labourers. To labourers who conglomerate increasingly in limited agglomeration points, the only way to secure living space is moral degradation. Labourers, tied by "invisible threads" to the agglomeration of capital now enjoying growth, suffer further impoverishment. This impoverishment is aggravated by the heavier demand for food due to an increased number of labourers. The heavier food demand raises the price of food, introducing more remote agricultural land into cultivation, which requires a greater cost to annihilate space. The burden of this cost is passed on to the labourers. Facing the reality of this impoverishment, more labourers, especially those located in an urban area where antagonism is most acute, join the united front of the labourers struggling for social change.

8.4 Stages 3 and 4: Overexcitement and the Crash

a. The role of commercial capital and outer transformation

As capital accumulation continues, this stage of moderate expansion is gradually replaced with the stage of "overexcitement and speculative fever" (Harvey, 1982, p. 303).

As the autonomous accumulation of capital in the sectors of the means of production continues, deviation from the "equilibrium accumulation path" (Tomizuka, 1975, pp. 93 and 104–105) derived from the Marxist scheme of reproduction comes to be gradually apparent in the macro-economy. All the means of production and the means to annihilate space now work to full capacity, and ever larger quantities of commodities are produced everywhere across space. As the movement of commercial capital is "within certain limit independent of the reproduction process and its barriers" (*Capital*, Vol. 3, p. 419), commercial capital that "undergoes a very great expansion" forms the "healthy" basis for a ready flow of returns and expansion of production" (*ibid*, p. 619). Reproduction proceeds "happily for a good while, stimulated by prospective demand, and in these branches of industry business proceeds very briskly, as far as both merchants and industrialists are concerned" (*ibid*, p. 420). The production of the huge mass of commodities does not immediately appear to be overproduction.

Nevertheless, "happiness" is nothing but an outcome of a process of "outer transformation" of the overproduced commodities to the sphere of circulation process, conducted at spatially different points from the location of the labour process. The industrial capitalists are deceived "all the more, in that it is possible for the producer to feel that the circulation process of his capital is occurring, that it is in flux, even though the circulation process of his commodities, which have passed into the hands of the merchants, is stagnating" (*Capital*, Vo1. 2, p. 225). The products leave the location of the production processes regularly, daily and uninterrupted; however, "at some particular imperceptible point the commodity lies unsold; or else the total stocks of producers and middlemen gradually become too high" (*Capital,* Vol. 3, p. 419). The attempt of capitalism to combine two antithesis, sale and purchase, is gradually producing its antagonistic counterpart.

The potential overproduction of capital is thus still hidden behind the process of a temporary "outer transformation". Commodities are still exchanged using commercial credit, and the spatial transfer of commodities is still carried out without much difficulty. All the attempts of capitalism to annihilate space seem to be working almost perfectly well.

b. Rising interest rates and speculative fever

In this phase, interest rates are still low. Marx states:

> this is actually the *only* point in time at which it may be said that a low rate of interest, and hence a relative abundance of loanable capital, coincides with an actual expansion of industrial capital. The ease and regularity of returns, combined with an expanded commercial credit, ensures the supply of loan capital despite the increased demand and prevents the interest level from rising. (*Capital*, Vol. 3, p. 619)

Taking advantage of the plenitude of loanable capital available on the market at relatively low rates of interest, which increases "The portion of profit that is transformed into profit of enterprise" (p. 627), "the fullest employment of industrial capital, i.e. the utmost taxing of its reproductive power irrespective of the limits of consumption" (p. 613) sets in. Also at this stage, "jobbers first enter the picture on a notable scale, operating without reserve capital or even without capital at all" (p. 619). Under this speculative operation, "a great expansion of fixed capital in all forms and the opening of large number of new and far-reaching undertakings" (pp. 619–20) takes place. Some of the numerous small capitalists engaged in technological research and development speculatively take a chance to expand their scale of operations by applying the speculative money capital, which is nowadays called "venture capital".

This is also the time when a great number of speculative undertakings to construct the built environment catering to the annihilation of space—railways and other means of transportation and communication networks—emerge. For example, "the period of prosperity of 1844–7 was linked in England with the first great railway swindle" (p. 538). The bottleneck of these means of transportation, which is gradually being felt by this period, also supports this "speculative fever" for the construction of the built environment. Investment in the built environment, which has a long gestation period, creates a mass of purchases without sales, which induces a higher price for the means of production. In addition, the excessive "absorption of floating capital" into the construction of the built environment acts "to reduce money capital" (p. 617). This tying-up of capital in a circuit similar to what Harvey later termed "the secondary circuit of capital" occurs for two reasons.

First, investment in immobile fixed capital cannot be exported due to its physical nature, "therefore in so far as its export is actually impossible … no capital is obtained by way of returns for articles exported, including returns in cash or bullion." Second, the merchants and manufacturers "who had tied up a part of their normal working capital in railway shares" have to depend on "borrowed capital to conduct their business" because "their floating capital really had been fixed [to the land]." The excessive speculative investment in the built environment induces depletion of the reservoir of floating money capital available both to the individual capitalists and society in general. When these capitalists need floating capital, it is no longer at hand. This creates "a high rate of interest" (p. 620) and makes the interregional transfer of money capital increasingly difficult.

A considerable amount of such speculative investment generates a new demand for land. This demand further raises the level of monopoly rent, and the growing amount of monopoly rent creates an opportunity for speculation in land itself. When the rent keeps going up continuously, landlords become reluctant to let out their land, since their expected income grows due to the increasing amount of rent rather than from the flat amount of interest accruing on the funds obtained by letting out the land. Thus, private ownership of a portion of absolute space now gains its utmost strength opposing the capitalists, and the capitalists' "nightmare" of confiscation of their fixed capital in the form of the built environment once again surfaces. Private landed property, which the capitalists legally protect to justify their private ownership of the means of production, now starts to betray the very protector. The profit rates of the capitalists are further eroded by the increasing amount of monopoly rent and an accelerated depreciation of the immobile fixed capital, to defray its premature confiscation by landed property.

c. Crash

The bottlenecks of labour, the means of transportation and communication, landed property and the built environment come to be most prevalent at this stage. As Webber (1982, p. 9) points out, "the old geography, based on an earlier logic of development, has become a fetter upon accumulation."

Faced with bottlenecks, the prices of labour power, the means of production and monopoly rent go up rapidly. The higher price of labour power is also an outcome of the struggle of the organised labour which gained strength during the period of prosperity. An increasing amount of additional capital is now absorbed into the process of maintaining the continuity of production.

The rising rate of interest, ground-rent and cost-prices of materials erode the profit of enterprise. The congested means of transportation and communication hinder spatial integration across the macro-economy, and the process of capital reproduction becomes progressively confined to the local level. This eventually leads to a minor form of crisis at the local level and consequential "place-specific devaluations". At this stage, unequal spatial development is mainly created due to the "fetter" imposed by the means to annihilate space and constraint of the built environment; behind this unevenness, the eve of economy-wide crisis now quietly approaches.

The various factors of capitalist production sound the ultimatum to the speculative fever: the *crash*. Through an absolute overproduction of capital, the reproduction process collapses to a great extent, and ends "the entire interconnection of the reproduction system [that] rests on credit" (*Capital*, Vol. 3, p. 621). Now, capitalists are forced to realise that all attempts at subsuming and annihilating space are in fact dysfunctional. The agglomeration of production and distribution facilities hampered expanded reproduction at the existing place owing to the "fetter" of the built environment or the contradiction in the socio-spatial dialectics. The means of transportation and communication, clogged or infested with incidents due to overuse at the last moment of prosperity, blocks rather than facilitates the reproduction process as a whole. The increased amount of capital required to maintain the continuity of production to ship products to distant markets lead to the very overproduction of capital as it has absorbed a considerable amount of commodity capital. The credit system, in encouraging a speculative fever and consequential fictitious demand collapses and paralyses the flow of capital circulation built on it. Ground-rent created out of the need of capitalism to protect the system of private property, grabs the profit of enterprise and even the immobile fixed capital privately owned by the capitalists themselves. Finally, the collapse of the credit system brings the land under speculation back to almost a portion of absolute space without value. Nearly all means of subsuming and annihilating space now betray their producers and rise against them. Capitalism finally realises the dialectics of the annihilation of space and the tough and unbeatable nature of absolute space. Distance, the attribute of relative space, returns as the absolute barrier to the reproduction process.

The loss that the crisis creates is "by no means uniformly distributed amongst all the particular individual capitalists" but its distribution is being "decided by a competitive struggle in which the loss is divided very unevenly and in very different forms according to the particular advantages or positions that have already won" (*Capital*, Vol. 2, p. 362). For example, places with greater agglomeration of the production capital of the means of production suffer more than those with the means of consumption, as the reproduction theory of capitalism suggests.

However, "under all circumstances … the balance will be restored" (*ibid*). The reproduction of capital now occurs on only a limited scale and a limited spatial extent. Here, only the last and most effective form of annihilating space, the elimination of pristine distance itself by agglomeration, assists capitalists to maintain linkages in the reproduction process. The place with the production capital for the means of production can continue reproduction to some extent, since the labourers, including those who lost their jobs due to the crisis, still need a means to survive; and this creates a moment for the beginning of another cycle. Much of the former immobile fixed capital having been disposed of through severe devaluation, and sometimes physical destruction, space now takes a shape closer to pristine. The power of the landed property opposing the capitalist class abates. It thus gives capitalism another opportunity to "restore the balance" in space and to produce its own spatial configuration on it, in a more intense and efficient manner.

8.5 The Tendential Fall in the Rate of Profit and Emergence of Monopoly Capital

a. Tendential fall in the rate of profit

The start of another business cycle accompanies the emergence of new technology with a higher organic composition of capital owned and operated by capitalists of a larger scale as well as a more extensive network of the built environment for the production and spatial integration. Another way of annihilating space, the credit system, is strengthened and streamlined to meet the needs of these larger capitalists. This is the process in which the social productivity of labour and the technical and organic compositions of capital increase in proportion to living labour, as well as the larger industrial and banking capital coming to dominate society.

Continuous technological development brings about a progressive decline in the proportion of variable capital to total capital, and a consequential rise in organic composition. Marx states:

> its development does … involve a relative decline in the relation of variable capital to constant, and hence also to the total capital set in motion. This simply means that the same number of workers or the same quantity of labour-power that is made available by a variable capital of a given value, as a result of the specific method of production that develop within capitalist production, sets in motion, works up, and productivity consumes, with in the same period, an ever growing mass of means of labour, machinery and fixed capital of all kinds, and raw and ancillary materials – in other words, the same number of workers operate with a constant capital of ever-growing scale. This progressive decline in the variable capital in relation to the constant capital, and hence in relation to the total capital as well, is identical with the progressively rising organic composition, on average, of the social capital as a whole. It is just another expression for the progressive development of the social productivity of labour, which is shown by the way that the growing use of machinery and fixed capital generally enables more raw and ancillary materials to be transformed into products in the same time by the same number of workers, i.e. with less labour. (*Capital*, Vol. 3, p. 318)

This growth of the mass of constant capital as well as total capital induces a "*tendential fall in the rate of profit*", where "the same rate of surplus-value … and unchanged level of exploitation of labour, is expressed in a falling rate of profit" (*ibid*, p. 317). As the following inequality is always true,

$$\frac{V+S}{C} > \frac{S}{C} > \frac{S}{C+V} \equiv p' \text{ (Matsuishi, 1983, p. 270)} \tag{8.1}$$

the decline of V/C (representing the organic composition of capital), which induces a decline of the value of leftmost fraction, always reduces the rate of profit, p'.

There are, however, several "counter-acting factors, checking and cancelling the effect of the general law and giving it simply the character of a tendency" (*Capital*, Vol. 3, p. 339). Marx left us with "a motley array of countervailing influences" that check and halt the falling rate of profit. They are: "(1) rising rate of exploitation; (2) falling costs of constant capital; (3) depression of wages below the labour power; (4) an increase in industrial reserve army." The array goes further: "the constant devaluation of a part of the existing capital … (planned obsolescence)", "transformation of a great part of capital into fixed capital which does not serve as agency of direct production", "investment in public works" as well as "increase in stock capital" which only receives dividends (Harvey, 1982, p. 179). Faced with the falling rate of profit, capitalists strive to implement these countervailing forces to save capitalism. Under contemporary capitalism, the countervailing forces take the forms of neo-liberalism and the New International Division of Labour, which has generated profound concomitant spatial manifestations.

b. Monopoly capital and financial oligarchy

The most important of these countervailing factors is the emergence of large-scale monopoly capital which can defray the falling rate of profit by accruing monopoly profits higher than that of normal capital both in rate and absolute amount.

As Lenin (1964 edition, p. 205) states, the transformation of "complete free competition" to monopoly, or the "rise of monopolies, as the result of the concentration of production, is a general and fundamental law of the present stage of development of capitalism" (p. 200). Here, "cartels become one of the foundations of the whole of economic life" (p. 202), and they attempt to monopolise every aspect of economic life. For example,

> an approximate estimate of the capacity of markets is made, and the associations "divide" them up amongst themselves by agreement. Skilled labour is monopolised, the best engineers are engaged; the means of transport are captured – railways in America, shipping companies in Europe and America. (p. 205)

Although "commodity production … continues to be regarded as the basis of economic life" (p. 206) and "appropriation remains private" (p. 205), the whole structure of the capitalist economy is now put under the "yoke of a few monopolists". As monopoly capital comes to dominate society, the credit system and its "administrator", banking capital, ceases to be "the humble assistant of accumulation" (*Capital*, Vol. 1, p. 778) but becomes "powerful monopolies" as well. Lenin (1964 edition, p. 210) states:

> as banking develops and becomes concentrated in a small number of establishments, the banks grow from modest middlemen into powerful monopolies having at their command almost the whole of the money capital of all the capitalists and small businessmen and also the larger part of the means of production and sources of raw materials in any one country and in a number of countries. This transformation of numerous middlemen into a handful of monopolies is one of the fundamental processes in the growth of capitalism into capitalist imperialism.

The concentration of banking capital and the more complete dependence of "industrial capital … on the bank" (p. 220) transform the spatial configuration of capitalism:

> we see the rapid expansion of a close network of channels which cover the whole country, centralising all capital and all revenues, transforming thousands and thousands of scattered economic enterprises into a single national capitalist, and then into a world capitalist economy… [or] the subordination to a single centre of an increasing number of formerly relatively independent, or rather, strictly local economic units. (p.213)

Through this "close network of channels", banking and monopoly capital, which together constitute "financial capital and the financial oligarchy" (p. 226), produce a built environment to their own advantage. Huge amounts of money capital accumulated in the hands of the financial oligarchy are invested in ways that need the continuous input of money capital without an immediate return of product. Land speculation and construction of the built environment which involves a long gestation period are typical examples.

Accompanied by a monopoly over the means of annihilating space and absolute space itself, the financial oligarchy accrues an ever-larger amount of monopoly profit:

> speculation in land situated in the suburbs of rapidly growing big towns is a particularly profitable operation for finance capital. The monopoly of the banks merges here with the monopoly of ground-rent and with monopoly of the means of communication, since the rise in the price of land and the possibility of selling it profitably in lots, etc., is mainly dependent on good means of transportation, which they have monopolised, to the interests of their real estate business. (pp. 236–237)

Nevertheless, despite the monopolisation, uneven development and crises cannot be eliminated. The belief that monopoly "can abolish crises is a fable spread by bourgeois economists who at all costs desire to place capitalism in a favourable light" (p. 208). Instead, "the growing concentration (of capital) leads in turn, at a certain level, to a new fall in the rate of profit" (*Capital,* Vol. 3, p. 359). The monopolisation of capital and monopoly profit may work for the monopoly capital as a countervailing factor for the profit rate to fall, but they never arrest the tendency of the profit rate to fall altogether. Monopoly capital may temporarily circumvent the problem and enjoy prosperity arising from a large amount of monopoly profit accrued, as "beyond certain limits a large capital with a lower rate of profit accumulates more quickly than a small capital with a higher rate of profit" (*ibid*). However, the overproduction of capital, even that of monopoly capital, can never be circumvented. As capital invested in "very large undertakings" like railways or other forms of the built environment, "where the proportion of constant capital is very high… do not yield the average profit rate, but only a portion of this, an interest" (p. 372), monopoly capital investing particularly in these "large undertakings" cannot avoid the problem of the fall in the rate of profit.

The portion of the economic sector related to the creation of the built environment in the whole capital in society gets larger, never smaller, as the development of capitalism requires more and more means of annihilating space. This means to the "mass of fragmented capital" of a smaller scale that do not constitute monopoly that they are forced "onto adventurous paths: speculation. Credit swindles, share swindles, crisis" (p. 359). Some venturous small capital which succeeded in speculative operations or by inventing technology useful to larger capital, may grow, but for most of this fragmented capital the ultimate fate is annihilation. The more the rate of profit falls, the higher is the probability and the intensity of the absolute overproduction of capital and crisis, as the margin within which the business cycle of capitalism can fluctuate gets smaller.

Since crisis is a sudden plunge of a higher rate of profit at a prosperous stage into an absolute overproduction of capital where profit vanishes, the plunge may be ever deeper and its consequences the more destructive the lower the rate of profit is at the starting point. This is especially detrimental to smaller capital.

8.6 Neo-liberalism and the Globalisation of Capitalism

a. Neo-liberalism as a capitalist "regime"

The tendency towards an increasing magnitude of fixed capital in the built environment cannot be arrested if the capitalist class, through the process of monopolisation, wants to expand the reproduction process and action space for the market ever further.

However, this process, coupled with the tendency to rely on automated production processes and cyberspace, inevitably expels the living labour and enhances the organic composition of capital, thus forcing down the very source of capitalist operation, the rate of profit. If "capital formation were to fall exclusively into the hands of a few existing capitals, for whom the mass of profit outweighs the rate, the animating fire of production would be totally extinguished. It would die out" (*Capital*, Vol. 3, p. 368).

Yet, global capitalists seek every possibility to avoid the "Twilight of the Gods—the Day of Judgement" (*Theories of Surplus-Value*, Part II, p. 544) of capitalism. Capitalists thus envisage overcoming this through transformation of the quantitative changes into a qualitative change. This has triggered the transformation of contemporary capitalism into the regime of neo-liberalism.

The term "regime" comes from the concept of capitalist regulation, which was first developed by French political economists such as Michel Aglietta (1979) and Robert Boyer (Boyer and Saillard, 2002). They claim that the invisible hand of the market mechanism alone is insufficient to maintain the capitalist mode of production. To maintain capitalism as the primary economic structure of society, the state must intervene by deploying its power to contain two fundamental "natural enemies" of capitalism: the crisis of over-accumulation and the class struggle that could undermine capitalism and create a socialist revolution.

In regulation theory, a particular politico-economic structure that keeps these two "natural enemies" simultaneously at bay is called a "mode of social regulation". Capitalism needs to be permanently supported by state power, which designs the regime to guarantee the long-term and obstacle-free functioning of capitalism.

The mode of social regulation most clearly demonstrated by the regulation theorists is "Fordism". The term "Fordism" came from Antonio Gramsci's reflections on American life and the philosophy of Henry Ford. Ford introduced the Taylorist mass production system, the efficiency of which allowed his company to pay his employees high wages so that they became able to afford automobiles (Gramsci, 1971, p. 302). This system proliferated across large monopoly capital catering for mass consumption throughout the industrialised world. Thanks to the high profit margins made possible by automated and efficient fixed capital, these monopoly capitalists were able to pay high wages as well as offer better working conditions, which in turn generated increased effective demand for the product that they produced, especially such durable consumption goods as automobiles, electric appliances and houses.

Workers did not achieve this without class struggles, of course. Powerful trade unionism, often acting in national and global alliances, had power to bring the capitalists to the table of collective bargaining for higher wages, job security, better working conditions and a shorter working day. When their demands were not met, the organised labour went on strike. The increased effective demand promoted sales of industrial goods and abated the risk of the crisis of over-accumulation. The working class enjoyed the fruits of this system, with their suburban homes full of durable consumer goods, leading to satisfaction with their lives and a conservative mindset. These measures generated the intense suburbanisation of cities. In the US, suburbanisation "entailed a radical transformation in lifestyles and produced a whole new way of life [with] new products—from suburban tract housing to refrigerators and air conditioners, as well as two cars in the driveway…" (Harvey, 2012, p. 9). This way of life generated among labourers a conservative mentality hostile to more militant class struggles that might develop into a socialist revolution.

After the oil crisis, however, it became increasingly difficult for the capital and state power regulating the regime to be able to afford Fordism. The collapse of the Fordist mode of regulation occurred for two reasons: the fiscal crisis of the national and local states because of the eroding of the corporate tax base, and the profit squeeze in the manufacturing sector. Both boiled down to the falling rate of profit in the capitalist economy.

Neo-liberalism thus took over Fordism. Neo-liberalism sought a radical transformation of Fordism and made intense and sometimes insane attempts to restore the profit-earning and capital accumulation opportunities in ways quite in contrast with those of Fordism. We can therefore position neo-liberalism as the successor regime of Fordism, since most of the properties of neo-liberalism are in clear contraposition to Fordism, while both of them attempt to realise the same objectives: the prevention of crisis and social revolution.

In the meantime, the neo-liberalist solutions instigated the countervailing forces to the falling rate of profit: reducing tax on corporate profit by adopting a more austere fiscal policy through cutting expenditure on public investments and introducing the market principle to the public sector, as well as various attempts to enhance the rate of exploitation and rapid obsolescence and therefore devaluation of the existing fixed capital (Table 8.1).

Table 8.1 Two contrasting capitalist modes of regulation. *Source* Mizuoka, 2013, p. 91, edited

	Fordism	Neo-liberalism
Capital accumulation	Mass production (Taylor System—mass consumption) that created high-profit margins	Gain through financial speculation and information technology. Holding back the tendency for the profit rate to fall
Social integration	Conservatism arising from high wages and concomitant higher standard of living, generous welfare schemes	Individualised competition to join "winners" group. "Equal opportunity" to compete and non-envy the outcome
Staple economic sector	Manufacturing. Finance assisting industrial investment	Finance and information technology. Financialization on industrial investment
Basic sanction	Expulsion from the community	Miserable life for those in the loser's group (for example, fear of absolute poverty and homelessness)
Capital-Labour relations	Strong trade unionism, leading to wage rises, job security, etc., achieved through collective bargaining	Trade unions co-opted to achieve competitiveness. Wage rises through individual competition among labour
Government functions	Income redistribution, social and economic development policies including provision of needs-based welfare, crisis prevention though Keynesian public investment	Controlling market conditions, ensuring competition. Promoting privatisation and deregulation. Policing by surveillance and stricter regulations for deprivation of the people
Social ideals	Mutual symbiosis; stable society through "cradle to grave" government social welfare policies	Cut-throat, alienating competition, self-responsibility and the "no-envy" principle
Social norms that endorse the regime	Social justice, fraternity, mutual assistance	Market fundamentalism, individualism, self-responsibility, limitless commodification
Spatial reach of industrial production	Mainly within the national economy	Globalization based on the New International Division of Labour
The outcome in reality	Relatively egalitarian	Widening discrepancy among socio-economic levels, supremacy of the rich over the poor

Ideologically, this regime transformation was endorsed by market fundamentalist thought, which advocated the free market based on the principles of neo-classical economics and a shrunken, but stronger, state power (Low, 1991, pp. 175–182). The worker was imagined as an independent agent engaging in market competition rather than a member of the working class in solidarity. The powerful unions were either liquidated or co-opted. The struggle for better wages and working conditions, formerly fought as a class, was shifted to individuals competing in the labour market: collective bargaining was replaced by cut-throat competition for employment against one's peers.

The capitalists and the state power, initially of the Anglophone world but later almost everywhere worldwide, enthusiastically subscribed to this silver bullet containing countervailing forces to the falling rates of profit. They ardently embraced Margaret Thatcher's dictum "There Is No Alternative" (TINA) to giving the market free reign, and set off to develop a whole new set of policies dismantling many elements of Fordism and the concomitant Keynesian welfare society, for capitalists to resurrect their opportunity to halt the fall in profits. Neo-liberalism survived for almost half a century and its principles have infused much public policy at national and sub-national levels.

Capital that accumulated in excess of effective demand, leading to the potential for crises caused by overproduction, was then channelled to the speculative financial sector, which became the mainstay of capital accumulation under neo-liberal regimes. Neo-liberal state power privatised many public bodies that had previously offered services to the people without the profit motive, which also opened up new fields of investment by commodification of what had never traded before: the symbolic meaning of places under "naming rights", the national railway systems, or even living children in Japan. Alienating competition was encouraged instead, claiming that it would bring vigour and efficiency to the economy.

People are touted to be no longer in need of working hard in the dust and dirt of a Taylorist factory to earn money, but could gain it on the whim of smart clicks on Internet speculation sites. Core countries encouraged financial capital to flourish, and its *laissez-faire* speculative activities, seeking capital across the globe, became rampant.

The augmenting financialisation of capitalism under neo-liberalism also functions as a countervailing factor. Much capital has left the less profit-earning manufacturing sector towards speculative "stock capital", some of which has been invested in urban and spatial developments. The countervailing force of the obsolescence of existing fixed capital has been implemented through rapid development of IT technologies. This leading-edge technological development has the important effect of accruing extra profits and founder gains for the capitalists who developed it successfully. The leading-edge technology consequently devalued the existing fixed capital, which also functioned as a countervailing force to the falling rate of profit.

"World cities" have emerged in North America, Western Europe and Asia as financial centres and the centres of IT innovation. In these cities, amidst the self-bounding "gated communities" of the rich, poverty-stricken people dropped out of the neo-liberalist competition to search for food in litter bins and sleep on the streets, in public parks or railway stations. This striking bifurcation of the urban landscape has become a quotidian scene in many world cities nowadays.

Yet the financialisation of capitalism itself eventually led to a new economic and social crisis based on fictitious capital formations and the era of instability since 2008, when the commercial banks lent "to speculators looking to appropriate rents, then fictitious capital look[ed] more and more like an infinite regression of fictions built upon fictions. Leveraging at ever higher ratios … magnifies the fictional amounts of money capital in circulation" (Harvey, 2012, p. 40). The strategy of macro-economic stabilisation through suburbanisation thus collapsed.

b. Expanding the spatial sphere of exploitation: the New International Division of Labour and global capitalism

Enhancing the rate of exploitation of labour to increase the rate of profit could be achieved in two ways: first, expanding the spatial extent of the labour market to lower-wage countries to exploit the reservoir of cheap labour in developing countries; and second, restructuring the domestic labour market to force labour to draw upon the neo-liberalist ideology, that is, more flexible and insecure labour contracts and the introduction of a stagnant surplus population, which functions as a dead weight on the wage rate.

The former is achieved through implementation of the New International Division of Labour (NIDL) (Flöbel et al., 1982). The NIDL is in fact a spatial manifestation of neo-liberalism. Labourers in less developing countries cannot cross the international boundary since they do not have appropriate visas or money to travel. This immobility of labour imposed by the state and financial power limits the action space of the labourers within a domestic market, which creates an ample pool of low-wage labour. The location of productive investment shifted towards peripheral countries with an ample low-wage labour pool with little job protection or rises in wages through trade unionism. This "global shift" indeed enhanced the increase in the rate of exploitation globally.

The spread of the NIDL goes hand in hand with the penetration of neo-liberalist "structural adjustment" policy into developing countries, as, after the 1980s, the IMF and World Bank demanded that these countries also accept neo-liberalist policies in exchange for assistance policy packages under the name of "structural adjustment". Also at the village scale, micro credit proliferated, which transformed village reciprocal communities into an instrument of debt guarantee. Many formerly socialist agricultural production cooperatives in these less developed countries have come under the ownership and management of the profit-making multinationals.

The global space thus has been neo-liberalised, as "almost every city in the world has witnessed a building boom for the rich—often of a distressingly similar character—in the midst of a flood of impoverished migrants converging on cities as a rural peasantry is dispossessed through the industrialization and commercialization of agriculture" (Harvey, 2012, p. 12).

The domination of neo-liberal regimes across the globe, however, triggered struggles in the 2000s. In countries under a democratic political system with one-person-one-vote regardless of wealth, neo-liberalism encounters an inherent paradox. The number of poor that neo-liberalism produced outnumbers the rich by far. The dissatisfied poor began to resort to democratic political processes to subvert the governments that imposed the neo-liberal policies upon them by voting for political parties that represent the people. This is exactly what happened in many Latin American countries in the 2000s. Faced with this paradox of neo-liberalism, the state power sometimes deploys outright oppression or conspiracy plots to overcome it. This indeed triggers further social instability in these countries.

Given this paradox, coupled with the crises and the rupture of social integration, global neo-liberalism never won. Taking advantage of this rupture, another attempt to seize global hegemony has been made from the former socialist camp: the coalition called the "Shanghai Cooperation Organization" (SCO), consisting of the People's Republic of China (PRC), Russia and some republics of the former USSR, many of which still have authoritarian political regimes, as manifested in the oppression of domestic minorities especially in the Uyghur, Tibetan and Inner Mongolian regions of China and in Hong Kong, as well as assassinations and detentions of the dissidents. All of this has drastically infringed human rights. Moreover, Russia has waged a war of aggression against its former socialist ally, Ukraine. Since the aim of President Vladimir Putin is clearly to alter the existing configuration of global collective absolute spaces of nations, upon which world peace under UN leadership has rested, the powers allying to the principle of respecting reified state boundaries are offering massive military aid to Ukraine in order to save and retain this post-WWII geographical legitimacy. The viability of the SCO has thereby become fragile.

Global geopolitics has now become more volatile with this struggle for renewed global hegemony. The PRC has also found considerable success in establishing a leading-edge IT base and a global project of spatial integration called "The Belt and Road Initiative", while the US is striving to contain it by reconsolidating its allies. Behind this current geo-political strife among the global dominant powers, peoples remain oppressed and exploited.

References

Aglietta, M. (1979) (translation). *Theory of capitalist regulation: The U.S. experience.* Translated by David Fernbach. Verso.

Boyer, R., & Saillard, Y. eds. (2002). *Regulation theory: the State of the art.* Routledge.

Flöbel, F. et al. (1982). *The new international division of labour: Structural unemployment in industrialised countries and industrialisation in developing countries.* Cambridge University Press.

Gramsci, A. (1971). *Selections from Prison notebooks.* edited by Q. Hoare and G. Nowell-Smith. International Publishers.

Harvey, D. (1982). *The limits to capital.* University of Chicago Press.

Harvey, D. (2012). *Rebel cities: From the right to the city to the urban revolution.* Verso.

Lefebvre, H. (1991). (translation). *The production of space.* Translated by Donald Nicholson-Smith. Wiley-Blackwell.

Lenin, V. I. (1964) (translation). Imperialism, the latest stage in the development of capitalism. In George Hanna (Ed.), *Lenin Collected works* (Vol. 22, pp. 185–304). Translated by Yuri Sdobnikov. Progress Publishers.

Low, N. (1991). *Planning, politics and the state: Political foundation of planning thought*. Uwin-Hyman.

Mandel, E. (1968) (translation). *Marxist economic theory*. Vol. 1. Translated by Brian Pearce. Monthly Review Press

Marx, K. (1971) (translation). *Theories of surplus-value*. Parts II and III. translated by Jack Cohen and S. W. Ryazanskaya. Progress Publishers.

Marx, K. (1977 and 1981) (translation). *Capital*. Vols. 1 and 3. Translated by Ben Fowkes. New York : Vintage Books.

Matsuishi, K. (1983). *Shihonron Kenkyu the study of capital*. Sanrei Shobo.

Mizuoka, F. (2013). Capitalist regulation and the provision of public transportation in Japan. In Nicholas Low (Ed.), *Transforming urban transport: the ethics, politics and practices of sustainable mobility*. Routledge.

Smith, N. (1984). *Uneven development*. Basil B1ackwell.

Tomizuka, R. (1975). *Kyokoron Kenkyu (Studies on the Crisis Theory)* (Enlarged). Mirai Sha.

Webber, M. (1982). Agglomeration and the regional question. *Antipode, 14*(2).

Chapter 9
Spatial Struggles for Emancipation

Contents

Abstract Subsuming space with the power discussed so far is never complete. In lieu of the conclusion, this chapter presents various spatial strategies in the social struggles regarding the different stages of space subsumption addressed in the order of the preceding chapters. The oppressed and subservient people fight back by exploiting such space that remains unsubsumed as 'stray space', using such process of space subsumption for their emancipation and empowerment as monopoly rent and deploying such less oppressive forms of space subsumption as action space. Section 8 presents a struggle against human rights infringements committed by Japan's state power as manifested in the child guidance centre, against which the author has engaged for several years.

9.1 Spatial Praxis to Produce Counter-Space

"Sovereignty implies 'space', and what is more it implies a space against which violence, whether latent or overt, is directed—a space established and constituted by violence" (Lefebvre, p. 280). Space has, first, been produced and dominated by the state and economic power. The transformation of society "presupposes confrontation" (Lefebvre, p. 422), and this confrontation includes struggle for the control of

F. Mizuoka, *Subsumption of Space*, Contributions to Regional Science,
https://doi.org/10.1007/978-981-97-7560-6_9

space. "Physical and social re-engineering and territorial organization of these sites is a weapon in political struggles" (Harvey, 2012, p. 118). Space therefore constitutes an indispensable moment and instrument for leverage in the struggle of the people against the power.

As it is already clear, the subsumption of space is in itself the process of creating the spatial configurations for the dominating power. Social space is created "to be *politically instrumental* in that it facilitates the control of society" and "underpins the reproduction of [existing] production relations and property relations" as well as the dominating "set of institutional and ideological superstructures" (Lefebvre, p. 349, emphasis original). Steve Pile states, in this regard, "authority produces space through, for example, cutting it up, differentiating between parcels of space, the use and abuse of borders and markets, the production of scales (from the body, through the region and the nation, to the globe), the control of movement within and across different kinds of boundaries and so on" (Pile & Keith, 1997, p. 3). Yet, those being dominated contest that space of and for domination. The configurations of produced space produced by the dominating power, both in the physical and mental forms, are something to be crushed and overcome by those controlled. The state and monetary power configures relational space, or the space of "disjoined unity, as at once fragmentary and homogenous" (Lefebvre, p. 388). The struggle between the dominant and the dominated triggers oppressed people to create alternative configuration of space, through "putting up resistance", inaugurating a "counter-space" (p. 349).

Therefore, there is an inherent dialectic in the subsumed space: "the political power which holds sway over "men", though it dominates the space occupied by its "subjects", does not control the causes and reasons that intersect within that space, each of which acts by and for itself" (Lefebvre, p. 413). Therefore, the domination of the power over space "exacerbates the conflict inherent in the political arena and in the state per se … and promotes a political critique which lends its weight to the trend towards the self-destruction of the 'moment of politics'" (p. 416).

The power thus cannot subsume space entirely. Contrarily, space can enhance the contradiction of the domination and becomes a tool for emancipation. Resistance is "the people fighting back in defence of freedom, democracy and humanity" in space. The actions for resistance "take place through specific geographies" (Pile and Keith, p. 1).

Consequently, in a class society, the configuration of space becomes always class-specific; different layers of space controlled by different classes in society overlap. State power, or in Lefebvre's example, the "Pater-Rex, later Imperator … thus reconstituted the space around him as the *space of power*" (p. 243); that is, the representation of space. On the other hand, "representational spaces would develop: women, servants, slaves, children—all had … their own spaces."

The configuration of space thus becomes dialectical, infused with struggles. It contains "a brutal condensation of social relationships" (Lefebvre, p. 227), or, to use Lefebvre's terminology, "*pratique spatiale*". "Inasmuch as global space bears the inscriptions and prescriptions of power", the struggle ensues from the contradiction and conflicts in the social relationships, attempting to create an alternative space of their own.

Lefebvre stated that the knowledge of space has a "prospective import", which is "the *project* ... of another space and another time in another ... society" (p. 92). Here, "another space" has dual implications: first, it is the alternative configuration of space or the "counter-space" (p. 367). Second, space can be deployed for the struggle to attain "another society". In this chapter, I deal with both in turn.

9.2 The Dominant Space of Power Versus the Counter-Space of the People

a. Abstract space: the spaces of the dominant power

The capitalist and state power "colonise" the space of ordinary citizens. Lefebvre conceptualised the confrontation in the production of space by stating that "new social relationships call for a new space, and vice versa" (p. 59). Explicitly, giving spatial irradiation to the conflicting social relations, "the representation of the space (*les représentations de l'espace*)", or the space of the dominant power, produced through contesting the space of representation (*l'espace de représentation*), which is the space of the daily biological reproduction of ordinary citizens.

The space of power superimposes itself over that of the daily lives of labourers and families. This confrontation arises in two contrasting issues: "abstract space and concrete space" and "a representation of space and the space of a representation".

The "abstraction" of abstract space (*espace abstrait*) derives from "abstract human labour" in *Capital* (Vol. 1, p. 142). Abstract human labour crystallises in impersonal monetary power, which create the space of private ownership through land-use coordination in a market economy. Such a thorough process of commercialisation and bureaucratisation of space, while mutually reinforcing, organises the relational space and the built environment as a space of "exchange value".

In the representation of space, the process of monetisation and the dominant power or bureaucracy are inscribed in the built environment. The bureaucracy conducts systematic monitoring and control over space, and inscribes the configuration of relational space and the built environment, which manifests legal and political organisation of society, onto pristine space. The technologies of civil and urban engineering, architecture and city planning are projected here, to legitimise the dominant economic and social order. This is exactly the ideology that supports the production of abstract space through the intervention of capitalist economy as well as the state power.

The representation of space is therefore the configuration of space formalised and framed by the dominant power and the relation of production. The space thus produced by state power or bureaucracy is polymerised onto abstract space. In these spaces, ordered and formalised by monetary and state power, space is no longer a simple container of the living being. It shackles those who seek alternative representation of space.

b. Counter-space: pursuit for escaping the territory under domination

The term "concrete space" emerges here. It is derived from concrete useful labour that constitutes use-value (utility). This is the "space of the representation", which critically observes the representation of the space, and gives a way to intervene in opposition to it. The alternative configuration of space can be produced through such contesting actions of the people as "dislocations through, for example, frictions of distance, the blurring of boundaries, and hiding and coming out" (Pile and Keith, p. 13).

The simplest way to escape domination is just to leave the territory dominated by the power. The ancient Nara period of Japan, when those who could not endure serfdom gradually escaped to estates owned privately by nobles, Buddhist temples or shrines was explained in Chap. 3. Consequently, the Imperial Court lost the villeins that supported it economically, and it collapsed.

Sack introduced another intriguing example in the ancient church (p. 111): "since territory was intimately connected with the definition of authority, a prime means for Church officials to resist authority was to leave their territory. Evidence for this practice are the numerous prohibitions against it."

In short, if the contiguity of absolute space and the propensity of the homogenising process enable the spatial migration of the people, it puts the dominating power on the verge of collapse. This is the consequence of the dialectics between formally subsumed absolute space and the power or market, and the negative property of physical contiguity which absolute space brings into the economic and societal power.

However, this primitive strategy of deploying the unsubsumed property of pristine space in an alternative way is readily suppressed once the power manages to establish a higher-order scale and puts that scale under its domination, as discussed in Chap. 5 (p. 89).

c. Struggles to establish a counter-space of the people

In cases where multi-scalar configuration of power domination is in place, movements to recover a firmer counter-space of daily life as "representation space" arise from the those dominated by the power through spatial praxis. This social action is essential, since "groups, classes or fraction of classes cannot constitute themselves, or recognize one another, as 'subjects' unless they generate (or produce) space" (Lefebvre, p. 416).

The counter-space is an alternative configuration of space which arises from everyday struggles, including secret and illegal aspects in social life, based on the autogenous bond with space as experienced by the subservient people. The counter-space is "lived space" set as the base for the opposition. It offers an opportunity to criticise and intervene in the process of configuring the relational space and the built environment. The people must turn back state power through the production of "counter-plans and counter-projects designed to thwart strategies, plans and programmes imposed" (Lefebvre, p. 383) from above, the dominating class.

The counter-space earmarks, initially, "what is *excluded*: the edges of the city, shanty towns, the spaces of forbidden games, of guerrilla war, of war." If "no counterattack is mounted" from those under domination, these excluded spaces are likely to be homogenised and absorbed (p. 373). Counterattacks must therefore be waged to show those in power that they do have limits "to integrate, to recuperate, or to destroy" (ibid) the space that has been excluded.

Then, the "counter-project" emerges to promote "a counter-space in opposition to the one embodied in the strategies of power" (p. 381). The counter-space inserts itself against, for example, "power and the arrogance of power, endless expansion of 'private' and of industrial profitability" (p. 382). The counter-space can also function as the container of "local powers" creating "independent territorial entities capable to some degree of self-management" (ibid).

The struggle is thus fought between the power that colonised and dominated space and the people whose space has been colonised and peripherised. The people thus stand up to produce "counter-space" or territories of local powers. Failing this struggle, the "dominated space will simply be weakened" (p. 374).

The people oppressed under domination thus challenge the restrictive divisions in the dominant configurations of relational space and the built environment. An "extraordinary *spatial duality*" would ensue, then, as a spatial manifestation of the "duality of political power" (p. 374). Here, the contradictions of society "simply emerge in space, at the level of space, and so engender the contradiction of space" (p. 358).

The objective of the struggle is to recover and regenerate the concrete space of daily life or the "counter-space" from the "abstract space" generated by the monetisation of society and the rampant infliction of state power. We should not belittle the struggles to create "counter-space", since they shake "existing space *to its foundations*, along with its strategies and aims" (p. 383, emphasis mine) and, of course, *shake the existing power structure* that the spatial struggle is fighting.

The physical power of the built environment as a representation of space imposes itself on the people as the manifestation of political power. The struggle in space appears as the opposition between conventional and counter versions of the spatial configuration as well as the built environment which in itself contains the duality of the contiguity and separation.

Thus, the theory of the subsumption of space as put forward in the previous chapters develops into a theory of spatial struggle, placing two different versions of the relational space and the built environment in opposing axes, if the alternative space is to be successfully defended. These opposing axes are the focus of resistance and struggle for counter-space and become the source of the space of representation.

Seen from the homogenising power of the dominant, the struggle means to create differences from the dominating space, and in preceding it, to ensure the right of struggle to create the spatial difference, which "implies no entitlements that do not have to be bitterly fought for" (Lefebvre, p. 396).

9.3 Struggles around Absolute Space 1: Contiguity and Bounding

a. Pursuit of contiguity: space for liberation and realisation

As discussed in Chap. 3 (pp. 28–29), the property of unlimited contiguity of absolute space that embraces every subject is homologous to the ideal of universal human rights, as represented in the slogan of the French Revolution: liberty, egality and fraternity. The strategic objectives here is, as Lefebvre states (p. 418), "reunification of what has been split apart".

The network that the dominating power produced is shared by the people as well. This is one of the empowering effects of absolute space, giving rise to a certain kind of dialectics. The proliferation of denser networks sometimes weakens the state power, since it reduces isolation and offers the people an opportunity for empowerment by creating a counter network of communication across space, as in the case of the Internet. Whence the "clamour … raised on all sides by those who want to loosen the grip of power, to decentralize, to manage (or self-manage) from the grass roots" (Lefebvre, p. 378). Through the expansion of alternative action across space through this alternative use of the network, the "state's tendency to establish centres of decision armed with all the tools of power and subordinated to a single main centre, the capital, thus encounters stiff resistance" (pp. 378–379).

There are examples of civil society organisations seeking empowering contiguity.

The coalition of member groups of The Right to the City Alliance of New York sought their definition of "public" space, that they can not only "truly access so-called public space, but can also be empowered to create new common spaces for socialization and political action" (Harvey, 2012, p. xvi). That is, the citizens' aim to grab power to produce commons that can be utilised by everyone should be a condition for emancipation.

Some global NGOs expand their action space to the global scale, so that they actually share global common space with the multinational enterprises for their counteractions. Here are two examples with different configuration of spatial scale.

Greenpeace, a civil society organisation for environmental protection, has been active globally on a wide range of environmental problems, from global warming to product liability of vinyl chloride toys, sometimes deploying illegal force and relying on the financial donations and funds from innumerable citizens concerned about the environment. Overcoming the fragmented systems of domestic laws and confronting environmental destruction by, for example, multinational enterprises on a global spatial scale, Greenpeace embraces the global action space and reminds multinational enterprises seeking to invest in areas least resistant to environmental pollution that there is no longer any "spatial fix" for the predatory use of the environment by confronting them globally.

Another civil society organisation is the "Kalabaw-no-Kai" for poverty-stricken citizens in the neighbourhood of Kotobuki in Yokohama. This society, whose official appellation is "Association in Kotobuki for Solidarity with Migrant Workers", continues to support international workers residing there, some of whom have no valid employment visas. This association may seem to work at a local spatial scale, unlike Greenpeace. Yet its standpoint is firmly at the scale of global contiguity. It questions why the action space allowed for the elite of multinational enterprises is off-limits to simple labourers? The Kalabaw-no-Kai aims at a globalism which universally empowers the human right to spread the action space to seek jobs over the global space, and has had positive results in the struggle to empower international labourers to have the right of action space. Therefore, just like Greenpeace, Kalabaw-no-Kai pursues a strong alternative to the global contiguity of space created by multinational capital and the power of the nation states. It also provides an empowering consultation service by volunteers to international labourers to establish contiguity in international labour migration with the universal human rights of workers guaranteed.

In short, the action space for neo-liberalism and the spatial configuration created by it having spread globally to subsume the global scale, the action space of the people in opposition should not be confined to the local scale. It should advance the movement on the scale of global contiguity, to struggle at the same global scale.

b. Spatial contiguity empowering self-realisation

It is necessary for those seeking alternatives to break the isolation created by bounding and the containment of social action to a limited territory inscribed by those holding power, to empower themselves through grabbing the universal and contiguous spread of the global space back to themselves through their actions.

At one time, all people on earth enjoyed the contiguity of the global space without visas or passports. Humans in the Stone Age could expand territory or action space provided there was the physical and technical means of space integration. Such universal contiguity is derived from the property of pristine absolute space of "liberty, egality and fraternity", which makes space as a field that realises self.

After people became confined into territories under oppression and control by power, they were deprived of this freedom, as the global space had been divided by the state power. The people can, however, get back their freedom and empowerment once they recover the spatial contiguity in some form and dare to overcome containment to the division set by the state power. Contiguity therefore works for the empowerment of those who are oppressed, and for gaining political and social leverage towards their liberation.

For instance, when the Hungarian government opened its border with Austria, the citizens of former East Germany, oppressed under the Stalinist SED (*Sozialistische Einheitspartei Deutschlands*, the Socialist Unity Party of Germany) regime, were able to acquire the contiguity of Europe that had been blocked by the "iron curtain". This contiguity eventually led to the fall of the Berlin Wall and put an end to the oppressive Stalinist regimes in Eastern Europe. The strategy of securing or restoring contiguity by the people and establishing it more clearly as an instrument for struggle is now taking place in various ways as a movement for emancipation.

In this context, Harvey pressed home the strategy (2012, p. 87), "for the populations to self-organise to provide their own commons". Grabbing back and extending and enhancing "the qualities of the non-commodified reproductive and environmental commons" (p. 88) is a political struggle which "has to be integrated wholly into anti-capitalist struggle in a very specific way" (p. 87).

c. "The tragedy of the commons" and the concept of *Gesamteigentum*

The Roman legal system presumes the existence of private economic subjects and a market where bounded space and the individualisation of territory were imposed by the state power. On the other hand, the Germanic legal system recognised the right of sharing the contiguous space as *Gesamteigentum* (collective ownership). An example of this type of ownership is the right of the members of a village community to share the forest wilderness which lay within their action space. However, the contemporary legal system with respect to space has been established based on the Roman system, and the right to the commons has been denied by many state powers.

If the rights of space are subsumed straight into the market economy, where each economic subject is independent and competes with others, it causes a contradiction of what Hardin called the "tragedy of the commons". Neo-classical economists love the metaphor to deny the viability of the commons; yet Harvey aptly criticised that "if the cattle were held in common, of course, the metaphor would not work. This shows that it is private property in cattle and individual utility-maximizing behaviour that lie at the heart of the problem, rather than the common-property character of the resource" (Harvey, 2012, p. 68).

Therefore, for multiple entities with collective rights to restore the contiguity of space as the commons, the alternative social system of reciprocity and redistribution within a community of outcomes using collective space must be installed and implemented. Once the principle of reciprocity has been installed as a legal provision, society does not require the bounded mosaic of territories for each subject as in the market economy. For example, if the rules for the use of commons are set clear, and the people concerned work cooperatively, then the resources in the "Grand Bank" are available, where spatial contiguity reigns. The alternative society indeed makes the alternative mode of subsuming space possible.

d. Overcoming the fetishism of separation and fragmentation created by the power

Space is "more often prohibitions" and most such prohibitions "are invisible" (Lefebvre, p. 319). The divided space of discrimination, isolation and prohibition that has been imposed by the state and capitalist power must be denied and restructured to restore emancipation from imposed division. This is the key to empowerment—the "action of political power, which creates fragmentation and so controls it—which creates it, indeed, in order to control it" (p. 321). In the contemporary world, the barriers confining people within the territory of their respective scale are mostly under rigid management by the authority dominating the fragmented territories. Ethnic groups who happen to be confined in a certain territory at the national scale regardless of their will are placed in the status of minority ethnic groups under the divided territory where their potential to exercise their human rights is rather impaired (dispowering).

In urban space, the minorities and the poor are spatially contained, and this containment is generated by the compulsion of the built environment. In "gated communities", wealthy people separate themselves with a high wall and a guarded gate through which only residents can pass.

The strategy of voluntarily regaining the contiguity of the space from those oppressed people through involuntary confinement will not be realised without overcoming the artificial separation imposed by the dominant power, which has colonised the space of their daily life and labour reproduction.

Ironically, however, the subjects or groups of the people in the dominated territory actively seek to separate the territory in some cases. It is sometimes an effective means to relinquish the domination by creating at the same spatial scale their own territory, which functions as a node for constructing alternative autonomy. There are many such cases in Europe undergoing the process, as in Scotland and Catalonia, or that have already materialised as in Kosovo, to obtain separation and establish a new state where the hegemony of existing higher-order state power can no longer exercise domination.

From the side of those oppressed, it is necessary to relativise the existing systems and claimed legitimacy of spatial configurations, including the fetishism of bounding and territory, which are institutionalised or take a physical or imaginary form. Through these efforts, the people can consciously overcome the fetishism and explicitly re-examine the legitimacy of separation. Overcoming the fetishism by re-thinking one's everyday routine is the first step to de-fetishise the absolute legitimacy of the existing multi-layered spatial configuration.

The fetishism of border and territory as "it has all been taken for granted in everyday consciousness" must be overcome. Labourers who cross borders without a valid working visa are recognised and treated undoubtedly as "illegal immigrants" by the power dominating either side of the border. However, the border of a national territory including the superimposed boundaries is indeed a product of the state power as a political artefact, not something natural and absolutely given, such as the delineations of rivers and mountains. By creating a national border, it even defines the ethnic minority groups incorporated into the territory circumscribed by the border as a "minority" whose protection is to be carried out only through "emphasizing ethnic identity and heritage." The border is never natural or eternal. Its legitimacy should be duly questioned and fought against through various forms of struggle.

As a way of struggle, those confined within a border of a state and capitalist power need to construct a system of counter-space of their own. The counter-space thus generated spontaneously from those oppressed, after overcoming the fetishism of space, relativises the existing division. For example, the collapse of the Habsburg Empire, which had seen many ethnic groups labelled as minorities, turned some minorities into majorities, and former majorities such as the Hungarian and German-speaking Austrians became minorities in Transylvania, Romania and South Tirol after the dissolution of the Empire. After all, minorities are nothing more than the products of historical contingency.

Therefore, a strategy here is to relativise the fetishism of bounding created by state power and formalise the autogenously created territories made under the long-term association of the social group and space more explicitly by the power of former minority people.

International borders after WWII were consolidated under the domination of the UN, but this has resulted only in the form of segmentation of existing independent states observed in former the Yugoslavia and former Soviet Union. Yet some ethnic groups, such as the Irish in Northern Ireland, insist on annexation of their territory to the country where the same ethnic group dominates as the majority. A solution to the ethnic problem and the realisation of self-determination can be found only in the spatial strategy of a fundamental reshuffling of existing national borders, as actually happened after WWI in Europe and as Kwame Nkrumah demanded for an independent Africa.

9.4 Struggles around Absolute Space 2: The Dialectics between *Wirkungsraum* and Action Space

a. Coercive *Wirkungsraum* and emancipatory action space

As suggested in the previous section, territories created out of the real subsumption of absolute space fall into either of two types, which have distinct properties and contradict one another.

Wirkungsraum is the type of space which needs state power or sometimes the power of the occupants themselves to ensure exclusive occupation of a territory. Without power, the territories are always vulnerable to trespassing, and to be taken over by others.

By contrast, action space is a type of space not controlled much by the dominant power but more anarchical, fluid and *laissez-faire*, controlled only by the physical property of pristine space.

As summarised in Table 9.1, action space is more amenable to the production of counter-space, by allowing more anarchical, flexible and spontaneous human actions, not controlled by the dominant power; whereas *Wirkungsraum* is more institutionalised, controlled and created by the explicit political process of bounding. Once created, the boundary of a territory forms an "iron frame" where free human actions are negated or constrained. The boundary of action space is set by a physical distance decay effect, where interaction over space diminishes with the inverse square of the distance, while the boundary of *Wirkungsraum* is set by a political process backed by state power.

Action space lacks the concept of "trespassing"; instead, it has property close to the commons, as different agents share a territory, and more than one action space can overlap with another. Therefore, action space is more empowering, while for *Wirkungsraum*, exclusive occupation and the ownership of a territory protected by power is the norm. The owner or occupier dominates the territory and trespassing by outsiders is subject to prosecution.

Table 9.1 Comparison of action spaceand *Wirkungsraum*. Source Mizuoka (2012) p.54 (edited)

Action space	*Wirkungsraum*
More anarchical, spontaneous and *laissez-faire*	More institutionalised, controlled and constraining by power
Boundary set by the physical "distance-decay effect", where interaction over space diminishes with the inverse square of the distance	Boundary set by political processes, including physical battle and subsequent peace negotiations or explicit economic transactions of landed properties
Created by repeated spatial actions	Created by the explicit process of bounding
Different agents share a territory, and more than one action space normally overlaps	Exclusive occupation by a body, social group or economic agency
Presupposes *Gesamteigentum*, which lacks the concept of "trespassing"	Presupposes private ownership of a territory and trespassing is subject to prosecution
Emerging out of free, flexible and spontaneous human actions, not controlled by the dominant power	Once created, the boundary forms an "iron frame", where free human actions are negated and constrained
Nodal configuration	Homogenous configuration
Empowerment and freedom	**Power domination and constraints**

In sum, action space is less institutionalised but more emancipatory; whereas *Wirkungsräume*, or bounded territories, is more fixed and coercive.

b. The dialectics of *Wirkungsraum* and action space in social struggles

Various action spaces come together in different types of spatial scales. The scale of metropolitan areas is formed by such factors as daily commuting and shopping ranges, range of longer-term labour migration, and the habitat of an ethnic group or groups of people using a common language.

Among these scales emerge many vertical inter-scalar relations. Some scales are almost totally dependent upon higher-order ones, as in the relationship between the state and the jurisdictions of local states; yet others are more independent and contradictory in relation to other scales.

A typical socio-spatial dialectic comes out of the contradiction between spontaneous action space and institutionalised *Wirkungsraum*. A bounded territory institutionalised by the dominant power is always exposed to fresh challenges from the actions embedded in the more pristine property of absolute space. People act beyond the spatial range of institutionalised boundaries, either out of ignorance or explicit intention. Action space can therefore erode and undermine the domination of power exercised in the bounded territory. A more anarchical and spontaneous action space thereby creates opportunities of empowerment or to challenge the dominant power represented in the institutionalised *Wirkungsraum*.

While those in power attempt to impede the freer action of agency or socio-economic flows by controlling the porosity of the territorial "iron frame" grid, the people may attempt to continue their actions by breaking through this frame and penetrating the boundary, often without authorisation. The exclusiveness and boundedness of the territory and the authority over it are thereby undermined. This process is more detrimental to the authority because it can lead to the collapse of the dominant power contained in the institutionalised territory itself.

The subordinated class, ethnic group or individual can intentionally deploy the contradiction between *Wirkungsraum* and action space to create *les espaces de representation* for its struggle against the authority. The struggling agent may form a united front based on the common nature in spatialised oppression to engage in collective actions, while in other cases it may be more disintegrated, such as the individualised labourers in the labour market acting across action space rationally to maximise their income.

Ironically, many of these individual cases come out of the rational economic behaviour of agents following the fundamentalist market economists. For example, in some spaces, illegal immigration seeks higher incomes or contraband trade for higher prices, which are considered punishable by the laws enforced by the dominant power, including that of a neo-liberalist type. Such free mobility comes into conflict with the state power that places an undue burden on the free mobility of labour or goods based on the rational *laissez-faire* behaviour of the people. A typical case relating to immigration is the flow of Chinese labour in pursuit of higher incomes from the PRC to British Hong Kong without authorisation from the British colonial authority in the 1960s and 1970s (Mizuoka, 2018, Chap. 3). An example relating to contraband is the cross-border import of daily necessities from Thailand to Burma, where goods for daily consumption are in short supply.

These actions of the people spontaneously alter the configuration of the territory imposed by the state power. The proliferation of these action spaces eventually undermines the territories institutionalised by power, and the very authority that survived by deploying the "iron frame" as its container would collapse.

This socio-spatial struggle is clearly demonstrated in the "Pan-European Picnic" on the Hungarian border in 1989. The pressure generated by thousands of East Germans gathering spontaneously led to the opening up of the border fence with Austria. This allowed East Germans to flee from the institutionalised wall that had confined them into the "iron frame" and had split their potential action space. The collapse of the Stalinist regime of the GDR immediately after this "picnic" also demonstrates clearly the significance of counteraction deploying action space from the produced spatial iron frame to the emancipation-seeking society.

9.5 Struggles around Relative Space: Counter-agglomeration, Counter-Networks and "Stray Spaces"

a. Introduction

So how can we get a territorial foothold of counter-space in the existing space?

The distance-decay effect dictates that the longer the distance, the weaker the strength of social interactions, including power. This effect can be exploited by contesting social groups in two ways:

First, people belonging to an alienated and subservient social group can empower themselves through agglomeration, physical living, or acting closer together. This is the spatial rationale for the emergence of urban districts comprising people of particular ethnic or sexual identities. Here, the alienated group may place itself in the existing space to assert their social positionings. The agglomeration of people from the group brings about the creation and consolidation of their internal network and political power, and hence, empowers them and strengthens their social position.

Second, there can be a pristine space that has not been subsumed by the spatial network produced by the dominant power. Subservient people may find a space in a weak grip and deploy it as an element of an alternative spatial configuration. In Lefebvre's terminology (p. 383), "deviant or diverted spaces", categorised in this book as '*stray spaces*', can be created. Stray space serves as an important element in producing *les espaces de représentation.* Since a 'stray spaces' are out of bounds of the 'iron frame' of the institutionalised territory, subordinated social groups can escape domination and deploy power intentionally to secretly develop an alternative agglomeration to aid their struggle. This can take the form of a hidden 'liberated zone' that serves as a launching pad for engaging in national or global insurgencies against authorities.

In this sense, counter-agglomeration and stray spaces serve as important elements in producing *les espaces de représentation.* The effectiveness of the production of such a space for a struggle depends on the strength of the state's spatial grip, as well as, ironically enough, on the ability of the subordinate group to pay monopoly rent.

b. Agglomeration as a Spatial Strategy for Empowerment

Agglomeration is the physical annihilation of space to eliminate the effect of distance decay. Oppressed people living close together facilitate the creation of a denser network, with nodes for communication and exchange. Due to its sheer size, the agglomeration occupies a certain expanse of territory as a 'liberated zone', within which a territory of self-reliance and autonomy is created. This can lead to the creation of a source of power, as discussed in Sect. 2 of Chap. 3, and a spontaneous bond between the body and space.

Castells (1983, Chap. 14) depicted the positive role of agglomeration in his research on the creation of a gay territory in the Castro District of San Francisco. He stated, "When gay men try to liberate themselves from cultural and sexual oppression, they need a physical space from which to strike out" (p. 140). For gay people, a network is essential to find sexual partners, which requires nodes such as gay bars. Around the 1970s, relatively wealthy gay households began to agglomerate in the middle of urban San Francisco. This was possible because of their wealth, which allowed them to afford the monopoly rent (Sect. 4, Chap. 5). This was necessary in order to overwrite the pre-existing property ownership of the urban districts where they desired to live. Their wealth also contributed to the gentrification of their territory. On the contrary, lesbians did not agglomerate, presumably because of the non-affordability of monopoly rent due to their income constraints. The resulting gay community in San Francisco empowered the residents since the district coincided with supervisorial District 5, from which the prominent gay statesman Harvey Milk was elected.

Counter-agglomeration thereby enhances the position of oppressed groups in society, creating space for emancipation and giving them the freedom to pursue an alternative way of life. Counter-agglomeration not only ensures their survival but can also eventually lead to the accumulation of the power necessary to mobilise and change the government. Nevertheless, the affordability of monopoly rent is a key condition for the materialisation of this strategy in existing urban areas.

c. Alternative Networks for Struggle

The need for physical agglomeration has waned recently with the development of remote modes of interaction through the Internet. Indeed, the Internet arises from a spatial network that covers a wide spatial range and totally annihilates time.

The network can be shared by both dominant and non-dominant people. If the network cannot be shared, those struggling against authority need to build their own networks to materialise their objectives. With this move towards building an alternative transport network, people can now materialise their own action spaces.

The subordinated people may need an alternative network of spatial integration that covers a longer spatial range. In this case, those struggling against the authority may need to build their own transport network to materialise their own objectives.

An example of this alternative network is the "underground train" that functioned in the Civil War era in the US. It transported blacks from the Southern slave states to the industrial North, where the slaves were "liberated" and converted into industrial labour for manufacturing plants run by northern capitalists.

Another example is the Ho Chi Minh trail, connecting the PRC, North Vietnam, Laos and Cambodia with South Vietnam to transport ammunition and other military supplies for the National Liberation Front in South Vietnam, then dominated by a US puppet regime. Some parts of the Ho Chi Minh trail accommodated military lorries yet others only bicycles, together forming a sophisticated network connecting North Vietnam with various "liberated zones" in the South. With this network of the "trails", the Vietnamese people managed to oust the US from Vietnam.

Compared with the means to integrate space produced by the state power, counter transport networks such as these are often shabbily built since the subordinated do not have sufficient funds to construct a durable transport infrastructure. Nevertheless, these counter networks have been indispensable and essential for the people in undermining the dominant power.

d. Stray space arising from primitive means of spatial integration

The network of the Ho Chi Minh trail was built through the tropical jungles in Laos and Cambodia, which were mostly out of the reach of the ground US armed forces.

The effectiveness of such a network with nodal bases for the struggle depends on the strength of the spatial grip by the state power as well as the skill and craft of the subordinated groups to hide such an emancipatory base from the authority's surveillance.

In the past, when the technology to achieve surveillance over space was primitive, this space out of the reach of surveillance by the state power was a ubiquitous element of space in many countries. For example, in former Manchukuo (currently the north-eastern part of China), the central government at Hsinking (currently Changchun) could never achieve perfect domination over the peripheral mountainous areas under the state power. The areas along the Soviet border were typically subject to infiltration by partisans engaged in the anti-Japanese struggle.

In the remote mountainous areas in Malaysia and Thailand until the 1960s, inspired by the Chinese revolution and the strategy of Mao Zedong, communist rebels established centres of struggle in the northern border areas, aiming to launch communist revolution in these countries.

Today, the possibility of finding stray space exists only in countries where the government is defunct or surveillance and control over the territory by state power is dysfunctional. A good example is Somalia in the Horn of Africa. For insurgent groups, it is a valuable space which offers a rare global stray space to establish their alternative centres for waging counterattacks on the globally dominant neo-liberalist power. This is the very reason that the neo-conservatives have labelled such countries a *failed state* and attempted to place them under political domination akin to colonial rule, as in the case of Afghanistan.

Stray space can arise out of the "paradox of spatial integration" (pp. 61–62). Some parts of a territory are bound to be left out from the networks of transportation and communication. The higher the speed at which transport technology is designed to move humans and goods, the more severe the spatial unevenness of the network becomes. The parts of territory left out of real subsumption thus remain imperfectly controlled by the dominant power. This aggravating unevenness means differences in the intensity of domination by the power in a bounded territory: the core area can be firmly under authority, while domination in the periphery may be weaker. Even though the dominant power attempts to extend its hold over every corner of the territory, the level of funds required to make the network denser to accomplish successful surveillance over an entire territory may be prohibitive.

Due to this imperfect spatial integration, some parts of the territory always remain weakly or not at all subsumed under the state power. This allows the people struggling against the dominant power to act relatively freely without much control or surveillance by the state power.

e. Counter-struggle by the state power to relinquish stray space

In ccontrast, the dominant power always attempts to have a firm grip over the entire expanse of its territory. It therefore strives hard to detect any insurgencies and attempts to relinquish stray space or any candidate for it. The power does so by developing more powerful means to achieve surveillance and control effectively the potential area for stray space.

The dominant power thus introduces surveillance systems like the ubiquitous sensorium of the God that Isaac Newton assumed for absolute space or panopticon architecture. A panopticon has "centrality, the transparency of the cell, and the invisibility of the inspector" which work to "intensify the effects of supervision by giving the inspector 'an apparent omnipresence'" (Sack, 1986, p. 186).

For example, it sets up a security camera at every corner of the city street, asks those entering wilderness areas to obtain permits or to register beforehand with the authority and deploys special operations forces on permanent standby to put down any attempt by the dissidents to transform a stray space into an alternative centre for insurgence.

Recently, advancing information and space technologies have contributed greatly to relinquish stray space further. Satellites have been launched to take high-resolution aerial photos from outer space to detect any suspicious activities in stray spaces. An IC-equipped fare card for public transportation, developed as FeliCa by Sony, was first used in Hong Kong as the Octopus Card and later proliferated to other cities worldwide (e.g. Suica by JR East in Japan) to continuously collect data on the action paths of any person. The data are stored in the database of the IC fare card company and are ready to be deployed by the authorities who wish to keep track of anyone's spatial actions. The dominant power has thereby equipped itself with an enhanced capacity to check and obliterate possibilities for a stray space.

The "iron frame" of space thus becomes ever more tightly controlled and structured, while the people become more powerless in creating these alternative territories in secrecy.

f. Stray space for capitalist power

Intriguingly, stray space is also deployed by financial capital, which holds ultimate power under a neo-liberalist regime. Financial capital can escape formal financial regulation exercised by the state power at the established financial core by transferring capital "outside the regulatory reach of national jurisdiction" or tax havens (Dicken, 2011, p. 396) to enjoy lax or little taxation and control over financial operations.

These tax havens are typically hidden in the periphery of global capitalism in terms of geography, off the beaten track of major financial nodes; yet they often remain under the sovereignty of the financially powerful core countries.

A typical example is the Cayman Islands in the Caribbean, which is now a self-governing British Overseas Territory. The strength of the City of London as the real global financial centre rests partly on the existence of financial consultants who are knowledgeable enough to advise their clients to take advantage of the loopholes in financial regulations present there.

The formal part of the financial economy repeatedly claims, at least for appearance's sake, the need to put tax havens under more stringent control. Yet a crackdown on these financial stray spaces has rarely been conducted. The dominant "global society" has never labelled such stray spaces as "failed", placing them under surveillance or relinquishment. Tax havens are indeed an integral part of the neo-liberalist financial economy, forming part and parcel of the dominant *représentation de l'espace*. Both types of stray space are produced purposefully in the periphery, yet only that emerging through the initiative of the subordinated is subject to a serious threat of extinction. The class nature of stray space is evident here.

g. The people's right to mobility

There is also a need for spatial struggle to guarantee and enhance the human rights of mobility for those who do not possess or cannot drive a private car. An automobile-dominated society creates discrimination in real subsumption of relative space according to the income group and makes relative space more fragmented for the poorer classes. The grass-roots movement claiming the "right to move" or "*droit au transport*" addresses this issue.

The *droit au transport* has been advocated in Japan by the Association for the Research of Transportation Problems and Human Rights (*Kotsuken Gakkai*). It issues a journal which has published research on difficulties in mobility among the grass-roots people in conjunction with citizen initiatives. The "Charter of Right to Transport" (Association for the Research of Transportation Problems and Human Rights, 1998) stipulates the principle of equality, security of safety, convenience and culture etc. in public transportation offered both by government and private industries.

A movement demanding the right to mobility was also active in Watts, Los Angeles. The revolt of black people who could not use cars and felt confined because of their lack of means of mobility instigated the opening of the public light rail line connecting the heart of the Watts district to downtown Los Angeles. With this movement, a tram line, not containing the poor within a certain closed urban district, but enhancing mobility open to the general public, was produced by the state power to achieve social integration. A similar situation can be found in the construction of the urban MTR in Hong Kong in the late 1970s by the British colonial government after a series of two riots waged by the ethnic Chinese people there (Mizuoka, 2018, pp. 164–170).

9.6 Struggles Around Relational Space: "Poor People's Optimum" and Christaller's Central-Place System

a. "Poor people's optimum"

Revisiting the first form of subsumption of relational space, it is essential for the surrounding demand space of a city, called a "*complementary region*" in the central-place theory, to fulfil supply from the central place. The complementary region must have a sufficient spatial extent containing demand (demand space) for the capitalists in charge of the supply of goods to the cities to sustain itself economically. The extent of demand space must not be eroded through its overlapping with the "complementary regions" of other cities. In this sense, the urban hierarchy in capitalism must take a shape which guarantees a size of demand space sufficient to guarantee profit. This may be called the principle of "the capitalists' optimum" in space.

Here, it is intriguing to examine whether socialist Christaller built a system that satisfies the capitalists' optimum or an alternative optimum. This section examines this point based on the model of territorial integration that Christaller himself built.

The maximum range which an ordinary person as a consumer can travel to obtain a good or a service plays a crucial role in determining this point. Under capitalism, securing sufficient demand space which generates sufficient profit is the condition for the sustainable central place hierarchy.

For capitalists, any welfare considerations, like the existence of persons who are spatially out of reach of a certain type of commodity due to their remote location from the supply centre, or the accessibility of people to the central places of various orders that supply goods offering essential economic functions to them, is out of consideration. Capitalist space is always against the "*poor people's optimum*", as postulated by Peet (1972, p. 3):

> planning for the provision of social services has been oriented towards either minimizing the costs of supply through centralizing facilities and achieving economies of scale, or towards maximizing access to services through decentralization... The starting point for our service-supply models should be the preferences of the people who most need services... Our theories of the location of economic activity are constructed from the premise that location decision makers attempt to maximize profit... [whereas] the objective is to drag economic activity away from locations optimal in terms only of economic cost and push this activity as close as possible to the jobless population.

Harvey (1973, pp. 70 and 88) states a similar point—"the forces governing location from the producer's point of view are not necessarily beneficial when analysed from the consumer's point of view"—and there may exist "conflict between the technological necessity for a few productive points and the physical necessity for a large number of spatiality distributed consumption points".

It was not until Berry and Garrison's (1958) work that the "central-place hierarchy" was reformulated to support the principle of the "capitalists' optimum". In Christaller's original formulation, the "central-place hierarchy" is, rather, a normative concept, built deductively out of his socialist norm that every person must be placed within the reach of the supply of all the kinds of commodities. This concept in Christaller's own central-place hierarchical model is best displayed in his explanation of the social process, whereby a lower-order centre is created:

> let us suppose that the upper limit of the range [this is the absolute spatial limit that a consumer can travel to obtain a good] of central good No. 21 is, under certain concrete conditions, 21 km from central place B. If there is now another central good No. 20 which has a range on only 20 km under the same conditions, then obviously, a ring 1-km wide is at the edge of the region which cannot be supplied with this central good by B alone. For supplying places within this ring, at least three other central places are necessary, which must lie equidistant from each other. (Christaller, 1957 edition, p. 202)

Here, Christaller states in effect that *the lower order centre must be always established if the people living in a region "which cannot be supplied with" a certain type of commodity need to be supplied.* Elsewhere, Christaller explicitly states that "in developing the scheme... we simply spoke of the 'range', and the fixed value of the upper limit of the range was set there" (*ibid*, p. 215). This shows his social norm towards the "poor people's optimum" instead of the profit maximisation of capitalists.

Christaller claims that the consideration of the minimum size of investment required of capital to be competitive ("lower limit of the range" in Christaller's terminology or *threshold* in modern central-place studies) does not alter the "constellation" of central places, but does alter the economic functions that exist at each order of centre. He states:

> with regard to the lower limit of the range of central goods, there is no new constellation in the net of central places but only a change in the size of the types. If in a region, the lower limit of the range for certain central goods is higher than normal, then the *central places are generally more weakly developed because the offering of such goods frequently falls off*. (*ibid*, p. 216, emphasis mine)

This suggests that the variety of commodities supplied from a particular order of centre may be smaller in the hierarchical system based on the "lower limit of the range", or the system created under the "capitalists' optimum", "than that created based on the "upper limit of the range", or the principle of the "poor people's optimum".

b. Comparison of the central-place systems based on two different social norms

The two optima, those of the poor people and the capitalists, can be compared mathematically.

As mentioned earlier in Chap. 5 (pp. 78–79), the fundamental difference between the two systems lies in whether the system is built upon the egalitarian condition to satisfy everyone with the provision of all kinds of goods or upon the capitalist system where all the suppliers should be provided with normal profits. Reflecting this difference in norms, the poor people's optimum (Christaller) is built on the range, whereas the capitalist optimum (Berry and Garrison) is on the threshold.

To examine whether these differences make the function of the centres of the morphologically identical ranks different between the two systems, I first consider under the special assumption that range and threshold are equal. For convenience, the range and threshold are to be commonly called here "the reach" of goods.

Both Berry et al.'s *A* centre and Christaller's *L* centre (hereinafter, *A*(*L*)) supply all the goods, including those of the sector with the greatest reach. For the capitalist system, the goods with the largest threshold, the area of a complementary region, is identical with the area of a circle with a radius of that reach.

Putting the area of the complementary region of *A* (*L*) centre a^2, R_n, or, at this time, the radius R_n of the reach of the good *n* is equal to

$$R_n = \sqrt{\frac{1}{\pi}}\, a \approx 0.5642\, a \tag{9.1}$$

On the other hand, the distance H_n from one vertex of the hexagonal complementary region to the centre of the hexagon is

$$H_n = \sqrt{\frac{2}{3\sqrt{3}}}\, a \approx 0.6204\, a \tag{9.2}$$

Since R_n is shorter than H_n, there are already unsupplied gaps for this good at each vertex of the complementary region. In the poor people's optimum, one lower *B* (*P*) order centre needs to be set up here. This lower-order centre becomes necessary when a good has a reach slightly less than

$$\frac{H_n}{R_n} \approx 1.0996\, R_n \tag{9.3}$$

On the other hand, for the capitalist optimum, it is the "hierarchical marginal good" *n-i* which gives rise to a lower-order centre. Since the area of this lower-order "complementary region" is 1/3 of that an order higher, the radius of the reach of good $R_{n\text{-}i}$, is

$$R_{n-i} = \sqrt{\frac{1/3}{\pi}}\, a \approx 0.3257\, a \tag{9.4}$$

In short, the length of the reach of the hierarchical marginal good which gives rise to the *B* (*P*) centre is about Eqs. (9.2)–(9.4) = 0.2946 *a* shorter in the case of the capitalist system as compared with the poor people's system. It is shorter about Eqs. (9.2)/(9.4) = 52.50%. With regard to the *C* (*G*) centre, in the poor people's system, as it was already clear from Eqs. (5.1) to (5.3), when the radius of reach is $1/\sqrt{3}$ times H_n, that is, when the good is 0. 3582 *a*, the lower-order centre is to be set up.

These relationships are extended and summarised in Fig. 9.1. Here, attention should be paid to the set of goods supplied from the centre of *C* (*G*). In the poor people's system, this point provides a group of goods with a reach less than or equal to 1.0996 (*n-i*) -Δ. However, in the capitalist system, some of these products are not supplied even from the *B* (*P*) centre, which is one order above. The supply from the *C* (*G*) centre starts only when the reach of the good is $R_{n\text{-}i}$. The goods with the largest reach supplied from this order differ for the systems for poor people and those for the capitalists.

The goods with the largest reach supplied from the poor people's system and the capitalist system are therefore greatly different. From Eqs. (9.2) and (9.4) above, the radius of the largest reach of the goods supplied at the centre in the poor people's system is

$$\frac{H_n}{R_{n-i}} \approx 1.9046 \tag{9.5}$$

times more than that of the capitalist system.

When the goods *n-j* at centre *C* (*G*) are supplied by the capitalist system, the goods with a larger reach are supplied even from the *D* (*B*) centre one order below in the poor people's system.

Thus, when the range and threshold are the same in size, the sets of goods supplied at the centres of each order differ under the poor people's system and are far more

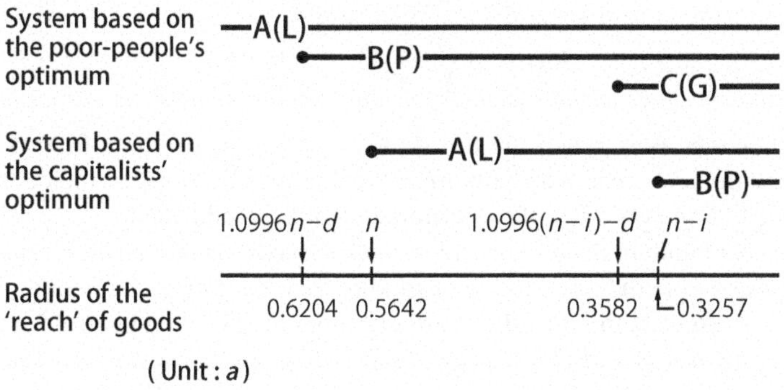

Fig. 9.1 Comparison of the reach of the goods under the capitalist and poor people's optima

affluent than that of the capitalist system. In the former system, people can enjoy a more affluent supply of goods.

Of course, the assumption that the range and threshold are equal can only be established by chance in reality, and there are various potential relations between the two. Next, then, more general relationships between the range and threshold are to be examined.

In a capitalist society, the acquisition of average profit in the long run is an absolute requirement. Therefore, for the establishment of the system under the poor people's optimum to be possible in the capitalist economy, it is necessary to satisfy the condition that the minimum demand space required for the sale of the smallest (in Fig. 5.2, good k just before giving rise to the K centre, which shall be called here "*hierarchy-specific lowest goods*") category of goods that the capitalist system does not supply is *not* eroded by each other in the poor people's system. To satisfy this condition, the area of the complementary region of the central system established on the poor people's optimum must satisfy the size of the demand space required for capitalist profit-making.

Now, considering the radius of the range of the "hierarchy-specific lowest good" in a central place at R_r, the area of the complementary region H_r shall then be

$$H_r = \frac{3\sqrt{3}}{2} R_r^2 \tag{9.6}$$

Suppose that the minimum required demand space H_r takes the form of a circle; then, the maximum radius of threshold R_{tMAX} that can be taken by the "hierarchy-specific lowest good" is

$$\pi R_{tMAX} = \frac{3\sqrt{3}}{2} Rr^2$$

$$\therefore\ R_{tMAX} = \sqrt{\frac{\frac{3\sqrt{3}}{2}}{\pi}} R_r \approx 0.9094\, R_r \tag{9.7}$$

In other words, only when the threshold has a radius of about 0.9094 times or less than the range, a necessary condition for the establishment of the central-place system based on the poor people's optimum shall be established.

On the other hand, in the poor people's system based on the range, if the threshold of the hierarchy-specific good is much smaller than the range that area of threshold is equal to, or exceeds the interstitial area not included in the threshold surrounded by the three central places that supply a good, then another lower-order centre that supplies the same good emerges at the centre of the interstitial area. In this case, the ratio between the range and threshold is determined by the length of the radius R_{t0} of the lower limit relative to R_r when the area of the portion indicated by the downward diagonal lines (S_I) and that of the portion indicated by the upward diagonal lines (S_2) are identical in Fig. 5.4.

The area of the equilateral triangle $A_1\ A_2\ A_3$ which includes the part not covered with a threshold is, as the point O forms the centre of gravity of the triangle,

$$\frac{\frac{2}{\sqrt{3}}\left(\frac{3}{2}Rr\right)^2}{2} = \frac{3\sqrt{3}}{4}Rr^2 \tag{9.8}$$

If $S_1 = S_2$, then
sectors $A_1B_{11}B_{12} + A_2B_{21}B_{22} + A_3B_{31}B_{32} = 1/2S_2$.
$(\because \angle A_1 + \angle A_2 + \angle A_3 = 180°)$.
$\therefore S_1 + 1/2\ S_2 = \Delta A_1\ A_2\ A_3$

$$\therefore\ S_2 = 2/3\Delta A_1A_2A_3 \tag{9.9}$$

Therefore, from Eq. (9.8),

$$S_2 = \pi R_{to}^2 = \frac{2}{3}\frac{3\sqrt{3}}{4}Rr^2 = \frac{\sqrt{3}}{2}Rr^2 \tag{9.10}$$

Solving this for R_t, we have

$$R_r = \sqrt{\frac{2\pi}{\sqrt{3}}} R_{t0} \tag{9.11}$$

Let $R_r = 1$ in Eq. (9.11); then, $R_{t0} = 0.5250$. That is, the system based on the poor people's optimum would not be feasible in capitalist society, unless the radius of threshold exceeds 0.5250 times of range, because a new centre R_{t0} would emerge in the interstitial area.

From the above analysis, the radius R_t of threshold has to stay in relation to R_r or the radius of range of hierarchy-specific lowest goods:

$$0.9094Rr \geq Rt > 0.5250Rr \tag{9.12}$$

Next, examine the same relation for goods in sectors where the range is slightly smaller than the “hierarchy-specific lowest goods”. For example, good k-Δ in Fig. 5. 2. This good has the maximum range of the goods among those not supplied in a centre, in the order below. Following the previous designation, it can be called the “hierarchy-specific highest good”.

Here again, the maximum possible extent of threshold that does not erode into each other is the area of the complementary region of an order below that central place. This can be expressed in terms of R_r:

$$\frac{3\sqrt{3}}{2}R_r^2\frac{1}{3} = \frac{\sqrt{3}}{2}R_r^2 \tag{9.13}$$

The radius of a circle of the same area is

$$\pi r^2 = \frac{\sqrt{3}}{2}Rr^2$$

$$\therefore r = \sqrt{\frac{\frac{\sqrt{3}}{2}}{\pi}}Rr \approx 0.5250\,Rr \tag{9.14}$$

The range of this good being R_r–Δ from the assumption, a necessary condition for the formation of the central-place system based on the poor people’s optimum is for the threshold to be 0.5250 R_r/ R_r–Δ times or smaller than the range.

Analysing a condition for a lower-order centre *not* to emerge, the area of the equilateral triangle corresponding to the triangle A_1 A_2 A_3 in the previous description is

$$\frac{3\sqrt{3}}{4}R_r^2\frac{1}{3} = \frac{\sqrt{3}}{4}Rr^2 \tag{9.15}$$

Substituting this into the relation obtained by Eq. (9.10) yields

$$S_2 = \pi R_{tMIN}^2 = \frac{2}{3}\frac{\sqrt{3}}{4}Rr^2 = \frac{1}{2\sqrt{3}}Rr^2$$

Solving this for R_r,

$$R_r = \sqrt{2\sqrt{3}\pi}\,R_{tMIN} \tag{9.16}$$

Assume that $R_r = 1$ in Eq. 21, $R_{tMIN} = 0.\ 3031$; then the threshold must have a radius larger than 0.3031 R_r/ R_r–Δ times that of the range.

Based on the above considerations, in the system for the poor people, the "hierarchy-specific highest goods", R_t must be within

$$\frac{0.5250R_r}{R_r - \Delta} \geq R_t > \frac{0.3031R_r}{R_r - \Delta} \tag{9.17}$$

From the above, examining the conditions for establishing the system based on the poor people's optimum in capitalist society for both the highest and lowest hierarchy-specific goods supplied in the central places of an order but not supplied in the lower-order central areas, Eqs. (9.12) and (9.17) are obtained. Putting them together, both equations overlap at only one point, where R_t slightly exceeds R_r by about 0.5250 times. The central-place system for the poor people is established under capitalism only in the very exceptional case where the threshold and range maintain this relation. In fact, in this value, a completely identical central system is formed in both systems.

Of course, in reality, it is rare that such conditions are met. As long as the purpose of capital is to obtain profits and secure effective demand in space, it is unlikely that a system based on Christaller's own socialism-inspired model will be established under *laissez-faire* capitalism, unless any social struggle for the poor people's optimum is waged.

9.7 Struggles Around Spatial Scale: Porosity and Scale Jumping

a. The porosity of boundaries and spatial fix

As discussed in Sect. 5 of Chap. 3, the porosity of boundaries creates contiguity in absolute space at higher scales. This contiguity gives rise to the action space at a higher scale, while at lower scales, bounded territories exist for the purpose of control. Thus, a multi-layered system of spatial configuration, consisting of mosaics of overlapping territories of multiple scales, emerges.

Each spatial position is thus assigned to more than one territory of various scale which overlap in a vertical hierarchy. Even if the power which dominates the territory in a certain spatial scale sets up a boundary, it is superimposed with a contiguous layer of other scales, undermining the boundary. Therefore, if an entity or a group can command a higher-order territory, it acquires the contiguity of absolute space and the concomitant new spatial instance at a different scale. This uncontrolled movement across boundaries gives the people at each scale the opportunity to fulfil diverse interests of their own. Thus, the relationship between spatial scales begins to take on some anarchy, depending on the strength of the power of the entity or group overriding the boundary.

For example, speculative financial capital can use various means to override the boundary of macroeconomic territories already experiencing a glut in capital and gain new opportunities for profit by investing in "green field areas" where capital is scarce and the profit rate is high. This action to overcome the boundedness set in absolute space for self-interest and avoid the problem of capital overproduction to postpone the crisis is called "*spatial fix*" by Harvey (1982 p. 427).

b. The production of lower domains for control

Those dominating the territory with political or economic power in a scale may, on the other hand, create controlled layers of the collective absolute spaces at lower scale within it to dominate and rule more effectively the people and economy under its jurisdiction.

The division of business territories as subordinate administrative units is a case in point. Although the lower-order territories are bound and separated from each other, the boundaries are always open to the higher-order scale controlled by the headquarters. The CEO at the headquarters draws the boundary so that the lower-order administration embodies the will of the corporate power covering the entire territory for their business.

The state power also deploys the borders as a barrier to manipulate the spatial movement of the people under control. It can manipulate the porosity of the boundary of the lower scale to limit the extent of action space of the people under its rule. The power that dominates the higher-order territory often uses the manoeuvre of divide-and-rule to make the subservient people spatially fragmented so that those the ruled would not come together to set themselves against the power. For example, the Bengal region, which most strongly advocated independence from the UK, was divided into two parts, independent India and East Pakistan, when British India became independent; thus, its overwhelming political power was prevented from influencing the politics of independent India. In the feudal Edo period of Japan, *sekisho* (check points) were established in various places, including Hakone, and *daimyo* (feudal lords) were able to pass freely, but the spatial movement of people was strictly controlled here, so that the people would not stand up to the Edo military government in unity nationwide.

c. The struggle in the multi-scalar spatial configuration

In a class or multi-ethnic society, the outcome of real subsumption of space is ridden with social struggles. The dominant/subordinate relationship arises along with the expansion of frontiers. Whether this multi-scalar spatial relationship emerges or not depends on the relative strength of power between these groups, which crush against one another.

The multi-scalar configuration of space is the outcome of this power struggle among these groups for domination or autonomy. When the dominant group wins, the spatial configurations thus produced are composed of multiple layers or scales, each of which is class- or ethnicity-specific. In this inter-scalar struggle, the subordinated people on a scale may attempt to attack—by deploying action space, for example—a scale produced by those with authoritative power to constrain them. In return, the dominant power fights back by institutionalising boundaries, keeping surveillance over them and attempting to retake control of the spatial configurations to forestall this struggle. The ultimate solution to those in domination may be that the power in one scale dominates another in the lower scale. At any rate, the interrelationship between the scales can be contradictory and struggle-prone, just as the dominant/subordinate classes or ethnic relations are always struggle-prone.

As the struggle of the people and the concept of local self-government advance in general, these lower-order territories can increasingly come to be the spatial base for local autonomy steered by the political entities in local scale, and eventually lead to the break-up of the higher-order scale of state power, as manifested in the prospective independence of Catalonia or even Scotland. At this time, the social struggle is in a sense transformed into that of the inter-scalar.

To forestall this struggle, the dominant power reinforces the boundary, keeps surveillance over the subordinate territories, and thereby attempts to maintain domination and control in the multi-scalar spatial configurations. Those in domination thereby aim to integrate the multi-scalar set of territories in a way that best supports their domination, with territorial integration or vertical coordination of multiple scales in an attempt to contain the challenge of subversion from the subordinated. Territorial integration is thus the way in which those in domination substantiate their power, piercing the overlapping scales.

Those in domination may not always be harsh and oppressive, and instead may attempt to co-opt the subordinated class or social group in the lower scale. The outcome may be one and the same scale being shared by different classes or ethnic groups, as in the case of the built environment.

d. Scale jumping: command of the higher-order scale for winning the struggle

According to Pile (Pile and Keith, p. 13), "different power relations may produce different power relations, and, further, that resistance may well operate between spaces authorised by authority." The struggle against the power that managed to set a battlefront at the global scale has different authority; thus it may have stronger leverage for winning as compared to those confined in the local scale.

As discussed in the previous section, the subordinated individuals or groups in space are in no way obliged to be confined within the assumed range of their action space. To empower themselves, they may opt to expand their spatial range of action beyond the spatial limit of the power that oppresses them; they then attempt to reach a higher-order spatial scale. This frees them from the oppressive power dominating in the territory at the lower scale and makes them able to access an emancipatory, often more empowering spatial range for struggle.

This spatial strategy is called *scale jumping*. Scale jumping has the effect of switching the spatial scale of action to a higher one so people are empowered more effectively and have a better chance of realising their political or social rights.

Scale jumping is especially effective with respect to the space of a nation, since the space of state power is "the space of the ruling class's hegemony over its people and over the nationhood that it has arrogated" (Lefebvre, p. 281). Once a subject manages to escape this hegemony of state power "which makes decisions in such a way as to ensure that the interests of certain minorities, of certain classes or fraction of classes, are imposed on society" (p. 281), the state can no longer impose its power on anyone in the society.

Scale jumping is a good manifestation of the dialectics between *Wirkungsraum* and action space. Contrary to the socio-spatial processes discussed in the previous sections, the production of the *espaces de représentation* is not required here. The people somehow manage to expand their spatial ranges and jump out of the existing scale at lower orders into a higher spatial scale to increase their influence and make their voices heard to a wider, global audience.

As evidenced in the Zapatista movement, the deployment of cyberspace can play a crucial role. Movements at the provincial scale in the rural state of Chiapas in Mexico exerted global influence and gained support from distant places through the Internet, the action space of which was essentially global. The scale jumping entails emancipation because it involves the spatial expansion of the struggle beyond the institutionalised boundary of the territory where the state authority exercises power to oppress the subordinated people. A state power cannot exercise it beyond its institutionalised boundary, while the subordinated can command a wider action space at a higher spatial scale, where their supporters exist, for their struggle.

Another example is local people who suffer from environmental pollution caused by a multinational corporation-owned plant. They remain powerless as long as they struggle against the multinational only at the scale of their own political jurisdictions. Even if they succeed in their struggle for stricter environmental regulations, the multinational corporation may simply resort to a "spatial fix" of moving its plant elsewhere to evade the stricter restrictions. In this case, those people need to acquire a spatial scale that matches with the action space of the multinational corporation. They need to jump the scale, sometimes skipping the national scale, to appeal, for example, to an alternative NGO with global reach, such as Greenpeace, and persuade it to mobilise its power against the global authority of the multinational corporation. When the multinational corporation can no longer resort to the "spatial fix", that is, switching territories on the same spatial scale to evade the struggle of the local people, the local people will achieve victory. The struggle of citizens against the human rights infringements by the child guidance centre of the Japanese government, discussed in the following section of this chapter, is another case in point. After all, "creation (or production) of a planet-wide space as the social foundation of a transformed everyday life" opens myriad possibilities (Lefebvre, p. 422).

There is nevertheless an important condition for successful scale jumping. The higher-order scale must be more emancipatory and devoid of the oppressive authority that exists at the lower scale. It is not always true, of course, that a higher-order scale is more emancipatory than the lower. This is typically demonstrated in case of present-day Hong Kong. It does not make sense, for example, for the democracy-seeking Hongkongers to jump from the local to the national scale under the Beijing authority. In some cases, "local and regional autonomy can be used whatever party stands to benefit from shifting the local and state decision-making to the particular scale that favours its own interests" (Harvey, 2012, p. 142).

In sum, those who command a spatial scale that has a more favourable emancipatory social ambience have a higher prospect of winning the struggle.

9.8 The Emancipation from Authoritative Space: A Case of Struggles Against the Human Rights Infringements by the Child Guidance Centres in Japan

The final section demonstrates a case of socio-spatial struggle that I have directly engaged in to demonstrate the combined class-specific processes of space subsumption for absolute and relative space as well as the properties of relational space and the concomitant strategies of spatial struggle.

a. Introduction: the body under social space of prohibition

Lefebvre states, "the fleshly (spatio-temporal) body is already in revolt" (p. 201). The human body has an inherent property of space, which is an object of appropriation, and therefore source of the revolt. Since the production of a territory by those in power always entails the spatial area of domination, "social space is the locus of prohibition" (p. 201). Anything against the will of the state power appropriating body of the people shall thus be extinguished. The space of pretended "welfare" becomes "prone to the sudden eruptions of violence" (p. 223) of the state power.

Yet the mosaic of social space or territory has the function of the dialectical opposite: "a subversion which 'breaks the tablets of the Law' (Nietzsche)" (Lefebvre, p. 201). A body strives to find its emancipation and empowerment through shifting the spatial scale, by transferring to outside of the state power that dominates the social space.

b. Oppression of bodies through the space produced by the state power

A good example is found in the struggle against the child guidance centres (CGCs hereafter) in Japan (Mizuoka, 2021). The system is quite similar to the removal of Aboriginal children to white families or orphanages run by whites under the White Australia Policy (Hollinsworth, 2003). This policy lasted until the early 1970s, after which Kevin Rudd, the prime minister of Australia, officially apologised in 2008. A similar policy called the "sixties scoop" (Stevenson, 2020) was implemented in Canada until the 1960s, by which indigenous children were removed from their biological families under the pretext of their well-being and adopted by white families. The latter victims are now demanding an apology and compensation. This is not a class struggle in the classical sense, yet it is indeed a struggle along "disputed frontiers" crossing "all sectors of society, extrapolitical as well as political" (Lefebvre, p. 418). Currently, a system most similar to the CGC in Japan is *barnevernet* in Norway. The operation of *barnevernet* has been severely criticised as infringing human rights globally (Bennett, 2019); and the Japanese CGC has generated almost exactly the same sort of problems.

In neo-liberalist Japan, under the welfare guise of "child guidance", with the claim of being the "last bastion for suffering children", children are removed and alienated from their families under venial or false abuse charges by the child guidance centre (CGC) and treated as a commodity. The children are then transferred to fill the beds of former orphanages left empty after the WWII orphans had come of age and left. These former orphanages are run by private corporations for profit with vested interests. Otherwise, these children are "sold" to infertile families either within Japan or overseas under the government's "special adoption" scheme for ca. JPY 2 million. It is de facto child trafficking.

Article 14 of the UN Guidelines for the Alternative Care of Children (2009) provides, "removal of a child from the care of the family should be seen as *a measure of last resort and should, whenever possible, be temporary and for the shortest possible duration*…" (emphasis mine). In the Japanese child guidance system, however, this is seldom respected and implemented. Colluding with the private corporations running former orphanages or alternative care facility, the policy to remove children from their families has been empathetically promoted by Japan's Ministry of Labour, Health and Welfare, which functions as if it is a harbinger of renewed authoritarianism in everyday governance.

Japanese people tend not to "get involved" with radical politics, but they prefer "to see things" (Pile and Keith, p. 25). Wilkinson and Pickett (2010, p. 52) pointed out, drawing upon a UN survey, that Japanese people had a fairly high level of public trust, as manifested in the rarity of violent uprisings, even in acute political situations. In spite of this social ambience, the families victimised by the CGC operations were very militantly mobilised, as manifested, for example, in two cases reported in the media of family members whose children had been kidnapped by the CGCs throwing Molotov cocktails into the CGC yards and bringing many court cases against the authority. A considerable number of CGC victims in Japan now more positively confront the state authority, aware that "the state can never play a constructive or supportive role in improving the daily life or the future prospect of anyone" and will put people and families "under surveillance, and if necessary criminalize and incarcerate all those who do not broadly accede to their dictates" (Harvey, 2012, p. 160). The anger of the Japanese families is quite rational and persuasive, because the CGC scheme in Japan infringes the sound and peaceful lives of the biological families, which are duly protected by the international human rights laws and supposedly nurtured by the traditional Japanese cultural value that has lasted for centuries.

Intriguingly, this CGC system of authority as well as the struggle of the people against this system have much to do with Lefebvre's claim (p. 410) that, "space is becoming the principal stake of goal-directed actions and struggles."

First, the relational space produced by the Japanese state power in removing the children from their families is quite similar to that of totalitarian states such as Nazi Germany or the Stalinist Soviet Union. Totalitarian states are unique in how they subsume space to produce a unique spatial configuration with two prominent elements.

The first element is a network of snitches controlled by the central authority, making the entire territory a ubiquitous "sensorium" of the state power encouraging the report of "abuse" from the citizens through hotline #189. The totalitarian system has its unique political space where "snitching" and "detention" are integrated, operated by the secret police with supreme administrative power incomparable to the regular judicial police which act on an arrest warrant by a court.

In the second element, Nazi Germany had concentration camps such as Auschwitz and the Soviet Union under Stalin had gulags in Siberia. In these facilities, persons captured by the secret police were detained in confined and isolated space in harsh environment under close surveillance for an extended period. The administrative authority unconditionally detained the body arbitrarily without an a priori third-party authorisation.

Political police detain people in many cases through snitching. No one knows when anyone around them will betray them and report them to the secret police. The spatial representation of this totalitarian system resembles a panopticon, "an architecture of surveillance and control" (Sack, 1986, p. 188), which makes the whole national space under surveillance of the state power just like a prison. The panopticon, devised by Jeremy Bentham, makes the power with constraints and violence omnipresent. It has an efficient and effective surveillance capability not only over the convicts but everyone, turning the national space into a space of "permanent, unfailing, ubiquitous" surveillance for collecting all sorts of information.

The Leipzig office of the former East German Stasi, which has been open to the public as a museum since the collapse of the GDR, exhibits a report submitted by a pupil to a teacher who was a henchman to the SED regime. The report confessed the pupil's dissatisfaction with life in East Germany. The teacher informed the Stasi about the pupil and the pupil's parents, with a copy of the report. The pupil and the parents were thus unknowingly placed under monitoring by the Stasi. As soon as the information would have added up to the threshold arbitrarily set by the authority, the family would be subject to interrogation or detainment on charges of treason. The CGC in Japan adopted a quite similar system called the "risk assessment" of families (Ueno, 2003, pp. 155–158) since the enactment of the "Child Abuse Prohibition Law" in 2000. The children are arbitrarily detained by the CGC, which has the authority of state power under Article 33 of the Child Welfare Act of Japan.

That is, Nazi Germany, the Stalinist Soviet Union, East Germany and the CGCs in Japan all had a common feature in that they produced the relational space consisting of the national scale with secret police at the centre which exerts tyrannical control over people across the nation through a political space made ubiquitous like pristine absolute space, together with the strictly bound space of confined and isolated concentration camps. This configuration of space is indeed the spatial manifestation of suppression and appropriation. It is homologous to the spatial organisation of the child guidance system in Japan for several reasons.

First, the state imposed a legal requirement to notify it of "abuse" cases using the hotline number 189 even there is no hard evidence, with secrecy guaranteed. The CGC accumulates the information thus collected in a single file under the heading of an individual child and gives points to the findings which may or may not be related to child abuse. Then, when the points add up to the threshold set arbitrarily and secretly, the child is removed from its family at the discretion of the director of the CGC, not through the regular judicial action with a warrant from the court.

Second, innocent children are then held for an extended period in the detention quarter of the CGC without even being allowed to receive compulsory education as stipulated in the Constitution. If children detained in the quarter of the CGC resists the warden, they will be disciplined by being confined to a small and detached space, which is a "place of disciplinary monotony" (Sack, 1986, p. 181) and forced to perform punitive tasks ordered by the warden. They would then be transferred to an alternative care facility (ACF hereafter), where they are kept under strict surveillance in detention, which lasts for two years yet is repeatedly renewed until they come of age. The visitation of family members to their own child is severely restricted or often totally denied by the CGC director. The child thus detained is treated as an "artificial orphan" by the ACF and used as an instrument by the private corporation running the ACF to obtain the government allowances to run its "welfare" business.

In short, the CGC system in Japan is supported by the same system of relational space as Nazi Germany and the Stalinist Soviet Union, with the only difference being that the latter is centred on the secret state police and the former is under the guise of "welfare". Yet state power allows in both cases for the confiscation and subsequent detainment of the human body without due court warrant. Once this system is extended to adults, it can immediately be transformed and used as a system of suppression by a totalitarian state.

The United Nations Committee on the Rights of the Child (UNCRC) (2019) thus recommended the Japanese government to thoroughly amend its child welfare laws; but the Japanese government has not completely complied with it to date.

c. The spatial struggle of a family seeking asylum in the Netherlands

In the summer of 2007, the daughter of a family in Nagasaki was removed from her mother by the Nagasaki CGC, alleging that the mother "abused" the daughter. Article 33 of Child Welfare Act (CWA) of Japan states that bodies composing a biological family can be arbitrarily broken apart by the CGC, in execution of the state power. This domestic law is clearly against Article 9 of the UN Convention on the Rights of the Child, and UN Committees under the umbrella of the High Commissioner for Human Rights have repeatedly asked Japan to amend it. In the global spatial scale, therefore, Japan thus remains a social space of prohibition, where a family cannot nurture its bonds peacefully and stably. The space in Japan is dominated by "power—it proceeds to repress in the name of power" (Lefebvre, p. 358) that intervenes in families.

The Nagasaki CGC planned to consolidate the separation of the family through the submission of an "Article 28 plea" which put the body of the daughter into an ACF. Although it is normally a breeze for the CGC to have the family court approve the plea, the first instance at the Nagasaki Family Court turned it down. Then, the CGC in secrecy transferred her away from the CGC detention quarters, with the daughter's whereabouts concealed. The CGC then appealed the case to the Fukuoka High Court, which approved the plea on the "evidence" fabricated by the CGC. The intimate bodily relation of the family was thus destroyed by state authority.

The mother then sought support from a human rights organisation to subvert the space of the state power by creating her own counter-space that would shift the power in space.

On 24 October 2008, during the organisation's activities to find the daughter, the grandfather spotted her (Jisou Higai #110, 2021):

"Grandfather! Why are you here? Did you come to pick me up?"

"That's right. Let's go home together. Your mother is right there."

The daughter decided to leave the ACF, the space of confinement where the authority is reified and made visible (Sack, 1986, p. 38). She ran away with all her might. At that time, a supporter said, "She ran for her life to see her mother. And I could see, indeed, that the CGC had made an irrational separation."

The daughter rejoiced at meeting her mother for the first time in about a year. The family recovered their bodily relation that had been destroyed through the undue infliction of the state power.

Suddenly, the ACF director showed up, and started to rip the daughter violently away from her mother. The mother exclaimed desperately, "Stop it!". The daughter's body began to distort under the masculine power of the ACF director. The daughter exclaimed, "It's hurting me; don't do it!" The grandfather and their supporters shouted at the director "You! The child is hurting! What are you doing?" The ACF director pretended he did not hear. Three supporters then grabbed his arm and stopped his assault on the daughter, who was freed from his grip for a moment and immediately jumped into a car through the door that her mother had opened.

The human rights organisation members and the grandfather were taken to a police station. A detective told one of the members that the ACF director had brought criminal charges against them. They were detained in the police station and interrogation began.

A detective asked, "They were fleeing to a foreign country, weren't they? Which airport did they go to?".

The supporters knew that transgressing the state boundary towards emancipation from the state power, Japan, was the most crucial moment to restore the bond of mother and daughter. They therefore lied to save the family.

"We've heard that they will take a direct flight from Kansai Airport in Osaka to Europe."

While the police were meddling with the long passenger lists there, the family safely left Japan through the passport control gate at Fukuoka International Airport in Kyushu for Seoul, South Korea, and then for the Netherlands. In Seoul, the mother rang up a head of the organisation who had supported their exodus from the space of prohibition. Yes, the family did manage to create their own counter-action space.

The family arrived at Schiphol Airport, Amsterdam, on 26 October 2008. Nagasaki police put them on the international wanted list through Interpol, prompting the Dutch authorities to place the daughter in custody upon arrival. Yet since there was no extradition agreement between the Netherlands and Japan, the mother was not sent back home. Acting across the global mosaic of fragmented collective spaces, the family now subverted the state power of Japan and turned the mosaic into the action space of emancipation to save their bodies in the intimate family relation.

After several proceedings, the Dutch court ruled on 29 December 2008 to allow the family to settle in the Netherlands together in exile. However, the members of the human rights organisation who remained in Japan were accused of "kidnapping the daughter" and were charged with criminal offences and sentenced to imprisonment.

Lefebvre aptly comments (p. 358), the "power—which is to say violence—divides, then keeps what it has divided in a state of separation; inversely, it reunites—yet keeps what it has divided in a state of confusion."

On 23 April 2018, when the daughter reached the age of 19, she returned to Japan to clear her name, after having hidden herself in the Netherlands for about ten years before the safety of her body from the arbitrary detention of the Japanese CGC was assured. She issued a statement, claiming, "What the CGC did to me was a crime… Please give me back my life and time with my family in Japan." It suggests that her body has been unable to build an autogenous bond with the social space of the Netherlands, which remains the place of displacement to her (Jisou Higai #110, 2021).

The mother, nevertheless, is still unable to return to Japan as she is still considered a criminal in Japanese prohibitive social space. After all, "every state is born of violence, and … state power endures only by virtue of violence directed towards a space" (Lefebvre, p. 280).

d. Another transgression: the CGC victims in Japan appealing their infringed human rights to the UN committees

To attain the "scale jumping" in solving the human rights infringements perpetrated by the CGC, the Japanese families whose children had been abducted by the CGC filed alternative reports directly with the UNCRC in Geneva in 2017. But since Japan has not ratified the Third Optional Protocol to the Convention (individual reporting system), CGC victim families cannot bring their individual cases directly to the UNCRC even today.

A human right group called the "Concerned Japanese Citizens for the Rights of the Child to Eradicate Child Guidance Centre Sufferings" (JCREC) invited the CGC victims across the nation to publish their sufferings in an alternative report on their human rights infringed by the CGCs. The JCREC put them together, added theoretical and historical explanations and submitted them to the UNCRC (JCREC, 2017 and 2018) in November 2017 and December 2018. The UNCRC duly considered the reports and issued its Concluding Observations in March 2019.

The UNCRC has paid due attention to the human rights infringements by the CGC since the late 2000s. This move constitutes an action for scale jumping.

The human-right problems in association with the CGC was first known outside Japan when a Japan branch of the Defence for Children International (DCI) invited Lothar Krappmann, a German sociologist and then the head of the UNCRC, to investigate Japan's compliance with the UN Convention on the Rights of the Child. Through interaction with people, he was astonished that the CGC issue was something that could possibly occur in a country which claims itself to be "advanced" in terms of human rights. This astonishment culminated in the concerns and recommendations in the Third Concluding Observations of the UNCRC on Japan issued in June 2010: "children who do not meet the behavioural expectations of school are transferred to Child Guidance Centres…" (Para. 62) and to "commission an independent investigation of the child guidance system and its working methods" (Para. 63).

The Japanese government totally ignored these recommendations. The UNCRC has thus become more engaged in tacking the CGC issue of Japan. Prior to the review session held in January 2019, members of the Task Force on Japan of the UNCRC offered an opportunity for an informal meeting with representatives of the JCREC at the Palais Wilson.

In the sessions held in February 2018 and January 2019, Olga Khazova, the vice chairperson of the UNCRC from Russia, raised intense questions about the issue. Having spent her childhood in the Soviet era and later obtained an LL.M. degree from Cornell University in the US, she must have had a sense of *déjà vu* from the totalitarian Stalinist regime in Japan's current CGC policy.

In March 2019, the UNCRC issued the 4th and 5th combined final observations, which devoted two entire paragraphs (28 and 29) out of 54 to the CGC issues. One significant achievement among them was that the UNCRC expressed its allegation of "a *strong financial incentive* for the child guidance centres to receive more children" (Para. 28(c), italics mine). That is, the "welfare" guise of the CGC was torn off and its neo-liberalist monetary incentives exposed.

The Anglo-American generic neo-liberalism proclaimed that it would shrink "government to the point where it could be 'drowned in a bathtub'" (Harvey, 2006, p. 150). Welfare provisions were to be either scrapped or privatised. However, in Japan, government ministers, especially the Ministry of Health, Labour and Welfare, sought to retain their vested interests and even enhance them via taxpayers' money, under the guise of "welfare", even if in reality it is contrary to it.

Currently, about two-thirds of a child guidance centre's annual budget comprises expense items supposedly catering to temporary custody, which is calculated as follows:

> Custody allowance (ca. JPY 350,000) multiplied by the expected number of children to be detained.

Every child guidance centre is compelled to cater to the expected number of children as stipulated in the annual budget; otherwise, the budget in the following fiscal year will be reduced. Therefore, the expected number of children to be detained is called the 'abduction quota' by the families victimised by the CGC.

Most ACFs originated as orphanages immediately after the World War II. Once the Japanese government began subsidising the cost of caring the children in custody in 1948, it turned to a vested interest to make money out of children. As orphans came of age and the beds became empty, ACF managers began demanding the government on sending more children into their care. The government ultimately set up a system in the late 1990s to streamline the process of the child guidance centre transferring the children removed from their families to the ACFs.

The natural consequence was to make the government as large and quaint as a monster using children as pieces of neo-liberalist money making. Thus, the Japanese people were being deprived of both money via the ever-heavier tax burden and their beloved children.

This variant of neo-liberalism may be called 'Neo-liberalism in the Oriental Way'.

The UNCRC committee members seemingly understood this Japanese "welfare" system's dispossessive and predatory nature, "to the point of daylight robbery" of children from their families, "particularly of the poor and the vulnerable, the unsophisticated and legally unprotected" (Harvey, 2012, p. 156). These UNCRC recommendations created a significant foothold for the victim families to dismantle the human-rights-infringing CGC system in Japan. The scale jumping strategy of the CGC victims of Japan has thereby met with splendid success internationally.

References

Association for the Research of Transportation Problems and Human Rights. (1998). Charter of right to transport. http://www.kotsuken.jp/charter/english.html.

Bennett, S. et.al. (2019). *Stolen childhood: The truth about Norway's child welfare system*. Emira Press.

Berry, B. J. L., & William, L. G. (1958). Recent Developments of Central Place Theory. *Papers and Proceedings of the Regional Science Association*, 4.

Castells, M. (1983). *City and the grassroots: A cross-cultural theory of urban social movements*. University of California Press.

Dicken, P. (2011). *Global shift: Mapping the changing contours of the world economy*. Guilford.

Harvey, D. (1973). *Social justice and the city*. The Johns Hopkins University Press.

Harvey, D. (1982). *The limits to capital*. University of Chicago Press.

Harvey, D. (2006). Neo-liberalism as creative destruction. *Geografiska Annaler*, *88B*(2).

Harvey. (2012). *Rebel cities: From the right to the city to the urban revolution*. Verso.

Hollinsworth, D. (2003). *They took the children*. Kingswood, S. Working Title Press.

JCREC (Concerned Japanese Citizens for the Rights of the Child to Eradicate Child Guidance Centre Sufferings). (2017). Severe Infringement on the Human Rights of Children and Families by the Child Guidance Centre and Alternative Care Facilities in Japan. An Alternative Report to the State Report 'Combined Fourth and Fifth Periodic Report of Japan on the Convention on the Rights of Child' June 2017. https://tbinternet.ohchr.org/_layouts/15/treatybodyexternal/Download.aspx?symbolno=INT%2FCRC%2FNGO%2FJPN%2F30000&Lang=en (accessed on 2 November 2024).

JCREC. (2018). Suppression of the Hard Facts and Deception on the International Community to hide the Infringement on the Human Rights of Children and Families. An Alternative Report Commenting on the 'Reply of Japan to the List of Issues'. https://tbinternet.ohchr.org/_layouts/15/treatybodyexternal/Download.aspx?symbolno=INT%2FCRC%2FNGO%2FJPN%2F33501&Lang=en (accessed on 2 November 2024).

Jisou Higai #110. (2021). Mother and Daughter's Flight to the Netherlands, 2008. Annex 6, The Human Rights Problems and their Current Situation of the Sufferings Caused by the Child Guidance Centres of Japan, an Alternative Report submitted to the UN Committee on the Human Rights. https://tbinternet.ohchr.org/_layouts/15/treatybodyexternal/Download.aspx?symbolno=INT%2FCCPR%2FCSS%2FJPN%2F44592&Lang=en (accessed on 2 November 2024).

Lefebvre, H. (1991). (translation). *The production of space*. Translated by Donald Nicholson-Smith. Wiley-Blackwell.

Marx, K. (1977) (translation). *Capital*. Vol. 1. Translated by Ben Fowkes. New York: Vintage Books.

Mizuoka, F. (2012). The dialectics of space subsumption, struggle in space, and position of localities. *Localities*, 2.

Mizuoka, F. (2018). *Contrived Laissez-faireism*. Springer.

Mizuoka, F. (2021). Human rights rationale behind the United Nations recommendations on the child guidance centres of Japan. *Hitotsubashi Journal of Social Studies, 52*, 31–49.
Peet, R. (1972). Some issues in the social geography of american poverty. R. Peet ed. *Geographical Perspectives on American Poverty*, pp. 1–4. Antipode.
Pile, S., & Keith M. eds. (1997). *Geographies of resistance*. Routledge.
Sack, R. (1986). *Human territoriality: Its theory and history*. Cambridge University Press.
Stevenson, A. (2020). *Intimate Iitegration: A history of the sixties scoop and the colonization of indigenous kinship*. University of Toronto Press.
Ueno, K. et al. (2003). *'Jido Gyakutai' no Kochiku (the Construction of 'Child Abuse')*. Sekai Shisosha.
United Nations. (2009). Guidelines for the Alternative Care of Children. Resolution adopted by the General Assembly on 18 December 2009. https://digitallibrary.un.org/record/673583/files/A_RES_64_142-EN.pdf?ln=en (Accessed 2 Nov 2024).
United Nations Committee on the Rights of the Child (UNCRC). (2019). *Concluding observations on the combined fourth and fifth periodic reports of Japan*. https://digitallibrary.un.org/record/3794942/files/CRC_C_JPN_CO_4-5-EN.pdf (Accessed 22 Nov 2024).
Wilkinson, R., & Pickett, K. (2010). *The spirit level: Why equality is better for everyone*. Penguin.

Afterword

This book shares the ultimate objective of critical geography as stated by David Harvey (2012, p. 153): “universal human flourishing beyond the constraints of class domination and commodified market determinations”. It is the outcome and fruit of a lifetime of my academic research. I have worked for half a century for emancipation and justice in academia and society, drawing upon past prominent contributions in this field, especially those of David Harvey and Henri Lefebvre. Yet this book is naturally not just a rehash of their arguments. I spotted an important concept that Marx presented in his manuscript for *Capital*, formal and real s*ubsumption*, and then reconstructed the existing theories and concepts of economic geography as well as the arguments of critical geography in dialectical order around this concept to explain the attributes of pristine *space* brought into a society under power and the struggles against it.

In this book, my past research on critical geography has been put together and edited into a systematic single body of a critical theory of space presented here. My past works upon which this book is based are as follows (in order of the year of publication):

- *Annihilation of Space: A Theory of Marxist Economic Geography* (Ph.D. dissertation submitted to Clark University, Massachusetts in 1986).
- “Chushinchi Riron (Central-Place Theory)” in Yoichi Asano et al. eds. *Chiiki no Gainen to Chiiki Kozo* (*The Concepts of Region and Regional Structure*). Tokyo: Taimeido, 1988, pp. 202–219. Published in Japanese.
- *Keizai Chirigaku: Kukan no Shakai e no Hosetsu* (*Economic Geography: Subsumption of Space into Society*) Tokyo: Aoki Shoten, 1992. Published in Japanese.
- *Keizai Shakai no Chirigaku* (listed in the Bibliography). Published in Japanese.
- “The Dialectics of Space Subsumption, Struggle in Space, and Position of Localities”, *Localities* (Pusan National University) 2, 2012, pp. 33–78.
- “Capitalist regulation and the provision of public transportation in Japan” in Nicholas Low ed. *Transforming Urban Transport: the ethics, politics and practices of sustainable mobility*. London: Routledge, 2013, pp. 85–110.

F. Mizuoka, *Subsumption of Space*, Contributions to Regional Science,
https://doi.org/10.1007/978-981-97-7560-6

I was born on 25 January 1951 in Aomori, Japan. My father was an engineer at a nearby US military base in Misawa. In high-school days I was fond of reading books on dialectical philosophy and Marxism.

When I was an undergraduate, the academic ambience of the critical geographers' circle in Japan was nourishing enough to encourage my critical spirit in geography. Until the early 1970s, Japanese critical geography enjoyed its heyday (perhaps along with its counterpart in France) relative to geographers taking a critical line worldwide. The core institution was the Japan Association of Economic Geographers (JAEG), established in 1954 (Mizuoka, 2006, p. 24) by contemporary geographers taking an alternative position to the academic authority. Taking advantage of the JAEG as a principal platform, Japanese critical geographers attempted to create original concepts of Marxist (economic) geography in the 1960s, a decade earlier than the advent of radical geographers in North America and other English-speaking countries (Mizuoka et al. 2005, pp. 458–459).

The work of Noboru Ueno (1972), quoted in Chap. 7 of this book, was of particular importance. Ueno attempted to integrate Marxist and humanistic approaches of geography into a single body of critical geographic theory, which was a significant theoretical achievement within the scholarship of critical geography. Drawing upon interpretations of Heideggerian phenomenology, Ueno explained the objective as intersubjective in interpreting produced nature (Mizuoka et al. 2005, pp. 459–461). Japanese critical geography, however, unfortunately had little global reach at that time. It is deplorable that this work of Ueno was hardly known among geographers overseas due to the language barrier.

The year 1973 marked a major turning point for radical geographies in both Japan and North America, but in totally contrary directions (Mizuoka, 1996). In that year, Toshifumi Yada, a settlement movement activist in his student days, published an article castigating past Japanese critical geographers, including Ueno, for subscribing to the "economic chorography school". Instead, Yada put forward his own "regional structure concept" (*chiiki kozo ron*). He then set out to identify relatively autonomous "regional economic circuits" within Japan. One could legitimately question if the identification of "regional economic circuits" in a national territory was on the agenda of Marxist geography at all. In fact, it is more a degraded copy of conventional, non-Marxist regional economics. Associating *chiiki kozo* with critical scholarship was thus imputed to Yada's previous critical scholarship on coal mining studies and his past association with the Japanese Communist Party, on behalf of which Yada published a couple of articles on energy policy using a pseudonym in the 1970s.

After all, Yada's accusations against the "economic chorography school" were more a political manoeuvre to establish his own faction than a serious academic endeavour. Nevertheless, Yada's ambition gradually attracted henchmen in Japanese geographers' circle while undermining the heritage of critical geography that Japanese geographers should have felt proud of at least until 1972.

While reading *Capital* and *Theories of Surplus Value* in graduate seminars at Hitotsubashi University, I initially joined Yada's study group, yet became increasingly sceptical of its critical nature. At a 1979 seminar organised by the National Association of Geography Graduate Students (of Japan), I therefore offered a friendly criticism of Yada's work, arguing that his *chiiki kozo* concept was a rehash of ideas presented by Japanese conventional regional economists in the 1950-1960s, and explaining that Yada's "concept cannot establish originality in the social sciences at large" (Zenchi-inren, 1980, p. 151). Much to my surprise, Yada replied vehemently, claiming that "Mizuoka [is] bent on pointing out obsoleteness to me [=Yada], who is striving for the systematic concept of economic geography ...[while Mizuoka has not] *without putting forward any of his own concepts*" (Yada, 1980, p. 156, emphasis mine).

While I was working as a visiting lecturer at the University of Hong Kong (1979–1981), in responding to Yada's critique I began to seek my "own concepts" which would be critical and robust enough to replace *chiiki kozo*. It gradually became my lifelong research agenda. To achieve this, I aspired to pursue a Ph.D. in order to establish a systematic conception of Marxist or critical economic geography. The radical geography emerging in North America in the 1970s appeared an attractive platform. Thus, financed by a Fulbright scholarship for study in the US, I entered a Ph.D. programme in geography at Clark University as it was a base of the North American radical geography movement through its publication of *Antipode*.

My doctoral dissertation presented my own critical economic geography in response to Yada's provocation. My argument, focused on the concept of space subsumption drawing upon Marx's formal and real subsumption of labour, forms the backbone of this dissertation. This concept flashed into my mind when I visited David Harvey at Johns Hopkins University in 1985. Richard Peet was my supervisor, and Harvey kindly volunteered to be on the dissertation committee.

After conferral of my doctoral degree, I was appointed in 1986 as an associate professor of economic geography in the Faculty of Economics of Hitotsubashi University, where Marxist economics still had a considerable influence. Harvey kindly wrote a strong letter of recommendation to the Dean for me. Here, I worked hard to introduce North American radical geography to Japan. I organised a group of Marxist economists and geographers to translate Harvey's *The Limits to Capital* and *Urbanization of Capital*, as well as Allen Scott's *Metropolis* into Japanese.

In the meantime, Yada began increasingly to pander to the state power, promoting the "National Land Axes" on behalf of the National Land Agency. In 1999, Yada and his henchmen plotted to amend the constitution of the JAEG in order to put this once critical organisation of geography under their domination. After a lengthy three-hour debate, I stood against this plot (Mizuoka, 2006, pp. 30–31) in association with a former president of the JAEG, Toshio Aoki. Unfortunately, after the amendment of the constitution, the critical heritage of the JAEG has almost been relinquished.

As such, this book represents my own struggle against this "counterrevolution" in critical geography in Japan as well as being a positive answer to Yada's demand made more than four decades ago, authentically reclaiming the heritage of Japanese critical geography. Through this book, I hope to share this Japanese heritage with the global community of Marxist geographers. It could also well be regarded as the "graduation thesis" of my entire academic life.

References

Harvey, D. (2012). *Rebel cities: From the right to the city to the urban revolution.* Verso.
Mizuoka, F. (1996). The disciplinary dialectics that has played eternal pendulum swings: Spatial theories and disconstructionism in the history of alternative social and economic geography in Japan. *Geographical Review of Japan, Series B, 69*(1), 95–112.
Mizuoka, F. et al. (2005). The critical heritage of Japanese geography: its tortured trajectory for eight decades. *Society and Space, 23*(3), 453–473.
Mizuoka, F. (2006). The demise of a critical institution of economic geography in Japan. *Critical and Radical Geographies of the Social, the Spatial and the Political (URP research paper 1)*, pp. 22–34.
Ueno, N. (1972). *Chishigaku no Genten (The Ultimate Origin of Chorography).* Taimeido.
Yada, T. (1980). On the criticism of Fujio Mizuoka. *Chiri, 25*(9), 154–156.
Zenchi-inren. (1980). The Zenchi-inren seminar report. *Chiri, 25*(7), 138–151.

Author Index

F. Mizuoka, *Subsumption of Space*, Contributions to Regional Science,
https://doi.org/10.1007/978-981-97-7560-6

T

U

V

W

Index

F. Mizuoka, *Subsumption of Space*, Contributions to Regional Science,
https://doi.org/10.1007/978-981-97-7560-6

SPRINGER NATURE

GPSR Compliance

The European Union's (EU) General Product Safety Regulation (GPSR) is a set of rules that requires consumer products to be safe and our obligations to ensure this.

If you have any concerns about our products, you can contact us on ProductSafety@springernature.com

In case Publisher is established outside the EU, the EU authorized representative is:

Springer Nature Customer Service Center GmbH
Europaplatz 3
69115 Heidelberg, Germany

The manufacturer's authorised representative in the EU is Springer Nature Customer Service Centre GmbH, Europaplatz 3, 69115 Heidelberg, Germany. If you have any concerns regarding our products, please contact ProductSafety@springernature.com

Printed and bound by CPI Group (UK) Ltd, Croydon, CR0 4YY
01/10/2026
02225910-0002